The Justification of Europe

The Justification of Europe

A Political Theory of Supranational Integration

Jürgen Neyer

UNIVERSITY PRESS

Great Clarendon Street, Oxford, OX2 6DP,
United Kingdom

Oxford University Press is a department of the University of Oxford.
It furthers the University's objective of excellence in research, scholarship,
and education by publishing worldwide. Oxford is a registered trade mark of
Oxford University Press in the UK and in certain other countries

© Jürgen Neyer 2012

The moral rights of the author have been asserted

First Edition published in 2012

Impression: 1

All rights reserved. No part of this publication may be reproduced, stored in
a retrieval system, or transmitted, in any form or by any means, without the
prior permission in writing of Oxford University Press, or as expressly permitted
by law, by licence or under terms agreed with the appropriate reprographics
rights organization. Enquiries concerning reproduction outside the scope of the
above should be sent to the Rights Department, Oxford University Press, at the
address above

You must not circulate this work in any other form
and you must impose this same condition on any acquirer

British Library Cataloguing in Publication Data

Data available

Library of Congress Cataloging in Publication Data

Data available

ISBN 978-0-19-964124-6

Printed in Great Britain by
MPG Books Group, Bodmin and King's Lynn

For my family

Acknowledgements

This book's argument owes a lot to the intellectual inspiration of Christian Joerges. When I started working with him at the Centre for European Law and Policy at the University of Bremen in the mid-1990s, I was amazed by the profoundness of his ideas and was permanently forced to place my own thinking in relation to his. The attentive reader will notice that many of his ideas have found their way into this book. It took quite some years, however, to accommodate his intellectual inspiration with my own disciplinary background and to forge both into a consistent argument. This process accompanied me on my scientific journey from Bremen to the European University Institute in Florence, the Ludwig-Maximilians-University in Munich, the Johann-Wolfgang-Goethe University at Frankfurt (Main), the University of California at Berkeley, the Free University Berlin, and finally the European University Viadrina in Frankfurt (Oder). This book is an effort to bring this long journey to a preliminary end.

I owe much to all the colleagues whom I met on the way and who discussed earlier drafts and reflections. A special thanks goes to my former and current collaborators and colleagues Katrin Auel, Christian Bühler, Ulrike Ehling, Tuomas Iso-Markku, Rachel Herp Tausendfreund, Jannik Pfister, and especially Julien Deroin who read and commented on parts of the manuscript or supported me in developing my ideas. Rainer Forst has been a major intellectual inspiration. The argument of this book is strongly inspired by his work on the 'right to justification'. I am also grateful to Peter Niesen, Nicole Deitelhoff, Felmon Davis, Detlef v. Daniels, Rainer Schmalz-Bruns, and Thosten Thiel, who spent a full-day workshop at the Wissenschaftskolleg Bad Homburg in discussing a first draft of the manuscript. Further acknowledgements go to Tanja Börzel, Deirdre Curtin, Erik O. Eriksen, Gunter Hellmann, Lisbet Hooghe, Mathias Kumm, Gary Marks, and Michael Schroeter, all of whom discussed at various conferences and workshops earlier versions of the argument. Finally, I owe a very special thanks to Jacqueline Haake, who has administered my office for the last five years with admirable efficiency and perfection.

This book would not have been written without the generous financial support of the German Research Foundation (DFG), the Thyssen Foundation, and the Volkswagen Foundation. A first DFG stipend in the years 2002 to 2006

Acknowledgements

helped to establish the intellectual ground for the book and provided the basis for a later Volkswagen and Thyssen stipend in the years 2010 to 2012. These allowed me to finish the manuscript and to lend it the precision required by the referees at Oxford University Press. I am also grateful to Scott Stock Gissendanner who did a terrific job in putting this manuscript into proper English and to Olga Eisele for doing the index and the bibliography. Finally, I dedicate this book to my family: to my wife Annegret and to my children, whom I love more than anything else.

Berlin, February 2012

Contents

List of Abbreviations x

Part I. Setting the Stage

1. The Challenge 3
2. Normative Realism 19

Part II. Understanding the EU

3. The Nature of the Beast 35
4. Towards a Supranational Democracy? 56

Part III. Setting the Standard

5. Justice in International Political Theory 73
6. Justice and the Right to Justification 85

Part IV. Reconstructing the EU

7. Structures of Justification 115

Part V. The EU's justice deficit

8. Imperfectly Justified Structures of Justification 151
9. The EU's Imperial Foreign Policy 169

Part VI: Conclusion

10. Conclusion 187

Bibliography 196
Index 211

List of Abbreviations

ACER	Agency for the Cooperation of Energy Regulators
ACP	Africa, Caribbean and Pacific
APEC	Asia-Pacific Economic Cooperation
BRIC	Brazil, Russia, India and China
BVerfGE	Bundesverfassungsgericht
CAP	Common Agricultural Policy
CEEC	Central and Eastern European countries
CFSP	Common Foreign and Security Policy
COREPER	Committee of Permanent Representatives
COSAC	Conférence des organes parlementaires spécialisés dans les affaires de l'Union
CSO	Civil Society Organization
DAC	Development Assistance Committee
DFG	German Research Foundation
EAC	European Affairs Committee
EAFRD	European Agricultural Fund for Rural Development
EAGF	European Agricultural Guarantee Fund
EC	European Community
ECHR	European Convention for the Protection of Human Rights and Freedoms
ECI	European Citizenship Initiative
ECJ	European Court of Justice
EDF	European Development Fund
EEA	European Economic Area
EEC	European Economic Community
EIGE	European Institute for Gender Equality
EMA	European Medicines Agency
ENP	European Neighbourhood Policy
EP	European Parliament

List of Abbreviations

EPACA	European Public Affairs Consultancies Association
ERA	European Railway Agency
ERDF	European Regional Development Fund
EU	European Union
GATS	General Agreement on Trade in Services
GATT	General Agreement on Tariffs and Trade
GFCC	German Federal Constitutional Court
ICA	Interparliamentary Constitutional Assembly
ICJ	International Court of Justice
IF	Integrated Framework for Trade-Related Technical Assistance
IMF	International Monetary Fund
IPA	Instrument for Pre-Accession Assistance
IPCA	Interparliamentary Constitutional Assembly
ITC	International Trade Centre
JITAP	Joint Integrated Technical Assistance Programme
MEP	Member of European Parliament
MERCOSUR	Common Southern Market
MP	Member of Parliament
NAFTA	North American Free Trade Area
NGO	Non-Governmental Organization
OAS	Organization of American States
OECD	Organization for Economic Cooperation and Development
OMC	Open Method of Coordination
OSCE	Organisation for Security and Cooperation in Europe
PHARE	Programme of Community Aid to the Countries of Central and Eastern Europe
QMV	Qualified Majority Voting
SEA	Single European Act
SPS Agreement	Agreement on the Application of Sanitary and Phytosanitary Measures
TEU	Treaty on the European Union
TFEU	Treaty on the Functioning of the European Union
TPRB	Trade Policy Review Body
TRIMS	Trade-Related Investment Measures
TRIPS	Trade-Related Intellectual Property Rights

List of Abbreviations

UN	United Nations
UNCTAD	United Nations Conference on Trade and Development
UNDP	United Nations Development Programme
USTR	United States Trade Representative
WTO	World Trade Organization

Part I
Setting the Stage

1

The Challenge

Why another book on legitimacy in Europe? Can anything meaningful be added that has not been written already? The list of insights and suggestions collected on the bookshelves is impressive. The European Union has been described as an 'unfinished democracy' (Eriksen 2009), deficient in terms of parliamentary rule, a proper party system, a European-wide media system, and a critical public discourse. It has been criticized for its lack of transparency and accountability, the distance between 'Brussels' and ordinary citizens, the ensuing negative effects on domestic democracy, the dominance of Member State executives in the constitutional and the policy-making process. The EU's constitutional bias in favour of negative integration and the EU's tendency to sacrifice democracy on the altar of integration have also been criticized.[1]

Despite these severe defects, much of the literature interprets the EU integration project as following in the footsteps of earlier nation building processes and understands the EU as an important step towards establishing democracy on a level above the nation-state (Habermas 2011). The institutional deficits of the EU are relativized by comparing them with the less-than-ideal practices common to nation-states. They are sometimes even defended for being comparably mild violations of transparency, accountability, and the idea of checks and balances (Moravcsik 2002). The European public discourse is said to have become increasingly relevant (Risse 2010) and European parliamentarism is interpreted as a 'multilevel field' that encompasses both national parliaments and the European Parliament (Crum/Fossum 2009). Deliberative elite processes and good administrative practices are praised and assessed as compensating for a lack of participation and representation (Majone

---

[1] The list of literature dealing with the deficiencies of the European Union and its failure to comply with the requirements of democracy is long and expanding every day. Most pertinent contributions that elaborate on the points raised in this paragraph include Eriksen (2009), Rittberger (2005), Mair/Thomassen (2010), Peter/de Vreese (2004), Sifft et al. (2007), Risse (2010), Bovens/Curtin/'t Hart (2010), Schmidt (2006), Zielonka (2007), Magnette/Nicolaides (2004), Lord (2007), Scharpf (2010a) and Majone (2010).

1998). A broad consensus exists in most of the literature that the EU's deficit in democratic governance can be overcome by a set of artfully designed institutional innovations (Hix 2008; Holzhacker 2007) or—even better—by the establishment of full-blown democratic European statehood (Morgan 2005; Verhofstadt 2006).

This book's claim to add something meaningful to this literature stems from its innovative analytical orientation. It starts from the assumption that the very problem of legitimate governance in the European Union does not originate in the failure at the supranational level to realize democratic principles, but that the supranational level is better understood as a mechanism for correcting democratic deficits emerging from the Member States. Europe's democratic deficit originates first of all in the Member States, not in its supranational layer. Under conditions of interdependence, and in the absence of a supranational regulatory body, all democratic nation-states suffer from the structural problem that the policies of one nation impinge on the policies of others, with no country having the ability to systematically internalize these repercussions. The democratic nation-state, so to speak, rules foreign lands and is simultaneously ruled by foreign sovereigns. It is a structurally inward-looking entity that is in need of an additional layer of governance for giving voice to those concerns that are affected by its decisions but are not included in its domestic decision-making practices. The EU can best be understood as constituting this additional layer. Its function is not to overcome but to complement the democratic nation-state and to transform its Member States' decisions' external effects into an input for a process of collective cross-border decision-making. Supranationality thus improves Member State democratic governance without necessarily being democratic itself. It is about 'democratizing' Member State democracies without aiming to succeed the nation-state as the primary entity of political authority in the EU.

The book is based on a methodology that is nearly unique in the integration literature. Normative approaches to the EU are often developed in an empirical void. They apply standards taken from mainstream democratic theory without taking the empirical facts of their object into consideration. The thereby construed 'democratic deficit' is used as an instrument of critique and eventually as the basis for identifying institutional measures that promise to make the EU more democratic. As will be argued in this book, any such approach is flawed from the beginning. Applying the democracy standard to the EU belies a fundamental misunderstanding of the EU's nature and ultimately means cooking up a bill of fare that the EU cannot digest. The democracy standard presupposes, minimally, individual political equality and a monopoly of coercion. Neither requirement resonates with the structure and practices of the EU. Indeed, both are wholly alien to the EU. This book chooses a different methodology. It closely connects empirical analysis and normative reflection and works not with an externally validated standard, but one that is internal to the EU itself. It is a methodology that finds normative inspiration in the structures of the EU and that uses this inspiration for critically reflecting on the EU's practices. The structural heart of the EU is seen in its combination of vertical legal integration and horizontal political integration. This dualistic structure was never meant to be an institutional frame for allowing the (non-existent) European demos to govern itself. It was from its very beginning oriented towards facilitating a constructive discourse among the European societies about conditions necessary to live together in interdependence. The EU is thus completely misunderstood if criticized as unable to live up to the ambition of establishing the sovereignty of a European people in a post-national state. From the Treaties of Rome to the Treaty of Lisbon, the EU has never tried to realize this aim. It is much better understood as an effort to constitutionalize cross-border justificatory discourses in an emergent multi-level structure. This is the appropriate starting point for a meaningful and non-utopian critique of its practices.

1.1. Assessing European legitimacy

The integration project always had and still has a great normative appeal. It has replaced a centuries-long European practice of nationalism and violence with the rule of law and collective policy-making. Inter-state violence has been overcome by tying together the Member States economically, legally, and politically. Exchanging military threats or even going to war is no longer a political option. Arguing and bargaining have become the uncontested modes of cross-border political action. The EU has also opened the borders of the Member States for the mobility of goods, services, capital, and citizens. It has spurred economic growth and cultural exchange across the whole continent. Constitutional tolerance (Weiler 2003) and the 'inclusion of the other' (Habermas 2000) have become the building blocks of a new European political culture. The formerly sovereign nation-states of the European continent have transformed themselves gradually into legally obligated Member States. The EU is thus not merely a project of economic liberalization. It has much higher ambitions. It holds governments accountable for the external effects of their actions by giving affected parties a say in the making of domestic policy. The EU is thus an instrument for extending not only governance but also legitimacy beyond borders.

Many authors share this affirmative assessment but nevertheless try to overcome the EU's structural deficits. The EU, as it is today, is often analysed as an unfortunate in-between—being neither state nor international organization—that is too powerful to be justified in the terms of international politics and institutionally too weak to be legitimized as a state. Affirming the EU thus motivates most normative writers to demand that it be transformed into a federal entity similar to a democratic nation-state. The EU is even frequently seen as a democratic federal state in *statu nascendi* that must develop into a full-blown democratic system if it is to overcome its lack of citizen support. This programme of developing the EU into a federal and democratic entity benefits from the deep-rooted conviction of many observers that legitimate governance is only to be found in democratic structures. But it is not without problems. Democracy has developed historically only inside, never beyond state structures. There is no single incidence of fully articulated democratic structures beyond the nation-state. A most important reason for the close relation between democracy and the state is that many of the policies of democracies rely on coercive capacities. A redistributive social scheme, for example, rests on the power to tax, which again is contingent on the power to enforce sanctions against parties unwilling to contribute their share. None of this can be guaranteed without a monopoly of coercion. Ever since Kant (1982) famously argued that coercion and freedom are inseparably connected, it is a well-established insight that democracy without a state is hardly more than a naïve utopia (cf. Habermas 1992: 168; Barber 2005: 94). The EU, however, is far from acquiring anything close to a monopoly of coercion. Its Member States all claim to be the sovereign guardians of their national constitutions and no large Member State has shown any readiness in the past to relinquish any part of its monopoly of coercion. Demanding the transformation of the EU into a state-like structure is therefore tantamount to calling for a major and highly unlikely political revolution in Europe.

A similarly serious obstacle to a democratized EU is that its very structure is built on the principle of difference, not of equality, among citizens. This is all the more serious when considering that the political inequality of EU citizens is not some unintended, unfortunate deficit in the organizational structure of the EU; rather, it is an expression of the historical character of the EU as an organization with significant international elements. Any effort to understand the organizational logic of the EU that does not take the European history of war and interstate conflict into account, and thus acknowledges its emphasis on national sensibilities, will fail. Intergovernmental equality is a normative backbone of the EU. It is not a democratic concept and is specifically difficult to reconcile with democracy's unequivocal emphasis on individual political equality. Thus, the EU is not undemocratic by mistake and it is not a democracy in the making. Rather, it is a deliberately different entity that intentionally violates one of the constituting principles of democracy.

If the EU, however, cannot become a democracy without forgetting the European past and changing its very organizational logic (and thus becoming a new political entity), then it is meaningless to measure it against a democratic standard. The banal result would provide no avenue for reform beyond rejecting the whole enterprise. Applying the democratic standard to the EU is nothing less than a categorical mistake. The important question to ask today is not whether the EU is democratic and if its practices differ from the ideal of normative democratic theory. The question to be asked is whether and under which theoretical premises the EU can be justified convincingly without resorting to a deep change in its institutional logic. We need to ask whether there is theoretical scope for a realistic normative theory that accepts the EU's most basic structures as a given and that engages in reform measures without, however, becoming mired in an unreflected affirmation of its practices. An approach is needed that can affirm the EU's structures while criticizing its practices at the same time.

This endeavour is far removed from an uncritical affirmation of the status quo. It is an intellectual project that formulates an ambitious normative standard with a view to political practice and critique. Only by developing and applying a normatively realistic standard can we expect our prescriptions for changing the EU to resonate with political practice and become politically relevant. This book therefore desists from the temptation to engage in visionary wishful thinking and is firmly embedded in a pragmatic analysis of the EU. It claims that only normative realism is a promising way for exporting theoretical ideas out of academia and into the political realm. It is thus an approach that is both theoretically and practically relevant.

This book embarks on this path by proposing to substitute the discourse on the democratic deficit of the European Union with a discourse on its justice deficit. Justice, not democracy, is the appropriate concept for questioning and explaining the legitimacy of the EU. In contrast to democracy, the notion of justice is not tied to the nation-state, but can be applied in all contexts and to all political situations, be they global economic structures or domestic election procedures or the EU. The proposition that we analyse the EU in terms of justice does not lower the normative standard set by champions of democracy. It corrects it. Justice, no less important than the idea of democracy, explains its normative thrust. Resetting the standard from democracy to justice relaxes the nation-state focus inherent in the language of democracy and opens the way for reflecting on new means to facilitate legitimate governance. It is a critique of methodological nationalism and asks for new solutions to new problems. Whilst the discourse in democratic theory most often focuses on parliamentary competencies and divided government, the discourse on justice centres on the right to justification, and puts primary emphasis on power asymmetries and on overcoming the obstacles to justifiable political outcomes (cf. Forst 2011). Realigning the standard from democracy to justice, and from here to the right to justification, thus implies a shift in analytical emphasis and a readiness to consider an innovative normative terminology.

An EU that gives full effect to the right to justification would look quite different from the EU of today. It would guarantee a high degree of individual freedom and safeguard that any restriction of that freedom is made dependent on good reasons. It would guarantee transparent decision-making procedures by providing permanent public access to all institutions with law-making authority. Neither the European Council nor the Council or the Commission would conduct their deliberations behind closed doors but would have to work under full scrutiny of the media. The practices of blame-shifting and scapegoating on the part of Member State governments would thereby be ended. National parliaments would have the administrative capacities and legal rights to keep their governments under close scrutiny and become active political participants in Brussels. The EU's sleeping beauty, the 'Conférence des organes parlementaires spécialisés dans les affaires de l'Union' (COSAC) would be transformed into an effective instrument for national parliamentary control of the EU's constitutional and legislative processes. Supranational structures would tie individuals, governments, and supranational organizations together in a multi-level structure of discourse in which the legal requirement to justify and provide reasons is codified and can be enforced by both supranational and domestic courts. In this structure, weak states would no longer be negligible participants in a game of the big powers and individuals would be involved not only as unseen subjects of governments. Weak states and affected non-governmental actors would have enforceable rights that would carry them as far as their arguments are good.

Although the argument of this book seems to put primary emphasis on justice and to downplay democracy, it is ultimately oriented at explaining the relationship between national democracy and transnational justice. Legitimacy in the multi-level system of the EU can only be properly understood if it encompasses the domestic and the international level. The normative promise of national democracy to foster self-governance will only survive Europeanization if it is supplemented by an organizational layer that fosters transnational justice. Only if interdependent national democracies are supplemented by a supranational layer of justificatory discourses can we expect nation-states to systematically respect the external effects of their decisions as a relevant factor for domestic decision-making (cf. Joerges 2006). Democracy entails that those who make the rules must be the same as those who must obey the rules. If this standard is to be respected, i.e., if we are not ready to accept the effects of other nation-states' decisions without having had the chance to make our concerns heard in 'their' decision-making processes, and if we are not willing to subject other citizenries to our decisions, then we have to work for a system of collective multi-level governance in which national democracies open themselves to the concerns of foreigners. Otherwise, the external effects of the internal practices of our democracy will impose illegitimate costs on foreigners and vice-versa. Under conditions of interdependence, therefore, transnational justice and national democracy mutually support and necessitate each other.

The EU is already on the right path towards accommodating these ideas. It promotes the cause of justice by providing an effective remedy for horizontal and vertical power asymmetries and for the arbitrariness of untamed anarchy. The constitutionalization of justificatory requirements by means of European law changes the mode of representation from preferences and power to arguments and reasons and thus transforms intergovernmental bargaining into transnational deliberations. It provides safeguards against the impact of vertical power asymmetries on the justificatory discourse and exerts a compliance-pull by increasing the costs of non-compliance to powerful and weak states alike. The EU already possesses the initial elements of such a 'justified structure of justification' (*eine gerechtfertigte Grundstruktur*) (cf. Forst 2007: 270–87). It not only allows for and demands justifications, the EU itself is to some degree the product of a justificatory discourse. Since the Treaty of Maastricht, a growing number of people are demanding the right to vote on new treaty proposals and to actively engage in EU reform. Further steps on the road to European integration have to pass through the bottleneck of an increasingly critical citizenry that demands justification and explanation and does not hesitate to reject proposals if the proffered reasons for their acceptance are not good enough. The Treaties of Amsterdam and Lisbon have strengthened the powers of national parliaments and thus have connected Member States' citizens closer to the European project. There is no doubt that Member States' governments are still the pre-dominant actors in Europe and much remains to be done before the EU can indeed be described as a justified structure of justification. The EU, however, has made significant steps, and although it is by no means perfect, it is no exaggeration to say that the EU has already achieved an approximation of this ideal. The EU is to be lauded for the extent to which it has progressed towards a justified structure of justification and to be criticized for not having reached this goal. The EU is not democratic and probably never will become a democracy. Supranationalism and democracy are established on divergent normative foundations that are hard, and probably impossible, to reconcile. Nevertheless, the EU is a necessary condition for the continued proper functioning of Member States' democracies. Reconstructing this potential of the EU is the aim of this book.

1.2. The EU in global context

The EU is without a doubt the region in the world where denationalization, economic de-bordering, and political internationalization are further developed than anywhere else. After centuries of war, the European nation-states have learnt their lessons and turned the formerly most violent continent into an area of international peace and stability. War among the members of this community is no longer an option. Common norms take on an important function for shaping action. They include the respect for national sovereignty, the rule of law, and human rights. Political relations are conducted cooperatively and by means of arguing and bargaining only. This unique success story is neither isolated from global processes nor is it beyond comparison to any other international organization, however. The arguments set forth in this book are consistent with the assumption that the EU gives expression to a number of trends and processes that can be observed elsewhere as well. In many respects, the EU can be seen as a vanguard of processes that are happening in other international institutions. Just like the United Nations, the International Monetary Fund and the World Trade Organization, it helps nation-states to establish common rules for administering interdependence and to establish collective problem-solving capacity. All of these institutions produce collective goods for their members and add policy capacities whenever the nation-state has lost potency. They are, so to speak, extensions of governance beyond the state. Most international organizations also have striking commonalities with regard to their modus operandi. The United Nations, the WTO, and the EU all give expression to an expanding body of an intergovernmentally agreed upon set of norms that have come to be widely accepted as 'law' (Abbott, Keohane, and Moravcsik 2000). This body of rules is growing daily and reaches ever more deeply into formerly national domains like monetary policy, human rights standards, or the technical details of economic policy. 'Legalization' has become a global process that characterizes not only the EU but also a large number of international organizations.

The state itself has not been left untouched by these processes. Nearly all international organizations are policy-specific with competencies that typically are limited to a narrow range of topics. By offering access to the international production of collective goods, they have stimulated a process of governmental fragmentation. National ministries develop cross-border contacts, often mediated by international bodies. International politics, and even more so European politics, is no longer solely or only predominantly conducted by the heads of governments or their foreign ministers and ambassadors. Rather, the various ministries and their subdivisions establish cross-border working contacts and are de facto responsible for most international rule making. Nor is this process of state fragmentation limited to governments. Courts in different states follow the practices of their colleagues in other jurisdictions, read their judgements, and learn from each other. They have, over time, established a transnational community of judges that regularly meet in conferences, share the same journals, and develop similar approaches to tackling legal issues. Parliaments are also no longer content to formulate and adopt domestic regulations but exchange delegations with each other and try to harmonize their legislative efforts. Private actors have also moved to centre stage in modern international politics. Rating agencies became crucial actors in the financial crisis of 2010–2012, standard-setting bodies harmonize goods and services, internet addresses are administered by a Californian company and private cross-border disputes are often settled with the help of non-state arbitration courts. Where power monopolies once existed, a complex network of power structures is emerging in which the state is only one of many power holders. Power is no longer wielded directly by the state alone but rather in interaction with private actors such that the state is demoted from 'power monopolist to power manager' (Genschel and Zangl 2007: 16). A 'new world order' (Slaughter 2004) of state fragmentation, cross-governmental interaction, and new political complexity makes up the reality of modern 21st century global politics.

All these processes are global in the sense that they have changed the rules of the game for all states that are part of the international community. Today, the regular exercise of state power involves, as a matter of course, being represented in international organizations, respecting binding international legal norms, and avoiding unnecessary affronts to the customs of international relations. The integration of national economies has led to a truly global market in which no state can single-handedly manage its economy, in which currency values are interconnected, and in which the stability of markets depends on global processes. Even an economy such as China's, which was inward-looking for a long time, is today so strongly interwoven with the economies of the United States and Europe that its rate of growth, its balance of payment, and the setting of its exchange rates cannot be understood without considering global factors. Indeed, the current geopolitical context cannot be characterized as anything but some kind of 'post-national constellation' (Habermas 2001).

The EU embodies these processes to a degree unmatched by any other region in the world. Europe is globalization in intensity. Domestic markets for capital and goods are melted into one unified 'common market', and trade in services and the mobility of labour are following suit. The EU also distinguishes itself from all other regions of the world in the extent to which structures of political decision-making and transnational structures of interest articulation have been established. The European Union possesses an institutional structure with a remarkably high concentration of intergovernmental and transgovernmental coordinating bodies, expert committees, and supranational authorities. The degree to which political authority has been transferred to these international and supranational institutions is unparalleled globally. The EU has acquired nearly complete jurisdiction over monetary policy and market regulation from its Member States, and its ever-expanding authority in the areas of environmental politics, foreign and security policy, domestic policy, and judicial politics clearly impinges on Member States' capacity to order their own affairs autonomously. The EU is a palpable manifestation of the limits to national autonomy and the most successful innovation in coordinated governance among nation-states. There exists nowhere else in the world a comparable level of cooperation and policy coordination between nations, and nowhere else has a group of nations agreed to transfer to any international organization a palette of competencies of such depth and breadth. Neither global organizations like the WTO and the United Nations nor other regional organizations such as NAFTA, APEC, or MERCOSUR even come close to replicating the institutional density and the level of authority currently characteristic of the EU. In this sense, the European Union is a unique institution.

Clearly, these innovations do not signal the death of the nation-state. The nation-state is still the only institutional framework in which democracy is firmly institutionalized, and it remains the main locus for citizen allegiance. Only the nation-state collects taxes and engages in extensive redistributive social expenditures. It is the only provider of domestic and international military security and is the main site for making decisions regarding fundamental ethical matters. But even as the nation-state remains a political authority of decisive importance, there also can be no doubt that the basic architecture of politics—and therefore the basic architecture of democracy, too—is being subjected to extensive changes influenced by internationalization and Europeanization. The democratic nation-state, with its characteristic mixture of representation, separation of powers, and checks-and-balances, is increasingly integrating into cross-border multilevel European structures in which new rules apply. To correctly assess political power today we must understand the nation-state as an integral component of larger multilevel systems.

Given the shift in political authority and in light of deep-seated reservations about the democratic bona fides of the newly emerging supranational political architectures, questions regarding the normative foundations and the appropriate institutional arrangements for European and international multilevel systems have become urgent. Should we be content with executive dominance and the primacy of diplomacy, or call for a thorough reform of these organizational forms? Can international organizations be constituted in accordance with the standards of democracy and justice? Which criteria and standards of democracy are to be applied? Can the organizational principles of the nation-state be applied to international organizations, or do we need completely new standards that are better adapted to the international environment? Is there a realistic chance that participation, equality, and public discourse might be nurtured not only within national democracies but also in the relations between states? Or will we have to live with the fact that the new reality of governance beyond the state is incompatible with the ideal of comprehensive democratic governance?

1.3. The structure of the book

This book deals with finding a normatively and empirically convincing answer to these questions for the European Union. The search is undertaken with a procedural theory of justice that claims to be both normatively sound and empirically applicable to the EU. This theory takes individual liberty as its normative backbone and understands governance arrangements as instruments for fostering this value. Its conceptual heart is established on a procedural theory of justice that highlights the individual right to justification, that is, the right of all of us to receive good reasons for any limitations that are imposed on our freedom by political institutions and political actions (cf. Forst 2011). National and supranational political institutions are legitimate to the extent that they promote the right to justification. The EU is understood to be an entity structurally similar to other governance bodies. Just like any other governance arrangement, it must meet the standard of contributing to justificatory practices between power holders and citizens and can be assessed according to the questions of whether and to what extent it complies with this condition. This argument and its implications for an empirical assessment of the EU are developed in this book in five consecutive steps.

After having discussed the major theoretical alternatives to an analysis of the EU as an institutional order of justification, the remainder of the first part of the book introduces and explains the methodology of normative realism. It is a methodology that combines insights from Walzer, Rawls, and Habermas, and connects empirical, theoretical, and normative reflections. It seeks to understand the established structures of the EU and to identify a normative potential inherent in these structures that can be used for meaningfully criticizing its practices.

The second part of the book implements the methodology explained in part one. It argues that the supranational character of the EU should be understood as a structural component of its identity and that it will neither advance towards statehood nor retreat into mere internationalism. Supranationality is employed here as a fixed condition that defines the identity of the EU, just as the identity of the state is defined by its legitimate monopoly of coercion and the international system is defined by the condition of anarchy. The concept of supranationality advanced in this book builds on the distinction introduced by Weiler (1981) between the legal and political dimensions of a polity. It reconstructs its institutional and legal order as a dualism of a hierarchical normative order and a non-hierarchical coercive order. Supranationality, so the argument of chapter three, represents nothing less than a paradigmatic shift in international politics. Supranationality combines elements of the domestic and the international order in a historically new way. It connects the horizontal power distribution characteristic of international politics to a vertically integrated legal order that tames many of the former's negative implications for justified politics. Supranationality thus does not adopt state-like structures but remains a voluntary order constituted by contract among sovereign nation-states. The Member States of the EU have given up their sovereign rights in a limited number of policy areas with the reservation that European law respects their legitimate concerns and constitutional traditions. Thus, compliance of Member States remains ultimately a voluntary act, deliberately repeated on each occasion of implementing European norms. Supranationality does not establish an independent coercive order above the Member States but remains dependent on their voluntary compliance. Supranational structures, then, are neither state nor interstate but are 'among' states. In this, they are indeed *sui generis* (cf. Ipsen 1987: 202).

The specific structural features of supranationality have wide-ranging implications for its legitimacy. Chapter four shows that a majoritarian form of democratic legitimacy is incompatible with the very logic of supranational governance. Most of the important structural elements of supranationality simply fail to harmonize with the essential principles of democracy. European supranationality is built on normative principles that are irreconcilable with the democratic prerequisites of individual political equality, of an encompassing public sphere, and of a broad political problem-solving capacity. European supranationality, in a nutshell, is structurally incompatible with the requirements of democracy.

The third part of the book sets out to establish a normative standard that is more compatible with supranational structures. It departs from the democracy discourse and turns to justice. Although theories of justice occupy a prominent and central position in international political philosophy, they scarcely have been noted in theories of integration or in empirical analyses of international relations. In order to acquaint the non-introduced reader to this literature, chapter five undertakes a tour de force through important currents of the most relevant literature on international justice. Different theories of justice are discussed and criticized with the aim of distilling a set of criteria for a theory of justice that is adequate for a non-utopian normative assessment of the EU.

The right to justification enters the stage in chapter six. It is introduced as a concept of justice that meets the criteria of normative realism. It has both critical bite and the capacity to reconstruct the most central structures, institutions, and practices of the EU. It is explained as a philosophically grounded political standard with universal applicability. The right to justification implies that persons or institutions that restrict our freedom are obliged to explain their reasons for doing so to an independent third party equipped with the competence to assess the merits of the arguments. Restrictions on our freedom are not unjust on principle; they do require, however, an explicit justification for why they should be considered necessary. Every person or institution that restricts our freedom owes us a justification and we have the right to demand it. The right to justification invokes not only a right to defend oneself against the illegitimate infringements on individual freedom by political authorities, but also has an activating component. We have the right not only to insist that others abstain from committing unjustified acts but can also demand political action if action is necessary for ending unjustified practices or conditions that result in freedoms withheld.

Part four of the book reconstructs the legal and political practices of the European Union in the terms of the right to justification. The EU is reconceptualized as a transnational discourse among citizens, institutions, member-state governments, international bureaucracies, and international courts characterized by a duty of rule-setting bodies to provide persuasive arguments justifying actions that impinge upon the freedom enjoyed by other parties. The non-coercive character of supranationalism plays an important role in fostering deliberative practices and thus encouraging the right to justification. Supranationalism is either an inclusionary and deliberative practice or will fail to convince its addressees that compliance is in their best interest. Supranationalism fosters this practice by providing positive incentives to transform bargaining into arguing and thus to positively respond to the demand for deliberative interaction. The beneficial impact of supranationality on political interaction is illustrated by regarding its contribution to softening the structural self-referentiality of democracies, the asymmetric distribution of power among nation-states, and executive dominance in European politics. In all three areas, supranational structures create a new opportunity for justice in that they make argumentative interaction more likely and require justifications of political acts. In the legal regime of supranational structures, political actors must ground their actions on consensual material and procedural norms and couch the legitimacy of their preferences in those terms. The sorting out of preferences inconsistent with shared material and procedural norms serves to discipline political discourse. Indeed, given the fact that national actors know that their preferences will have to be justified on the supranational stage on the basis of collective norms, processes of domestic preference setting are from the outset biased toward those preferences that will meet collective standards. This disciplining effect of supranational structures has major implications for the mode of political representation. Whilst states in international politics represent territory, people, economic power and military prowess, states in a supranational regime represent arguments. Even the biggest state will find it hard to succeed in conflict with the smallest of the Member States if the latter has the power of legally valid arguments and the support of the EU institutions on its side. Supranationalism thus changes the mode of political representation and makes justificatory discourses likely. In order to be compatible with the requirements of a legal community, power must be dressed in the clothes of persuasive arguments and abstain from all actions that fail to comply with the legal standards. The ability of a state to assert itself in European negotiations is no longer a matter of bargaining power only, but rather a matter of who proffers the most persuasive argument.

Deliberative processes of justification are not limited to the EU's horizontal interactions among the Member States but encompass also vertical relations between individuals, governments, and citizens. Affected citizens have a right to hear the rationale underlying governmental and supranational actions and are promised access to legal remedy of unjustified policies. The EU is far from perfect in implementing these ideas. It has institutionalized, however, a number of measures that give expression to the Member States' awareness of their necessity. The recent strengthening of the role of national parliaments in the EU, the European Ombudsman, and the European Citizenship Initiative are innovations in European governance that clearly distinguish the EU from all other international organizations. They place the EU in a political structure that is closely tied to domestic democratic procedures and significantly reduce its intergovernmental bias. Thus, supranational governance is unlike international governance, for it does not take place in a democratic vacuum with an intergovernmentally co-opted 'civil society'. It becomes rather a component part of the national democratic discourse. The ability of societies to foster transnational justice through the establishment of discourses centred upon law and justification, indeed, becomes a central precondition for the fulfilment of democracy's promise at the national level.

Part five of the book moves beyond reconstructing the EU in the terms of the right to justification and addresses the question of whether the EU is not only true to the structure of justification, but whether it also complies with the requirements of a *justified structure of justification*. Full compliance to the ambitious normative requirements of the right to justification commands that the structures of justification are themselves the product of justificatory practices. They must be subjected to contestation and critique, be questioned and challenged, and be always only temporarily affirmed without closing the option of new contestation. A justified structure of justification must be responsive to the changing preferences and normative dispositions of its societal principals. This discussion sheds a critical light on EU practices of constitutional development and highlights some of its inherent strengths and continuing weaknesses. It is shown that the EU has the potential to achieve a justified political structure but that this potential is still limited by the dominance of intergovernmental bargaining and the insufficient integration of national parliaments into the constitutional process. Chapter eight takes this deficiency as a starting point and inquires into the adequate role of national parliaments in the European political process. How can they be empowered and made constructive actors in the European multilevel system? The chapter argues that national parliaments could fulfil a most useful function if they were given a more active role in the European constitutional process. Such a role could be realized if the 'Conférence des organes parlementaires spécialisés dans les affaires de l'Union' (COSAC) were transformed into an Interparliamentary Constitutional Assembly (ICA) that would act as a transmission belt between member-state citizens and the European level. It should have the competence to review all practices and competencies of the EU, to propose amendments to the Treaty or any other legal documents of the EU. The new ICA would safeguard that the EU's constitutional development reflects not only governmental preferences but be, through its members, in permanent close contact with the national parliaments and thus the democratic sovereign of the respective Member States. Turning COSAC into an ICA would be an important institutional reform and would help to justify European structures of justification. These structures would no longer be unduly shielded from critical scrutiny by the requirement of intergovernmental unanimity but become subject to permanent critique and eventual reform.

Chapter nine takes a closer look at the role of the EU in world politics and asks whether, and to what extent, the EU's external actions live up to the idea of a justificatory discourse. The idea of the EU as 'empire' is introduced and further developed by distinguishing between benevolent and ruthless forms of imperialism. After reviewing a number of foreign policy practices, it is shown that the EU's readiness to apply justificatory practices in foreign policy is far less developed than in domestic policy. For living up to its ambition of being a non-imperial empire, it should take its external effects more seriously and make them an integral component of all future draft legislation.

The final chapter summarizes the argument and formulates a cautiously optimistic view of the future of justified politics beyond the nation-state. The optimistic half of the argument is that supranational structures provide, indeed probably for the first time in history, a realistic chance of justified politics outside of the structures of the democratic nation-state. This is not mere wishful thinking; it is well founded theoretically and can be observed in the empirical reality of supranational structures as they exist today. Supranational law is at work in the decision-making procedures of the EU, directing political discourses into a framework in which justification is required and facilitated. This framework represents an important accomplishment, for it is a basis upon which a future extension of the practical scope of the right to justification can be established.

The cautious half of the argument has two elements. The first element is the caveat that it is no accident that supranational structures exist primarily in economic policy. The willingness to accept the restrictions of justificatory discourses presumably arises only under conditions of interdependence. Powerful rational actors will only accept the bounds of law if they expect a beneficial pay-off. Such advantages are apparent whenever it can be anticipated that optimal outcomes can be reached only through coordinated, collective action. Only under these restrictive conditions is it rational for the powerful state to comply with the same rules as they apply to weaker actors. In this manner, the hand of force is gloved with self-restraint and a political space for justice is created. The second element of the cautious side of the argument is that the hope for greater justice depends on using a concept of justice that is limited to procedural matters. More ambitious concepts of justice seldom find general acceptance in a world characterized by normative heterogeneity. Generally acceptable, however, is the argument that political rules are only legitimate if good reasons justifying the limits they place on freedom can be produced if demanded. These kinds of rules emerge in political processes that set governments, non-governmental organizations, and the wider public into a pattern of interaction with outcomes that are determined not by power asymmetries but by the better argument. This vision is realistic, not utopian. It does not presuppose altruistic orientations, it is not blind to real-world power asymmetries, and it does not promise heaven on earth. It is a vision that accepts the rational self-interest of political actors as a given and claims that weak and strong actors alike have a rational interest in adhering to political order that promises to combine national democracy, supranational justice, and the capacity to produce collective goods that even the most powerful individual nation-state cannot attain autonomously.

2

Normative Realism

The literature on the European Union is full of theories for describing, analysing, and criticizing the EU (cf. Rosamond 2000; Wiener and Diez 2005; Neyer and Wiener 2011). Broadly we can distinguish three types of theories that deal with the EU. A first set of theories comprises normative reflections and employs general moral or ethical principles for criticizing the practice of politics. Normative theories are often either deliberately non-empirical (cf. Schmalz-Bruns 2007), or they use empirical insights only for illustrating normative concerns (cf. Bohman 2005) and for demonstrating that they find some resonance in practice (Morgan 2005; Dryzek 2006). Normative theories are strong in sketching ideal worlds and in motivating us to reflect about alternatives to the practices of politics. Normative reflections function as an important corrective to non-reflected affirmations of reality and safeguard against an uncritical acceptance of the world as we see it. The major shortcoming of purely normative approaches, however, is a direct outcome of their strengths. By deducing reform proposals from normative ideals, they often remain far removed from the actual practices and everyday experiences of the people, have little concern for the practicability of their proposals, and thus easily tend to remain politically irrelevant. They simply do not resonate with reality. What do we do, for example, with the suggestion that a global democracy is desirable if powerful states continue to refuse to relinquish to the supranational level their monopoly of coercion or their sole authority to tax and spend? We can, of course, insist on the uprightness of our normative intuition and blame the big powers for ignoring our normative insights. This laudable position cannot be criticized on any morally sound grounds. It is, however, rather irrelevant from a political perspective. If politics is the art of the possible ('*die Kunst des Möglichen*') and if political science has the ambition to contribute not only to our knowledge about the world but also to its improvement, then we have good reasons to construct normative ideas that have a firm foundation in the practices and structures of politics.

On the opposite side of the range of approaches to reflecting about the EU (or the political world in general) we find the empirical strategies. Empirically oriented work either explains political practices or sheds light on aspects that have been neglected or overlooked so far in the literature. They are very important for helping us to understand politics and to identify its structural elements. In European studies, empirical approaches have, for example, underscored the importance of intergovernmental bargaining (Moravcsik 1998) and of the multi-level character of the EU (Hooghe and Marks 2001). They have pointed to the ubiquity of informal networks (Elgström and Jönsson 2009) and have highlighted the constitutional asymmetry of the EU's institutional set-up (Scharpf 2009). Empirical approaches have shown that EU policy-making is not only about bargaining but strongly influenced by arguing and deliberation (Lewis 2005; Puetter 2012). Empirical approaches, however, have little added value if they are not somehow inspired by normative reflection. How do we know whether new empirical insights are relevant if they do not refer to categories that have some normative relevance? Understanding the constitutional asymmetry of the EU, for example, only becomes relevant if we attribute some importance to social policy and have a normatively based concept of a fair distribution of wealth. Likewise, understanding the empirical relevance of informal networks and of policy deliberation only becomes relevant if we share a concern for issues such as accountability or legitimacy. Empirical approaches build on normative reflections and have little value to add if not rooted in categories of moral significance. Conversely, sound normative approaches that aspire to political relevance are well advised to ensure that their standards are not utopian in the sense that they demand impossible changes.

2.1. The major contenders

Some of the most interesting contributions to the literature on the European Union are established on the insight that the world of norms and the world of facts must be in close nexus for the making of relevant argument. They have provided generations of researchers with a theoretical framework for both normative and empirical analyses and have served as focal points for much of the scientific debate.

2.1.1. *Federalism*

Federalism is a prime candidate for illustrating the close nexus between norms and facts in political theory. As a political theory, it always has been and still is a major tool for understanding and justifying the EU. Federalism entered the debate on the EU's constitutional architecture already in the 1950s and ever since has been a recurring theme in constitutional reflections (cf. Burgess 2000). The 'federal vision' (Nicolaides and Howse 2001) tries to strike a balance between offering citizens central institutional sites for deliberating and deciding on common rules without, however, merging Europe's political and cultural plurality into a unified entity. As an approach to politics, it is critical of any concentration of power. It aims at the dispersal of power across multiple levels and territorially divided units. Recent formulations of the federal vision emphasize the EU's character as a 'polity of polities' (Bohman 2005), justify it as a 'demoi-cracy' (Müller 2011), and describe it as 'federalism without a federal state' (Weiler 2000). Federalist thinking, obviously, is neither purely normative nor purely empirical but includes strong elements of both. On a normative level, advocates of demoi-cracy argue that '(w)ithin the Union, Others are recognized as such, rather than being assimilated (or worse); and yet "the Others" are engaged with, via policy cooperation, mutual learning and even legislating in common' (Müller 2011: 197). The European demos is praised as a 'People of mutually respectful Others' (Müller 2011: 188) who consciously recognize each other and who actively seek to preserve their differences over time. The EU is understood as the embodiment of the principle of 'constitutional tolerance' and the European system of rule is applauded for not relying on command and control but on an 'invitation to obey' (Weiler 2000). Although much of this sounds highly normative, it is far from empirically uninformed. The principle of mutual recognition is the normative cornerstone of the EU's market-shaping practices and can be well observed in its everyday legislative output. It is the legal manifestation of the moral idea of tolerance and respect for the ways that others have chosen to live.

Federalism and its recent re-formulations, however, stand in uneasy relationship with a number of structural conditions of the EU. The limited common policy-making capacities of the EU and its complete lack of coercive capacities make it look more like a confederation than a proper federation. Nor does the policy-driven integration of Member States follow the federal logic of a symmetrical territorial integration. The EU consists of a variety of divergent government structures, each of which empowers different authors and obligates different addressees. The European monetary system has been adopted by only seventeen Member States and excludes heavyweights like the United Kingdom and Poland. The European foreign and security policy is conducted by all ten new Member States plus most (but not all) old Member States. Denmark has been granted an opt-out. Turkey is linked to the EU by an Association Agreement; Croatia, Macedonia, Montenegro, Serbia, and Bosnia Herzegovina by Stabilization and Association Agreements; and Norway and Iceland cooperate closely with the EU on the terms of the European Economic

Area (EEA) (cf. Lavenex 2011). The Schengen Agreements created a political space that was entirely separate from EU structures until the 1997 Amsterdam Treaty, which incorporated them into European Union law. The United Kingdom and Ireland, however, have been granted the right to opt out of the framework, and Bulgaria and Romania have been denied access to it. The EU has no difficulties, however, accepting the non-EU members of Switzerland, Norway, and Iceland into provisions on the free movement of people. The common market policy, furthermore, covers not only all European Member States but stretches in fact into the EU's neighbourhood policy (ENP) and thus establishes EU rules outside of EU borders (Zielonka 2006).

These illustrations show that the EU's mode of integration structurally violates the basic principle of federalism that all policies formulated at the central level apply to all of its territories. No federation in the world would allow, for example, an opt-out of foreign or monetary policy. The EU's constitutional structure looks, in fact, much more like an onion (De Neve 2007: 507) or, in terms familiar to political science, like an empire (Beck and Grande 2011) than a federation. Layered spheres of participation, inclusion and unevenly distributed influence are the principles according to which European governance is ordered. These principles can be observed in the EU's de facto discrimination between different classes or degrees of membership. There are first-class members like Germany, the Netherlands, or Austria, with full legal rights in all aspects of European governance. Others, such as Switzerland, Norway, and Iceland, are only second-class members with the right to consume much of the benefits of European integration (e.g. the common market) but without the right to fully participate in decision-making. Third-class members like Turkey and other of the EU's neighbours to the east and the south, finally, are loosely associated with the EU but have limited access to its market and no rights to participate in decision-making.

2.1.2. *Statism*

Whereas federalists tend to celebrate the diversity of nation-states in Europe, statists aim at overcoming it and analyse the EU as a nation-state in *statu nascendi*. The integration project is interpreted as the logical next step in the historical expansion of democracy from the nation-state to a postnational constellation (Habermas 2011). From this perspective, greater integration is a gain not only for the European Union but indeed for democracy itself. Most statists are well aware that national parliaments are successively losing their competencies and that democratic institutions at the nation-state level are becoming increasingly irrelevant. Yet, that insight is either ignored or discounted as a necessary cost that must be accepted for the sake of continuing integration. Many German political observers from Jürgen Habermas to Joschka Fischer call for the establishment of a 'United States of Europe' (Fischer 2010). The European Union is seen as a waypoint on the road to a new European nation-state with a single parliament, federal instead of intergovernmental institutions, and a single foreign policy apparatus in command of a European military force. Supranational law is attributed with a salutary and civilizing effect, serving to promote democratic political order and the rule of law above the nation-state level (Habermas 2011). The EU is viewed as a necessary and legitimate step in the realization of the 'politically organized global society'. To call this process of ever-closer union into question is deemed beyond the pale for reasonable individuals. Indeed, the refusal of Member States to give up their democratically controlled authority over the integration project is compared to the rejection of democratic reforms by the now defunct Mubarrak regime, and it elicits warnings of dramatically negative outcomes for European politics (Brunkhorst 2007: 16). Most statists are well aware that increased integration means sacrificing democratic accountability, at least in the short- to medium-term. European governance is dominated by executive actors, and the European Parliament has little to say in policy areas beyond market regulation. National parliaments—still the central strongholds of democracy in Europe—are but onlookers in the processes of European integration. Truly convincing arguments have yet to be presented on how to fix these congenital democratic deficits of the EU. In many ways, we seem to be headed in the opposite direction, as the budgetary authority of national parliaments, truly a central pillar of parliamentary authority and perhaps the most fundamental expression of popular sovereignty, is being threatened by plans to stabilize the Euro. For many supporters of integration, a loss of domestic parliamentary budgeting authority in EU Member States is taken as an unfortunate but necessary form of collateral damage in the battle to save the Euro, not as a fundamental loss for democracy. Indeed, when presented with a choice between strong domestic institutions of democracy and European integration, advocates of the European super-state often decide against democracy and for *la raison d'État* (Morgan 2005).

Statism is an approach to analysing the EU that is clearly deficient in both normative and empirical terms. First of all, whilst European integration does indisputably make a contribution to international peace and economic wealth, these effects are not in themselves sufficient reason for justifying the EU. A fully convincing justification must employ democratic standards and relate the EU's legitimacy to more than its policy output. It is misleading to argue, with Habermas (2011), that because governance capacity is requisite for good democratic government, building additional governance capacity at the European level is equivalent to building democracy. Governance capacity is never good in-and-of itself; it is only desirable when subsumed under democratic control and firmly in the hands of the sovereign people. Democracy must precede state power rather than the other way around. A second crucial problem of the statists' position is the nearly complete lack of popular support for the idea of a single European government. The idea of merging into a fully integrated Europe lacks any significant appeal today in countries as crucial for the integration process as the United Kingdom, France, or Poland. The intergovernmental structures of the EU are seen by most Member States not as a problematic hindrance to European governance capacity but rather as a necessary protection of their democratic autonomy. The idea of a politically unified Europe is so clearly divorced from political and social reality that it has, at best, only philosophical relevance. As a project of political theory, the European super-state has in fact failed.

A serious empirical misunderstanding also underlies the idea of a European state. The EU is often understood, falsely, as a project that covers the full range of Member States' competencies. Yet, the processes of European integration always have been limited to specific policy areas and will remain so for the foreseeable future. It is not states that are integrating but only specific domestic policy areas. The neo-functionalist process of quasi-automatic spillover occurs only in market policy; it cannot be found in the fields of culture, taxation, domestic and foreign security, or social welfare. Similarly, we see no portent of the emergence of a single European public discourse above and beyond what are still quite separate national discussions of European politics (Vetters, Jentges, and Trenz 2009; Risse 2010). The essential core of the EU is now, just as it ever was, an intergovernmental and policy-specific regime that is centred on market integration. This regime is characterized by intentional decisions and a deep concern for the autonomy of democratic decision-making in the Member States. Constitutional tolerance, mutual respect for national regulatory traditions and political cultures, and constructive cooperation are its central organizational principles, not standardization and unification. In sum, the EU is not like a state, nor is it likely to become one. It has neither an effective monopoly over the legitimate means of coercion nor does it have a clearly defined centre of authority. 'It is a polity without coherent demos, a power without identifiable purpose, a geopolitical entity without defined territorial limits' (Zielonka 2008: 473–4). The idea of Europe as a super-state, even if only a nascent one, is thus fundamentally flawed. The concept of the state is inadequate for understanding the EU: 'To continue to use it is like the futile attempt to open a door with the wrong key' (Beck and Grande 2011: 23).

2.1.3. Technocratism

A third influential approach to understanding and justifying the EU is technocratism (Featherstone 1994; Wallace and Smith 1995). It is an approach that figured prominently already in the founding period of the EU. Jean Monnet expected the integration process to proceed in pragmatic bits and pieces, by piecemeal technical steps, and driven by a logic of bureaucratic integration. His approach to integration, the famous 'Monnet method', was inspired by functionalism and the suggestion that spill-over processes in areas of low politics should lead over time to an ever growing number of integrated policy areas (Haas 1964). Democratic politics and parliamentary involvement should have no prominent role but be guided by technical deliberations, bureaucratic expertise, and an understanding of politics as pragmatic problem-solving. Although pragmatism and the Monnet method have come under attack recently for their allegedly non-democratic character, they still provide an important signpost in the debate on how to constitutionalize the EU.

The most prominent recent application of technocratism can be found in the work of Giandomenico Majone (2005). According to Majone, the EU is best understood and justified as an independent regulatory agency that serves as a 'fourth branch of government'. Its function and purpose is not to succeed the nation-state as the most important locus of policy-making, but to complement it with supranational institutions that allow technical deliberations undisturbed by the partisan disputes of majoritarian politics. The main task of the EU is to produce technically sophisticated problem-solving in politically non-salient areas of cross-border relevance such as product and process regulation (Majone 1998). Redistributive policies and all politically salient issues that involve fundamental normative questions should remain the prerogative of Member States. The institutional structure that Majone has in mind has inspired the recent wave of newly established regulatory agencies in the EU. They are designed to be as independent as possible from majoritarian politics and to be supervised by the ECJ rather than the European Parliament. Parliamentary involvement is to be limited to establishing standard-setting agencies and to codetermining their functional tasks. Parliaments are to refrain from getting involved in the everyday work of setting and changing technical standards. According to Majone, redistributive policies have no adequate place in the European order. They are a type of policy that has direct effects on private property and thus individual liberty. Redistributive policies thus demand full democratic legitimation and should be deliberated and decided upon by national parliaments alone.

The Majonean interpretation of the EU as an independent regulatory agency has important analytical strengths. Understanding the supranational layer of European governance as a corrective to the functional limitations of its Member States helps to safeguard against misinterpreting the EU as successor of the nation-state. It is also useful for explaining the limited role of the EP in European politics and the flourishing of European regulatory agencies (Egeberg and Trondal 2011). The website of the EU today lists a total of twenty-four regulatory 'policy agencies' that organize a wide range of regulatory tasks. Among all of them are lightly functionally specific such as the Agency for the Cooperation of Energy Regulators (ACER), the European Institute for Gender Equality (EIGE), and the European Railway Agency (ERA).

The Majonean suggestion is not without problems, however. Many issues that look technical at first sight in fact involve significant ethical and redistributive issues. Setting standards very often implies an asymmetrical distribution of costs and benefits. Whilst some benefit when their standards are 'Europeanized', others have to adapt their production processes and products and bear the ensuing costs. Standard setting also often necessitates an answer to the political question of how much safety we want and what price we are willing to pay for it. Ethical questions also figure prominently in regulatory decision-making. Should regulators apply the precautionary principle or the principle of scientific evidence? Are genetically modified organisms to be accepted or are there pressing normative concerns that should prohibit their production categorically? What about the size of cages for chickens and the conditions of legitimate animal experiments? None of these questions are simply technical matters for 'experts'. The suggestion of constitutionalizing the EU as a collection of independent expert deliberations is hard to harmonize with the democratic idea of politics as being open to permanent public contestation and as being structured by parliamentary rule. The Majonean idea is also in open contrast to the fact that the EU already today has a number of competencies in home and justice policy, that it has growing influence on public finances, on domestic expenditure, and on the foreign and security policies of its Member States. All of these issues are of central importance to democratic governance and cannot be handed over to politically unaccountable experts without depriving democracy of much of its substance.

2.2. The methodology of normative realism

Federalism, statism, and technocratism are all equally strong on one point: they combine explanatory power with normative ambition. All three theories derive much of their central status in the debate from their dual relevance for normative and empirical analyses. They are more than only empirical or normative approaches but are better understood as complex political theories that propose a certain meaning to the integration project and explain some of its important empirical features. Although strong in ambition, all three of them fall short due either to empirical irrelevance or to overly modest normative aspirations.

In the following chapters, this book will submit an alternative political theory that combines the strengths of the three theories while avoiding their shortcomings. Before starting, it will be helpful to reflect on some important methodological issues that arise when combining normative and positive theory. Mainstream social science methodology strictly separates normative and positive statements in order to safeguard against interference of norms with facts or vice versa (King, Keohane, and Verba 1994). It is often argued that blurring the line would lead to a distortion of reality by infusing the subjective normative orientations of the observer into the collection of data. The following section develops an approach to analysing politics that deliberately violates this recommendation and seeks explicitly to combine normative reflection and empirical analysis. It is built on the insight that norms and facts are equally important parts of social and political reality and that both must find their place in a convincing political theory. The approach claims to be both realistic in its normative claims and bold in its ambitions. It takes great caution to be clear at any step of its argument of the status of its propositions and to avoid any un-reflected transcending of the distinction between normative critique and empirical analysis. Such a 'normative realism' is critical not only of empirically naive idealism but also of affirmative empiricism. It assumes that all empirical observations reflect normative decisions about what is important and what not, and that, intentionally or not, all normative statements reflect a certain understanding of the empirical facts. The choice for the normative realist therefore is not between normative and empirical theories, but between theories with a different composition of normative and empirical claims. Positive theories must take norms seriously and normative theories need a proper assessment of the empirical facts. Normative realism thus rejects the claim that researchers must make a clear-cut decision of whether they want to engage in normative reflection or in empirical analysis. Sound political analysis is not either normative or empirical but integrates both ways of reflection. Its empirical analysis should be normatively reflected and its normative propositions should be supported by an in-depth analysis of real-world institutions. It should promote a certain conception of how the world ought to be and demonstrate the non-utopian character of this idea by providing evidence for its practicability.

Identifying the adequate methodological steps for implementing these insights is not easy, however. A prominent way of combining normative reflection and empirical analysis is so-called 'immanent' social critique. Walzer (1983a, cf. also Sabia 2010), for example, holds that the proper way of doing normatively inspired social theory 'is to interpret to one's fellow citizens the world of meaning that we share' (1983a: xiv). In his view, the members of a political community share 'sensibilities and intuitions' about the justice and injustice of various patterns of distribution (Walzer, 1983a: 28). The task of the normative political scientist is to empirically elaborate these sensibilities and intuitions, thus preparing the ground for a potentially powerful critique of reality. This critique can help in explicating to the people what they actually hold to be valid, and in exposing the hypocrisy and divergence between the thoughts and actions of the people. Although helpful as a starter for informing the methodology of a normatively realistic argument, Walzer's approach to normative theory is not without its deficiencies. An initial problem is its affirmative use of empirical analysis. Walzer does not provide any criteria for assessing whether the ideas and beliefs of people are indeed normatively sound, but instead uncritically accepts them as part of the structure of ordinary morality. He accordingly reconstructs a morality without offering criteria for assessing its normative validity. This becomes not only problematic in cases in which societies hold moral ideas which strongly violate basic human rights, but also in cases of societies which are characterized by a number of contending moralities and strongly diverging views about proper behaviour. In modern societies, and even more so in the multinational EU, it is often impossible to identify a singularly valid morality among the large number of differing normative conceptions. Walzer readily admits this problem. He argues that if 'radically different cultural traditions' offer competing standards, 'then it might be (morally) necessary to work out a political accommodation' (Walzer, 1983b: 44). It is unclear, however, how that should be done in a morally convincing way, if political accommodation is defined per se to be beyond morality. In short, Walzer's suggestion is helpful for criticizing the difference between a given idea and a real-world practice, but is unable to give a convincing assessment of whether this difference is a normative problem or not.

A similarly prominent suggestion is the concept of a 'reflective equilibrium' between theoretically founded moral principles and an empirical assessment of the normative dispositions held by an individual or a public at large (Rawls 1999a). The concept promises to strike a fair balance between empirical insights and normative reflection by putting equal emphasis on moral principles and pragmatic judgements: 'By going back and forth, sometimes altering the conditions of the contractual circumstances, at others withdrawing our judgments and conforming them to principle, I assume that eventually we shall find a description of the initial situation that both expresses reasonable conditions and yields principles which match our considered judgments duly pruned and adjusted' (Rawls 1999a: 18). As opposed to the priority Walzer gives to facts, the notion of a reflective equilibrium gives no prima facie supremacy to one or the other. A reflective equilibrium should identify those norms that result from challenging existing beliefs by arguments and implications that derive from the panoply of developed positions in moral and political philosophy (Rawls 1999a: 43). A reflective equilibrium is thus a cognitive disposition that we arrive at by asking for a permanent weighing of abstract principles with considered judgements. The idea of a reflective equilibrium has the great strength of taking norms and facts equally seriously and of being in compliance with the general advice of normative realism. It is not without problems, however. A normative theory that builds on initial judgements is easily discredited because many of our beliefs are just the result of historical accident and bias. We today have reasons for our moral convictions that are no less firmly established than those that we held yesterday or even a hundred years ago. They do, nevertheless, often differ quite substantially with regard, for example, to gay marriage or gender equality. So, how (and under what conditions) can we trust our considered opinions? In addition, it is very difficult to translate the concept into a specific methodology and to identify the steps to be taken in the process of weighing principles and judgements. According to Daniels (2011: 2), we can arrive at a reflective equilibrium 'by working back and forth among our intuitions about particular instances or cases, the principles or rules that we believe govern them, and the theoretical considerations that we believe bear on accepting these considered judgments principles, or rules, revising any of these elements wherever necessary in order to achieve an acceptable coherence among them'. Although the suggestion of working back and forth makes good sense for processes of intellectual reflection, it is far from obvious how this could be translated into a non-arbitrary process of doing practical research. If intuitions and principles are in conflict, how do we know where to draw the adequate balance? How do we know whom to follow if none of the two can claim ontological superiority?

A third way of combining normative reflection and empirical analysis is the method of rational reconstruction. It is a method that takes much inspiration from the work of Habermas and his critique of quasi-objective scientism on the one hand, and radical subjective hermeneutics on the other (Habermas 1983, Pedersen 2008). The method of rational reconstruction is centred on the assumption that proper science should seek to combine interpretative and explanatory elements and must be descriptive and normative simultaneously. Truth is not to be found in any one of these approaches alone nor in any single theory. More promising for conducting meaningful research is to engage different theories and methods with each other and to distil valid findings from their discussion with each other. An important element of the method is the distinction between explicit and implicit (or tacit) knowledge (cf. Polanyi 1966). Habermas argues that people often interact on the basis of a tacit knowledge, i.e. knowledge they do not know they have. They possess tacit knowledge, for example, of grammatical rules and apply them to their speech without being aware that they are doing so. Likewise, they use language not only for expressing wishes and preferences but also as a medium for facilitating social agreement (Verständigung) without, again, always being aware of this. They are, to put it in the famous words of Hegel, subject to the 'List der Vernunft' (artfulness of reason) that forces them to act according to a logic that is beyond their conscious control. An important task of science is to make this tacit knowledge explicit and thus to uncover the hidden normative content inherent in political and social practices.

The method of rational reconstruction combines a number of strengths that are important to the endeavour of this book. It allows the establishment of an argument that accepts normative reflection and empirical analysis as equally valid resources of knowledge and to engage both in a constructive discourse. The method also fits neatly onto the Rawlsian notion of a reflective equilibrium by inviting us to work back and forth between empirical analysis and normative reflection. Third, it connects well with the insight of Walzer that proper normative science should not be completely distanced from its object of observation but that it should take the historical experiences and lessons learned inherent in social and political practice seriously. Finally, but no less importantly, it helps to structure the development of the book's argument. Transposing the method of rational reconstruction into a research design leads us to unveil the deep normative structures of the EU and to explain their relevance for the practice of politics. It holds that the EU's structures have a normative content that guide political actors' decisions without them necessarily being aware of it. Rational reconstruction aims at uncovering this implicit knowledge and explaining it as the modus operandi of the EU. The argument to be developed makes explicit that political actors in the EU are competent to engage in justificatory discourses and to facilitate the necessary institutional prerequisites for these discourses. They do so because they have learned the historical lesson that simple international bargaining leads to a suboptimal production of public goods such as peace and prosperity, and that a well-functioning European public order is dependent on processes of mutual accommodation, inclusive policy deliberation, and policy outcomes above the lowest common denominator.

This argument will be developed in this book by applying a five-fold procedure that works back and forth between empirical analysis and normative reflection (Figure 2.1). It starts by laying the empirical groundwork for its normative analysis by describing the EU as a supranational entity that rests on a firmly established dual order. In a second step, the book turns to normative analysis and develops a standard for assessing the EU's legitimacy that is compatible with the EU's dualism and that accepts this structure as a given, fixed identity. From here, the book switches back to empirical analysis and uses

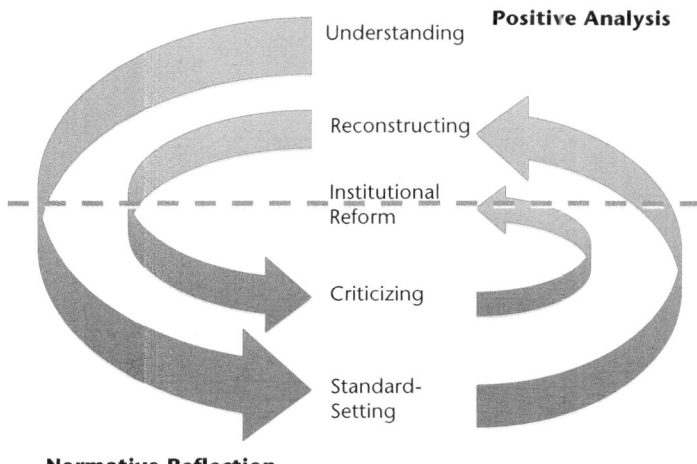

Figure 2.1. The Methodology of Normative Realism

normative standards for reconstructing the EU's institutional order and for reconstructing the tacit knowledge inherent in the EU's regulatory structure and its political practices. The fourth step of the argument employs the critical force of the argument by showing where and how the EU falls short in terms of living up to these standards and what should be done about it.

Part II
Understanding the EU

3

The Nature of the Beast

What kind of political animal is the EU? Is it always different, depending on which policy and point in time we analyse? Or can we identify certain elements that are fixed over time and that define its identity? Some argue that the EU is a 'moving target' that is continually changing and adapting to new challenges and to changing Member States' preferences. Are they correct in asserting that the EU should thus be understood as a political project rather than a specific polity? Or are those correct who claim to have identified some basic structures that survive the ups and downs of the integration project? It is firmly grounded knowledge in the literature that supranationality is structurally different from both a state and an international organization. It is described as being 'more than a regime' but 'less than a state' (Wallace 1983: 510–11). But what does that mean in positive terms? Is there any meaningful term that can capture the essence of the EU as a legally integrated not-state polity?

This chapter establishes an important empirical assumption for the remainder of the book, arguing that supranationality is a third type of political order structurally different from both states and international organizations. It has identifiable defining characteristics that set it apart categorically from its alternatives. These defining characteristics lie in its unique dualistic character, i.e. in the combination of a vertical legal order with a horizontal political order. It is true that this structure has only emerged over time and that it can, of course, change in the future, too. Vertical legal integration, the precedence of European law over national law and the direct effect of European directives was not written into the Treaties of Rome. They evolved over time and had to be accepted by the Member States and national courts (Alter 2001). Nonetheless, since the landmark European Court of Justice (ECJ) decisions of the 1960s, already fifty years old, vertical legal integration is a persistent condition of the EU. It also goes without saying that the future is uncertain and that the further ahead in time our objects of speculation are, the less certain we can be about the correctness of our propositions. If the European legal order retreats into a set of merely horizontal norms without supremacy or direct effect, or if Member States agree to delegate their competences unconditionally and equip the EU with the power to enforce European law by means of coercion, then the idea of the EU as a dualistic order would lose its empirical foundation. From all we know today, however, nothing like this is probable. Pooling instead of delegation has been the primary mode of integration in the EU since its very beginning and little has changed since then. We see neither significant steps towards the establishment of centralized coercive capacities, nor is there any sign of efforts to reduce the competencies of the Commission and the ECJ. Quite on the contrary, the structures of the EU are somehow in balance between what is practically useful and what is politically compatible with the democratic constitution of its constituent units, the Member States.

3.1. Reductionist theories of supranationalism

It is somehow surprising that the dual character of the EU is overlooked by the two most prominent political science approaches to understanding supranationality. Neofunctionalism and intergovernmentalism suggest highly reductionist images of the EU that highlight only one of the two pillars of the EU's institutional order while downplaying the other. Neofunctionalism, to start with, defines supranational integration as 'the process whereby political actors in several distinct national settings are persuaded to shift their loyalties, expectations and political activities toward a new centre, whose institutions possess or demand jurisdiction over the pre-existing national states' (Haas 1958: 16). Integration is conceptualized here as an ongoing political and social process leading to a new political structure extending beyond state borders and eventually replacing the nation states as the most important institutional site for the conduct of politics. The driving forces of this process are so-called spill-over processes (1958: 283) that emanate from the 'hiding hand' (Haas 1968: xiv) of functional imperatives and are implemented by the technical rationality of a bureaucratic elite. Haas' definition of supranational integration has provided a central point of reference in the debate on the nature of the EU for many decades. Its strength is that it combines procedural and structural aspects of supranational integration. It combines an emphasis on change with a specification of the telos of change. It also implies no contra-factual supranational state-building but is very much in line with reality by referring only to the establishment of a legal authority. More problematic is Haas' suggestion of an automatically continuing process of integration. It is an idea that is hard to reconcile with the insight that cost-benefit calculations, deliberate decision-making, and critical public scrutiny of policy-making are integral parts of politics. It has likewise little openness for the modern democratic idea that public policy-making should be accompanied by and integrated in a vivid public space. Neofunctionalism breathes much of the post-war spirit that saw international politics as a political realm that is (and should be) shielded from democratic control and participation.

Liberal intergovernmentalism is an approach that is diametrically opposed to neofunctionalism. It is established on the assumption that the EU was made by, with, and for governments. According to its leading proponents, the European treaties are best understood as not reflecting a functional logic but rather as the outcome of the rational preferences of the Member State governments. The EU is, first of all, oriented toward strengthening Member States' governments by providing them with institutions that are detached from domestic scrutiny and allowing them to pursue policies that would be hard or even impossible to realize in the domestic arena (Wolf 1999). The so-called democratic deficit is thus not an unintended defect of the EU, but rather an integral part of its *raison d´etre*. A second important purpose of the EU is to make intergovernmental agreements more credible (Moravcsik 1998). Democratic governments are not independent policy-makers but are controlled by the national media and the parliament. They may be voted out of office and change their policies as a result of new political orientations. Both factors militate against the long-term credibility of international commitments and have served in the past as a hindrance to long-term cooperation. It was only by tying themselves to the mast of supranational law and by setting up common institutions for monitoring and dispute-settlement that the Member States were able to add the necessary credibility to their contracts for making European integration possible.

It is clear that intergovernmentalism does not accept supranational institutions as autonomous actors. They are understood as agents of their principles, the Member States, with very limited discretionary power (Pollack 1997). International institutions are established and maintained by governments only if and when they promise to produce a positive return on investment, i.e. if and when the costs of additional discipline to comply with international law are outweighed by its benefit in terms of domestic autonomy and more reliable cooperation. Governments have thus not become weaker in the process of European integration. They are still firmly in the driver's seat of the process.

Intergovernmentalism serves as a healthy balance to neofunctional technocratism. It is an approach that is not any less reductionist than neofunctionalism, however. Whilst neofunctionalism neglects politics, liberal intergovernmentalism has no room to account for 'integration through law' (Cappelletti, Seccombe, and Weiler 1985). It overlooks the problem that to conduct policies in the language of law implies that Member States accept the discipline imposed by law. It necessitates switching from bargaining to legal reasoning, and thus engaging in a mode of interaction that shields much policy content from political interventions. At the same time, it opens the rule-making process to judicial activism (Burley and Mattli 1993). Courts do not merely arbitrate among competing governmental claims and are not confined to explaining the law. By applying general norms to specific cases, they add new elements to the legal order and sometimes change it quite substantially. Especially the ECJ has won a reputation in the past for teleologically applying EU law and for using every chance to promote closer integration in the EU. Time and again, it has interpreted EU law as implying the establishment of a supranational legal order. Neither the supremacy of EU law nor direct effect or mutual recognition was codified by the Member States at any place or any time in the Treaties. They are clearly the result of an activist ECJ, now established as a major actor independent of the Member States.

The brief discussion of prominent approaches makes clear that any artificial reduction of supranationalism to either political or legal integration distorts rather than clarifies. Legal integration and political integration are two closely interwoven pillars of supranationalism. The EU is not integrated by either law or politics but by both. Joseph Weiler (1981) has famously coined the notion of a European 'dualism' that combines elements of 'normative supranationalism' and 'decisional supranationalism'. Normative supranationalism refers to the relationships and hierarchy that exist between Community policies and legal measures on the one hand and legal measures of the Member States on the other. It is an element of supranationalism that emphasizes the legal order of the EU and the competences and decisions of the ECJ. Decisional supranationalism relates to the institutional framework and decision-making processes by which Community policies and measures are initiated, concluded, and executed (Weiler 1981: 271). As opposed to normative supranationalism, decisional supranationalism underlines the importance of intergovernmental politics, and of arguing and bargaining about the substance of legal norms. Following this suggestion of conceptualizing the EU as a dualistic institutional order *sui generis*, we clearly see that it is neither (more than) a state nor (less than) an international organization. It is not more or less but simply different (Table 3.1). Supranationality is a third type of political order that combines a unified legal order with a pluralistic political

Table 3.1: Ideal types of political systems

		Legal order	
		Pluralistic	Unified
Political order	Unified	/	State
	Pluralistic	International	Supranational

order. It combines the legal order of the state with the political order of the international system. It accepts that states retain their legitimate monopoly of coercion while at the same time demanding acceptance of the supremacy of European law over domestic statutory law. Christian Joerges has articulated this innovative character of the EU most clearly. It is 'an alternative to the model of the constitutional nation-state which respects that state's constitutional legitimacy but, at the same time, clarifies and sanctions the commitments arising from its interdependence with equally democratically legitimized states and with the supranational prerogatives that an institutionalization of this interdependence requires' (Joerges 2006: 790). States retain political sovereignty but apply common legal norms domestically.

It is important to emphasize that supranationalism is not a territorial but rather a functional concept that is applicable to certain policy fields only. Not the EU *in toto* but rather its regulatory policies in specific areas like currency or trade are supranational. The EU remains a 'multi-sectoral condominium' (Weiler 1981: 279) which leaves untouched, or only coordinates in, a large number of policies such as defence, education, redistributive policy, foreign and security policy, and asylum and migration policy. In all of these areas, the EU follows an international rather than a supranational logic.

Supranational structures represent a radical departure from the model of international organization in that they dispense with the dichotomy of domestic order versus international anarchy. They combine the unified legal order of the nation-state with the pluralistic political order of international relations. The members of a supranational order are not subordinate to a superior power but are voluntary members of an overarching legal community. It is misleading therefore to translate supranationalism as 'over and above' individual states. Taking both components of political and legal integration into account, we can better understand supranationalism as constituting an order 'among' Member States. Thus, supranationality differs fundamentally from both the state and from the international system. Understanding it presupposes an analysis of both pillars, knowing them to be interdependent.

3.2. The European legal order

At first sight, supranational and international legal systems do not seem very different. In both cases, all legal authority lies with nation-states, aside from competencies explicitly conferred. Similarly, international and supranational norms are both legally binding, for in both cases the state has obligated itself contractually to recognize them. Although the claim to validity associated with legal norms is beyond question in both international and supranational systems (*pacta sunt servanda*), they differ fundamentally in the degree of autonomy granted to the national level in deciding on the applicability of international legal norms. In an international legal system, the responsibility for determining which part of an international norm is applicable domestically lies normally with domestic authorities alone. National parliaments must ratify international treaties and governments must adapt their policies if the treaty is to become a legal and political reality. Hardly ever do international norms have direct effect so as to be directly applied by domestic courts. In a supranational legal system, the applicability of legal norms does not depend on domestic implementation but is produced by the supranational level itself. Supranational norms claim general precedence in the case of conflicting domestic norms. In addition, legal norms apply directly to domestic addressees and transfer rights and duties independently from domestic legislation and implementation. They are enforced, furthermore, not by the domestic addressees themselves but by supranational authorities.

3.2.1. *Primacy*

Primacy of European law over Member State law is contested but is nevertheless the most basic condition of a supranational legal order. It is difficult if not impossible to have a unified legal order if no hierarchy of norms exist. The Member States of the European Union did, however, require fifty years to codify primacy. The first significant step in this process was undertaken by the ECJ in the early 1960s. In a decision typical of a long line of subsequent teleological interpretations of EU (then EC) treaty law, the court declared that EC law must take precedence over national law if it is to be effective at all: '(T)he law stemming from the treaty, an independent source of law, could not, because of its special and original nature, be overridden by domestic legal provisions, however framed, without being deprived of its character as community law and without the legal basis of the community itself being called into question' (C-6/64, 1964, ECR 585, at 593). In subsequent decisions, the ECJ specified the supremacy of EC law and extended it to a duty to set aside provisions of national law which are incompatible with Community law (C-106/77, 1978, ECR 629), and to interpret and apply national law, insofar as possible, so as to avoid a conflict with a Community rule (C-106/89, 1990, ECR I-4135).

The Member States reacted with surprising calm to these bold statements of the ECJ. Some Member States even wrote the precedence of Community law into their constitutions. The Constitution of Ireland, for example, contains a clause that, '(n)o provision of this Constitution invalidates laws enacted, acts done or measures adopted by the State which are necessitated by the obligations of membership of the European Union or of the

Communities...' (Art. 29.4.6). Other Member States' supreme courts have accepted that Community law takes precedence in principle and only added the reservation that fundamental constitutional principles of the Member State must be respected. The German Federal Constitutional Court (GFCC) was hesitant for a long time to give such wide latitude to European law. In 1974 it claimed that the European political order does not live up to the standards of the rule of law and that its protection of fundamental rights was still deficient (BVerfGE 37, 271). It therefore claimed the competence to review European legislation with a view to its compatibility with national constitutional law and to limit the applicability of EC law to those cases where it did not object. It took more than ten years for the GFCC to relax this critical attitude towards the primacy of EC law somewhat and to credit the EC with adequately applying the principles of the rule of law and guaranteeing fundamental rights. It was not before 1986 that the GFCC assented to no longer exercising its jurisdiction to decide on the applicability of secondary Community legislation and that it assumed all EC legislation to be in compliance with fundamental rights contained in the Basic Law (BVerfGE 73, 339).

Today, the acceptance of EU law as having precedence over national law is uncontested, by and large. The Member States tried to codify precedence in the draft Constitutional Treaty, by stating that '(t)he Constitution and law adopted by the institutions of the Union... shall have primacy over the law of the Member States' (Art. I-6). However, the Constitutional Treaty never entered into force. When the Treaty of Lisbon was negotiated in 2006, the political mood in Europe had already become slightly more sceptical with regard to closer integration and no longer allowed for a similarly clear codification of precedence for EU law. The Member States did nevertheless agree to attach a declaration to the Treaty that 'recalls that... the Treaties and the law adopted by the Union... have primacy over the law of Member States'. The declaration also refers to an opinion of the legal service of the Council 'that primacy of EC law is a cornerstone principle of Community law'. It explains that 'the fact that the principle of primacy will not be included in the future treaty shall not in any way change the existence of the principle and the existing case-law of the Court of Justice' (Declaration of Precedence). Here we see the crucial contrast to international law, which is recognized as enjoying full primacy of application virtually nowhere. Even in states with a monist legal tradition, which acknowledge international legal obligations as having direct effect, international legal norms are still subject to the *lex posterior* principle and can be displaced by any subsequent law.

It is clear, however, that the primacy of European law must not be misinterpreted as referring to an unconditional supremacy of European law over national law. In legal theory, the difference between primacy and unconditional supremacy is well established and explained by two arguments (cf. Avbelj 2011). The first argument holds that the supremacy of EU law is conditional on a number of criteria. EU law is only to be accepted as supreme by the Member States if it complies with the conditions of subsidiarity, proportionality, and respect for the Member States' identities. Compliance with the three conditions is not only safeguarded by the ECJ but remains a relevant issue for the national supreme courts, too. The 1993 decision of the GFCC on the constitutionality of the Treaty of Maastricht (BVerfGE 89, 155) is a clear example of such a check. The court was asked whether the provisions of the Maastricht Treaty would not lead to violations of democratic principles wide-ranging enough to threaten the quality of German democracy. By accepting the complaint (although rejecting the argument), the Court underlined its role as a guardian of the national constitution and as a competent body for assessing whether the new Treaty would be compatible with the German political order. The court also made clear that supremacy of European law ends where fundamental democratic rights are violated. Every supranational legal norm is still subject to an assessment of its compatibility with constitutional law. According to the GFCC, the final legal authority over the constitutional organs of Germany cannot lie with the ECJ but must remain within its own competence. It cannot allow norms with the status of ordinary law to obtain primacy over constitutional law, because the validity of ordinary laws is derived from the very constitution that they would then have the power to alter. Under the same logic, the GFCC cannot allow itself to be subordinated to the ECJ, which was created through international treaty and thus on the basis of ordinary law, in matters of constitutional interpretation. Indeed, the GFCC could hardly decide in any other way. As long as it has the responsibility of guarding the constitutional order of Germany, supranationality will only obtain primacy in non-constitutional legal areas.

At this point, we have already entered into the second argument regarding the limits of the supremacy of European law. Primacy does not mean that supranational law is generally above national law (albeit in limited fields) but only that it prevails in case of conflict. Supranational law does not invalidate a conflicting national law but only requires its disapplication. It takes conditional precedence rather than being supreme in the sense of being over and above national law. It would be wrong therefore to assume a clear hierarchy between the national and the supranational legal order. Primacy does not establish a new form of supranational sovereignty above the nation-state but only regulates the interaction between the two sovereign levels of the EU and its Member States. The ECJ can neither invalidate national law nor can national courts invalidate EU law. The European legal order has not yet found a definite solution to the question of who has the competence to distribute competencies (*Kompetenz-Kompetenz*) (Schilling 1996; Weiler and

Haltern 1996) because each supreme court is supreme within its own sphere and cannot claim to extend its authority to any other legal order. The EU's legal order is thus a legal order unified not by hierarchy but by consent. It rests on a Member State pillar and a supranational pillar. Both pillars must interact and cooperate on the basis of partnership. They must mutually recognize each other's continuing legal autonomy (Avbelj 2011: 752) without, however, neglecting the necessity of working together in a spirit of mutual loyalty.

3.2.2. Direct effect

A second important element of supranational order is that its norms have direct effect. Direct effect means that individuals can invoke supranational legal norms before national courts. Legal standing for private parties is an implication of the general rule that rights and duties belong together and that citizenship must be established not only on a duty to comply with the law but must also entail rights. The ECJ used this nexus in a decision in 1963 for arguing that citizens of the Member States must have the right to sue their governments if they violate individual rights stemming from EU law. In its decision in the case Van Gend en Loos, it interpreted the Community as 'a new legal order of international law for the benefit of which the states have limited their sovereign rights'. It went on to argue that '(i)ndependently of the legislation of Member States, community law ... not only imposes obligations on individuals but is also intended to confer upon them rights which become part of their legal heritage. These rights arise not only where they are expressly granted by the treaty, but also by reason of obligations which the treaty imposes in a clearly defined way upon individuals as well as upon the Member States and upon the institutions of the community' (C-26/62, 1963, ECR 1, 2).

The ECJ bestowed upon the citizens of its Member States legal rights and obligations, thus turning them into full legal entities under European law. In combination with the preliminary ruling procedure, the direct effect of European law proved to become a most effective instrument for fostering legal discipline. The procedure provides that all private parties who can claim to have been damaged by a national domestic law apparently in contradiction to European law can sue their national government in a domestic court. The national court of last resort must refer the case to the ECJ, which then makes a preliminary ruling and refers the case back to the national court. The important aspect of this procedure is that it establishes a close link between the ECJ and national courts and brings the latter into a position to implement European law even against their governments and national legal provisions if they are incompatible with European regulations. This mode of court interaction produces outcomes that are legally binding not only under European but also under domestic law. Indeed, if a national government were to ignore a decision made by a national court on the basis of this procedure, it would, in principle, be violating its own constitution.

The preliminary ruling procedure connects the international and the domestic legal order to a degree unmatched by any other international organization. In the WTO, legal standing for non-governmental actors is substantially weaker (Lukas 1995). The link between international and national law is not determined by international law (as in the EU) but is a matter of national regulation only. In the USA, for example, the 'supremacy clause' of the constitution prohibits any direct applicability of international law, including WTO law. The European Union, too, has articulated reservations about the direct application of WTO law. Although Article 216(2) TFEU stipulates that the fulfilment of all international agreements is obligatory for the institutions of the European Union and for its Member States, the ECJ is rather ambiguous in the interpretation of its legal implications. In Portugal v Council (C-149, 1999, ECR I-8395), the ECJ argued that the Community judicature could not be made responsible for ensuring that Community law complies with the WTO provisions. Demanding otherwise would 'deprive the legislative or executive organs of the Community of the scope of manoeuvre enjoyed by their counterparts in the Community's trading partners' (ibid., 46). The Court interpreted the WTO as an agreement based on reciprocal and mutually advantageous arrangements. If the EU were to unilaterally accept direct application of WTO law, opposing parties in disputes with the EU would have much less incentive to compromise. This would in turn greatly weaken the EU's hand in negotiations.

It is also emblematic of the WTO's diplomatic pedigree that the access of private persons to the dispute resolution mechanism is highly restricted. Non-governmental parties have only indirect access to dispute resolution in that they may request their national delegations to present their complaint to the WTO. In the USA, this process is regulated through Section 301 of the Trade Act of 1974. In the EU, it is regulated through Council regulation 3286/94. In both cases, private parties enjoy only the right to approach either the US government or the EU Commission with a request to investigate an allegedly unfair trade practice and, if these public authorities so decide, to instigate a dispute resolution process on their behalf. The United States Trade Representative (USTR) and the EU Commission retain full authority to evaluate the complaint and to decide whether to proceed to dispute resolution. The only possibility for non-governmental actors to get directly involved in the process is to obtain a hearing before one of the disputing parties or to be made a member of the official state delegation. These participatory options are commonly used, but individuals have no independent standing to initiate a dispute against a WTO signatory state. The much greater restriction on non-governmental parties' involvement in trade disputes within the WTO framework makes quite clear that its institutions are still grounded upon the diplomatic traditions of international trade regulation. It thus conforms with a pluralistic rather than a unified legal system.

3.2.3. Independent application of the law

A third important element of a unified legal order is an independent process of law application. The effectiveness of international law is structurally hampered by the problem that governments rarely sue each other, out of diplomatic courtesy and strategic calculation. Normally, a conflict between two or more states is resolved through negotiation and political compromise. The hesitancy of states to use courts for settling disputes has much to do with their fear of retaliatory action. Bringing the incident to an international court may only serve to incite legal retaliation later. Thus, it is not surprising that small states, especially if they are dependent on political, military, or development aid, rarely bring legal action against big states in international courts of law. One suit can provoke another and lead to a spiral of counteractions that prevents rather than furthers conflict resolution. Practice shows that legal conflicts can last many years, all the while poisoning political relations between the parties involved. Well-known examples of such cases are the disputes between the EU and the US over the European banana regime and the dispute between Boeing and Airbus about state subsidies.

In national legal systems, the suppressive effect of the latent threat of retaliation is neutralized through the establishment of a public prosecutor. The state acts here as a neutral third party which is obliged to prosecute suspected criminal acts and to free injured parties from the onus of initiating a trial as a plaintiff. In the European Union, the European Commission has been entrusted with a very similar task. It acts as a 'Guardian of the Treaties' and has the task of bringing Member States before the ECJ for breaching EU law. Although the Commission puts strong emphasis on maintaining a relationship of trust and cooperation with national administrations (Curtin and Egeberg 2008), it nevertheless uses its powers extensively and does not shy away from starting legal conflicts with powerful Member States. At the end of 2010 the Commission's infringement database contained nearly 2100 active infringement cases with around 35 per cent of all cases originating from the Commission's own initiative (European Commission 2011). The Commission is also responsible for monitoring compliance by Member States with judgements of the ECJ. For safeguarding that the Commission is not too restrained in the exercising of its powers as guardian of the Treaties, any organ of the EU, including the Member States, can sue the Commission if it fails to act.

The Justification of Europe

The significance of an independent third party for the integrity of a legal order becomes obvious if we take a closer look at the WTO. The WTO provides for a dispute settlement system that has been praised by many observers as a huge step towards a 'constitutionalization of the WTO' (Cass 2005) and a triumph of the rule of law over the asymmetry of power resources. It automatically applies a binding arbitration procedure in cases where one party of the treaty believes that its rights are being violated by another party. If an initial consultation phase between the two parties does not yield results that are acceptable to both parties, either of the two parties can ask for the establishment of a dispute settlement panel with full authority to decide on the disputed case. In contrast to the old GATT procedure, an arbitration decision no longer stops being legally binding when only one of the affected parties raises an objection. Rather, it remains legally binding unless all parties, including the party whose position was upheld by the court, object to the decision (Hudec 1999).

Although the system is promising in its institutional architecture, it fails to deliver in practice the expected results. Empirical evidence shows that litigation still works very much in favour of developed states and that developing states' record in extracting concessions is rather weak (Busch and Reinhardt 2003). An important reason is that the WTO does not provide any independent third party with the task of guarding and enforcing compliance. Any Member State whose rights have been violated by the actions of another Member State must take the initiative to demand a settlement of the dispute. The WTO thus is still very much a self-help system. For small states, this obligation of injured parties to start a dispute can be highly problematic (Young 2005). A complaint brought against the European Union or the USA can lead to retaliation in the form of cuts in military or development aid, or suspension of market access. Small states, especially those dependent on exports, thus benefit much less than larger states from the way the system authorizes trade law disputes. In many cases, the damage done to general political relations resulting from a WTO dispute would cause more harm to national trade than the actual breach of law at issue (Hathaway 2004). Many trade disputes are thus resolved informally through negotiation rather than legal settlement—or they are not settled at all.

3.3. The European political order

The European legal order shows a number of striking similarities to the legal order of an ideal typical nation-state. It gives precedence of European law to domestic statutory law, has direct effect, and can rely on a third party who acts as an independent prosecutor. The European institutional order must not be confused with a state order, however. The EU still has many elements of an international organization, and there is little chance that the dominant role of the Member States will be significantly reduced in the foreseeable future. As opposed to a (federal) state, the transfer of competencies to the European level implies no loss of sovereignty for the Member States but is better understood as expressing a willingness to exercise sovereignty jointly (Lepsius 2000). European law is an instrument of the Member States, not the other way around.

The primacy of the Member States is most obvious in the fact that the integrity of the European legal order is not guaranteed by a central authority with coercive capacities but that compliance with European law remains an 'autonomous voluntary act' on the part of the Member States that must be 'renewed on each occasion of subordination' (Weiler 2000: 13). For this reason, Member States' loyalty to European integration should never be taken for granted, and the European order must not be understood in legal terms only. British angst about an overbearing Brussels or the GFCC's fear that the integration process might undermine democracy in Germany must be taken seriously as political qualifications on legal compliance. If the European legislative process becomes unaware of political sensibilities and if legal norms are interpreted without taking the political preferences of the Member States into account, the legitimacy of the EU and thus the readiness of the Member States to apply European law might suffer damage. The fact that legal norms are routinely followed should not lull us into a false sense of security regarding the robustness of the European legal framework. The European institutional order is still caught between a unified legal order and a pluralistic political order.

3.3.1. *The masters of the treaty*

A first important caveat to equating the European order to that of a state is that the European Union always was and still is strongly shaped by its Member States. It is an institution that was founded by the Member States and that from its very beginning was directed to cater for the interests of the Member States. The historian Alan Milward (1992) has described the early phase of European integration succinctly. The EU was founded by the Member States for rescuing the nation-state from the global challenges it faced after 1945. European integration was not designed to replace its Member States by a European federal superstate. Its founding fathers were first and foremost interested in rebuilding their countries as nation-states and saw European integration not as an alternative to the nation-state, but as the guarantor of renewed legitimacy. The real motivations of the EU's members were not to foster an 'ever closer union' but were instrumentally directed at promoting their economic interests and pooling political power (cf. Moravcsik 1998). European Union law was not to replace the respective national legal orders but was only 'to discipline the actors within the Community in their interactions and to guide strategic interaction into a deliberative style of politics' (Joerges 2007: 14).

The dominant role of the Member States in the integration process thus dates back to the fact that it was 'created of, by and for national governments' (Kahler 2004: 155). It was the Member States that established an additional layer of governance for promoting national interests, not a European institution that subordinated Member States. The intractable importance of the Member States in the EU has much to do with their internal democratic political orders. All Member States are democracies and all of their governments are constitutionally and politically obligated to conduct policy-making in the interests of domestic actors. Democracies are not oriented around maximizing supranational governance but aim rather to deliver political products to their domestic constituencies. The fact that all governments are selected by means of domestic voting guarantees that governments remain firmly tied to the goal of serving domestic interests and give only second-order importance to international or supranational issues. Under the rules of democratic politics, actions that do not please domestic concerns stimulate opposition and are politically costly. National democracies are therefore structurally inward-looking, even if their constitutions include provisions that emphasize the openness of the political system to European integration.

It is also of crucial importance for understanding the EU that all of its Member States have their own national histories, myths, and narratives. Most of them are proud of their past achievements in overcoming political oppression and establishing democratic systems. The political mind-set of the French is impossible to understand if one blots out the storming of the Bastille, the achievements of the revolution, legacy as *'la Grande nation'* and its unique culture. The United Kingdom is still very much removed from 'the continent' due to its history as the leader of a global empire and its pride in having spearheaded parliamentary rule. Merging into a continental Europe is for most Britons as hard to imagine as it is for Scandinavians. Many Central and Eastern European countries have just recovered from Soviet occupation and are eager to revitalize national traditions and to remember their national political past. Explaining to, say, Poles or Czechs, that they regained sovereignty from Moscow only to hand it over now to Brussels is a delicate task. Some argue that Germany is the exception to the rule. Its recent past experiences of fascism and nationalism have taught Germans the lesson that they should guard against surges of national feeling and find a new political identity in a united Europe. That lesson, however, was learned by the post-war generation only and is fading as time goes by. Germany's self-image is increasingly that of a normal nation-state, possessing all the rights and all the legitimacy to take care of domestic concerns as other states. The president of the GFCC recently explained that further steps towards integration are incompatible with the German Basic Law and that they may require a new constitution (Vosskuhle 2011). In most of the Member States, the nation provides not only the 'imagined community' (Andersen 1991) but also a community of communication, of remembrance, and of experience (Kielmannsegg 2003). The European nation-state therefore is not an outdated historical artefact but an entity that will be with us for the foreseeable future.

The role of the Member States in the EU is also of crucial importance due to their monopoly on the use of legitimate force, which is essential for implementing European legislation. The EU itself cannot issue a guarantee that its norms and regulations will be met with compliance. The preliminary ruling procedure goes only a short distance towards that goal. To achieve a supporting ruling, private parties must be ready to litigate, which is costly in terms of time and money. It is a procedure that tames anarchy but does not overcome it. Nor does the EU have its own administrative apparatus capable of implementing its norms and adapting them to technical and scientific progress. Without the administrative capacities of the Member States, EU law would remain blind to emerging problems and lack the necessary expertise for dealing with them. The EU, finally, cannot rely on any substantial European-wide public discourse that would allow its leaders to follow shifts in public opinion and to understand the concerns and preferences of Europe's citizens. All this must be provided by the Member States. It is the Member States that are of vital importance for lending their coercive capacities, supporting the European legislative process with technical and scientific inputs, and for conducting the domestic political discourses that allow politicians to identify democratic preferences. Without the Member States, the EU is hardly more than a technocratic regime without the resources to conduct effective policies.

The European institutional setting clearly reflects the dominant position of the Member States. The most powerful institution in the EU is not the ECJ, the Commission, or the European Parliament, but the European Council (Tallberg 2007, Puetter 2012). Its role was only recently strengthened by the Treaty of Lisbon, which finally recognized it as an official institution of the EU. It is no longer confined to setting policy guidelines for the EU, but has now the authority to define its own strategic priorities. Among the powers of the European Council is the ability to adopt decisions with regard to the suspension of membership of a state and the setting of criteria to be met by a state wishing to join the EU. It has the power to instigate Treaty reform and determines the composition of the Parliament and the Commission. It appoints the president of the Commission, the Commission, the High

Representative, and the Executive Board of the European Central Bank. The European Council coordinates programmes of legislation across all areas of EU policy and defines the strategic objectives and interests pursued in the CFSP. All major political initiatives of the past such as the negotiation and conclusion of new treaties and the various enlargement phases of the EU have been conducted here. The strength of the Member States in agenda setting and giving strategic orientation to the EU via the European Council is replicated in the normal legislative process with the strong position of the Council. It pools the combined expertise and know-how of the administrations of the Member States and it has the power of final decision regarding the adoption of legislation in most areas of EU policy. It is thus the most important institution in the law-making process. An interpretation of the EU that does not take its strong intergovernmental character into account is meaningless.

3.3.2. Delegation and pooling

The strong role of the Member States in the EU is reflected in the strict limits of the Treaty on the EU's supranational institutions' political and legal authority. The EU is like all other international organizations based on conferred powers, and as such can act only on tasks delegated to it by its principals, the Member States. Although the EU today has competencies in home and justice policy, and even primary (although rather nascent) authority in foreign and security policy, it is still very much a market regulating regime. It is true that it encompasses a wide spectrum of policies, among them the harmonization of standards for products and processes of production, environmental policy, foreign trade, and competition policy. Most of these policy areas, however, are closely related to market regulation. As a general rule, the further policies are removed from market issues, the weaker the EU's competencies are. In areas that are detached from market making, such as national budget policy, defence policy, or asylum and migration policy, EU authority is either subject to a unanimity requirement or restricted to legally non-intrusive means.

Market-making policies are so strongly integrated because they cannot be meaningfully conducted by the Member States individually. Economic policies pursued by one Member State effect the probability that other Member States can attain their economic policy goals. Clearly, no single Member State can realize the goal of a unified market without the cooperation of all other Member States. Limits on the free movement of goods must be lowered or abolished by all Member States if this goal is to be realized. Common social regulatory standards for products and production processes must exist for providing consumers with an adequate level of protection and for preventing cost discrepancies among producers in different Member

States. The same logic applies to the need to adopt common environmental standards. If the burden of dealing with environmental pollution is shouldered only by some Member States whilst others free ride on their efforts, the market is distorted and nations that voluntarily contribute to the public good of a clean environment are punished by the reduced competitiveness of their industries. In competition policy, equal standards for public subsidies to private business must exist if a level playing field among companies from different Member States is to be established. In external trade with third parties, the Member States must coordinate their policies due to the lack of intra-EU barriers to trade and the ensuing problem that a trade restriction issued by a single Member State is automatically annulled because importers can use more liberal neighbouring Member States as gateways to the common market. By the same logic, EU authority in foreign and security policy and in redistributive social policy is weakly developed. The larger Member States especially do not expect to gain much from a pooling of competencies due to the absence of a clear international threat and the limited military capacities of smaller Member States. The EU is embedded in an international system in which no significant military threat to the EU exists and in which Member States' national interests can be secured by 'mini-lateral' ad hoc 'coalitions of the willing'. Likewise, richer Member States have especially weak incentives to establish a European redistributive regime that goes beyond the already existent system of structural funds. Such a regime would most likely lead to financial flows from the richer to the poorer Member States and would offer no obvious benefits to net contributors.

The conferral of competencies to the EU is also structurally limited by the greater importance of pooling relative to delegation as the dominant mode of integration (cf. Moravscik 1998: 73–6). Pooling describes a process whereby sovereignty is exercised collectively. Member States agree to use their individual powers only collectively and to abstain in principle from unilateral action. Pooling applies to most aspects of the EU's mode of policy-making. It is codified in Art. 294 TFEU, which specifies the 'ordinary legislative procedure', and applies to all aspects of the internal market, to environmental policy, agriculture, fisheries, transport, structural funds, the entire budget, and the former third pillar. Legislative acts adopted according to Art. 294 require a qualified majority of the Member States to agree to a proposal of the Commission. The major reason for using acts of pooling instead of a full delegation is that pooled competencies remain under control of the Member States. Pooling is a middle way between establishing common policy-making capacities and emphasizing the sovereign control of democracies over legal norms applicable in their territory.

Pooling must thus be distinguished from acts of delegation. Delegation means the conferral of powers to a third party that has the competence to use them independently of its Member States principals. Proper acts of delegation are rare in the EU and mostly apply when Member States require a clear guarantee that all treaty partners will honour legal obligations. They are, in the words of Moravcsik, acts of 'making commitments credible' (1998: 76). The competence given to the ECJ to decide on the lawfulness of the actions of EU organs (including the Member States) is a prime example. Without equipping an independent third party with a delegated power shielded from political intervention, no EU Member State could be assured that European law would be applied by all equally. Likewise the monopoly of proposing EU legislation granted to the Commission is intended to ensure that no proposal enters the legislative pipeline that is openly biased in favour of a single Member State or a group of Member States. The broad authority given to the Commission in the application of competition law also reflects the concern that political intervention on the part of single Member States might allow states to subsidize national champions and to tilt the economic playing field.

The same logic that applies to the conferral of competencies between Member States and EU institutions also applies to internals acts of delegation. Article 290 TFEU requires the Council to transfer policy-implementing powers to the Commission. At the same time, however, the Council has provided for close scrutiny of the Commission and supervision by special 'comitology' committees. These committees supervise and control the Commission in the exercise of its competencies (Bergström 2005). Even within the authority conferred to it, the Commission's actions are closely monitored by the Member States. For example, although the Commission has a particularly large discretionary power in trade policy, and although no Member State is allowed to conduct an autonomous trade policy, the EU is not free to negotiate with third parties independently of member-state control. It must first acquire a mandate from a specialized committee that produces detailed guidelines for the Commission when negotiating.

3.3.3. *Decision-making without coercion*

With the adoption of the Single European Act (SEA) in 1986, Member States intended, *inter alia*, to streamline decision-making practices and to provide the EC with the momentum necessary for realizing a common market. An important element in the SEA was the formal codification of an end to the Luxembourg compromise of 1966, which had reintroduced unanimous decision-making to the Council, and the return to qualified majority-voting in all areas related to the common market. In practice, however, majority voting is only rarely applied. Even when the treaty explicitly provides for the application of majority voting, Member States tend to carry on negotiations until a unanimous agreement has been forged. Very early on it became clear that '[v]ery few important policy-setting decisions are taken without the agreement of all twelve governments to a Commission proposal' (Peterson 1995: 73). Observers of the Council of the European Union noted an 'instinctive recourse to behave consensually', meaning that the Council strived for maximum support, not a minimum number of votes needed to pass (Hayes-Renshaw and Wallace 1995: 565). More recent empirical analyses confirm this impression. In the years 1994–2002, unanimous decision-making in the Council has occurred in 81 per cent of all decisions on average, although more than 70 per cent of the items on the agenda formally could have been adopted by qualified majority voting (Heisenberg 2005: 72). Mattila even reports that an estimated 90 per cent of the Council's legislative acts are passed unanimously (Mattila 2009: 844). The same applies to the other institutions involved in the European Union's legislative process, the Committee of Permanent Representatives (Lewis 2005), many of the comitology committees (Joerges and Neyer 1997), and even the European Council (Puetter 2012). The Member States most often negotiate until there is consensus, even when a vote-based decision rule formally holds. Voting rarely occurs except in a few areas where decisions must be adopted under tight time constraints such as during the annual budgetary cycle and on internal staffing matters: 'Most decisions, even on routine issues, came to be made by letting deliberations and negotiations run until an agreement finally emerged' (Nugent 1999: 168–9). In the interactions of the Council and the European Parliament, too, a striving to reach broad consensus can be observed. The joint legislative processes by which the large majority of the European Union's legal acts are passed require multiple readings in the Council and Parliament, as well as the utilization of a conciliation committee for situations in which the two institutions cannot agree.

The same phenomenon can be observed in the WTO (cf. Ehlermann 2005). Depending on the matter at hand, majorities of two-thirds or three-fourths may decide in matters of interpreting or altering agreements or in determining whether individual members may be absolved of specific treaty obligations. Member States are also granted the option of making so-called 'authoritative decisions' as provided in Article IX (2). Such agreements can be used to explain, modify, or wholly change the legal provisions of the treaty. Formally, this actually empowers members to change international trade law without calling a formal round of negotiation. In fact, however, members have never made use of this procedural option. Not even in the 2002 debates over the use of generic anti-AIDS drugs in Africa did members make recourse to an authoritative decision rule, despite the fact that the passage of an exception to the TRIPS Agreement could probably have saved thousands of lives.

There are a number of reasons why voting is so rarely used in inter- and supranational institutions. Starting with the most fundamental reason, majority rule is a delicate issue in international politics. As a decision-making procedure, it grants other states the right to make binding rules for one's own territory and thus infringes openly upon the idea that valid law is to be adopted only by a national parliament. Countries with strong parliamentary traditions, such as the United Kingdom and Denmark, are thus the least enthusiastic about expanding the scope of majority rule within the EU. A related reason for the hesitancy to apply majoritarian procedures is that the Member States are well aware that the integration project is based on voluntary acceptance of the EU by its Member State principals and that legislative acts must not endanger their good will. If Member States were to adopt an attitude of viewing EU law mostly as a costly burden rather than a political benefit, the whole integration project would suffer serious damage. Member States probably also take into account that burdens imposed on other Member States might backfire in the future, as those states may choose to behave in a similarly inconsiderate manner. The Member States are furthermore well aware that decisions adopted in spite of open opposition impose burdens on EU institutions that often cannot be borne. Governments who have been overruled by the majority sometimes drag their feet when it comes to enforcement; implementation is often delayed, left incomplete, or totally neglected (Börzel et al. 2010). The enforcement capacities of the EU are too limited to cope successfully with such opposition. They differ fundamentally from domestic structures and are anything but impressive. In domestic politics, the state's monopoly on the use of legitimate force is an ever-present guarantee of compliance with the law in case non-coercive instruments fail. It compels conforming behaviour independently of whether the addressees of a regulation support or abhor the law. Supranational structures have no such recourse to coercive mechanisms and no way to guarantee that their regulations will meet with compliance. Most mechanisms through which supranational law is enforced are starkly political in nature and must be understood as instruments of bargaining, rather than coercion.

The way infringement proceedings are organized gives clear indication of the political nature of the EU's enforcement mechanisms. Infringement proceedings consist of three separate, chronologically ordered phases. In phase one, the European Commission demands a statement from the Member State regarding an alleged violation of treaty obligations. Only if this statement is not forthcoming or is found unsatisfactory may the European Commission address a 'reasoned opinion' to the Member State explaining the reasons why it believes the Member State has infringed upon EU law. If the Member State does not react to this statement by correcting the infringement, the European Commission may, in the third and last phase of the proceedings, bring the case before the ECJ and request a trial. Infringement proceedings do not have much in common with classic court proceedings. They are better understood as a legally formalized framework for political cooperation between the Commission and the Member States that employs legal action only as an option of last resort. The political, rather than judicial, nature of the process finds expression in the fact that the European Commission alone decides whether to initiate proceedings or not, whether it finds the Member State's reaction to the reasoned opinion acceptable or not, and whether to bring a controversial case before the ECJ. The European Commission is also free to choose the most agreeable timing for each of these decisions.

The political and even openly diplomatic character of the infringement procedure is clearly expressed in the Commission's regular reports on the application of EU law. For years now the Commission has issued the disclaimer that it can only monitor, not guarantee, the implementation of legal acts. In its recent report, it 'confirms the need for increased focus on effective instruments to ensure the enforcement of EU law' (European Commission 2010: 9). Indeed, the mechanism of infringement proceedings falls far short of the ideal sanction, as these proceedings often prove to be quite lengthy. Obtaining position statements and granting grace periods in the attempt to resolve conflicts without sanctions adds up to long delays, hindering the timely and effective implementation of European law. Eighteen or more months can easily pass between the time when the EU Commission determines that European law has been violated to the point at which a suit is filed with the ECJ. In its annual survey on the application of Community law, the Commission dutifully notes many hundreds of failures to implement its regulations.

From all these stumbling blocks built into the infringement proceedings it is clear that it is not geared towards compelling compliance. It seeks amicable solutions and puts much effort into avoiding legal action. The whole proceeding clearly demonstrates the awareness of the Member States that the unified legal order of the EU can only coexist peaceably with the EU's pluralistic political order if the Member States interact in good faith and if they take the concerns and problems of other Member States seriously. Where compliance with the law cannot be compelled by means of coercion, political authority can be expanded only insofar as the addressees of sovereign acts are amenable to compliance. Otherwise, the attempt to expand the scope of regulation will meet with resistance, and non-compliance will become the norm. Supranationalism does not and cannot mean overcoming the need to discuss and compromise; this need is integral to supranationalism itself. For it is not and never can be a form of authority vested with an inherent right to use force. It is an incentive structure based on voluntary obedience. Its effectiveness is directly dependent on its validity among Member States. Supranational authorities must take seriously the necessity of securing support for legal norms, as do national governments. Supranationality must win acceptance as being legitimate or die trying.

4
Towards a Supranational Democracy?

This chapter argues that democracy is the wrong category for assessing the normative qualities of European supranationalism. The concept of democracy emphasizes attributes of a polity that are irreconcilable with supranationalism. Supranationalism depends on normative principles and institutional mechanisms that are clashing with democracy's most basic principles. Polities are either supranational or democratic, but never both at the same time.

Addressing the question of whether the EU is capable of becoming a democratic entity without losing its supranational identity must start from a definition of what democracy is meant to be. The term democracy is in politics (and only too often also in academia) used very loosely for covering many different ideas and practices, ranging from the 'democratization of the WTO', meaning in practice a better integration of well-organized special interest groups, to any reform of political structures intended to strengthen deliberation, transparency, and accountability (de la Porte and Nanz 2004, Kissling and Steffek 2008, Nanz and Steffek 2005). This indiscriminate use of the attribute 'democratic' is misleading because it confounds indicators for measuring the normative quality of a decision-making procedure with an assessment of the structures of a polity. Democracy is only partially understood if equated with a certain procedure. It is much more than that. It is primarily a structure of authority. Democracy also is much more than only good governance. It refers to a practice of society-wide deliberation that is integrated in a structure of coercive authority. It is not only about inclusion and participation but also about rule and authority. It combines elements of input-legitimacy, throughput-legitimacy, and output-legitimacy. Its analysis, therefore, must not be restricted to performance issues but must encompass also the polity's most basic structures.

It is not easy to objectively identify the proper indicators for such an analysis. Different theories of democracy suggest different indicators. Liberal theories emphasize individual liberty, deliberative theories underline communicative interaction, and communitarian theories focus on shared values and local community-building. In addition, discussing the relative merits of these theories is difficult without taking into account the context in which they are to operate. Some societies may cherish communitarian values and be ready to limit the range of individual liberties; others would be loath to do so. Finding an objective definition of 'democracy' is thus difficult, and the term must always remain subjective to some extent. Most authors would agree, however, that the three principles of political equality (Dahl 2006), public discursiveness, (Habermas 2000) and substantial problem-solving capacity (Scharpf 1999) are essential for a democracy, independent of political and cultural contexts or theoretical orientation. They are a set of principles that resonate well with the distinction between input legitimacy, through-put-legitimacy, and output-legitimacy, and mirror the famous Gettysburg definition of democracy as being 'of the people, by the people and for the people'. A large number of contributions to democratic theory recognize all three principles explicitly, and to the knowledge of this author, no well-established theory rejects them outright.

This section argues that the EU does not strive to realize any of the three conditions of democratic governance. Although the Treaty of Lisbon makes several references to democracy, a thorough analysis of the treaty's normative structures and the EU's practices reveals that these references are merely declaratory in nature and do not address political equality, public discursiveness, or substantial problem-solving capacity in any meaningful way. The assertion raised in Art. 2 TFEU that the EU is founded on the principle of democracy is in clear contradiction to its broader organizational logic. The EU also makes no significant efforts at fostering a European-wide public discourse, but is content with a multiplicity of Member States' discourses running parallel to a European layer of expert discourses. The EU's policy ambitions, finally, are strongly biased in favour of negative integration; its members lack the political will to establish sophisticated problem-solving capacities in areas of positive integration. The EU thus does not merely have a democratic deficit, it is so lacking in the crucial elements necessary for democracy that it cannot be analysed meaningfully in those terms.

The final section of this chapter shows that the EU nevertheless has many positive effects on Member States' democracies. Although it is neither democratic nor does it aim to establish supranational democratic governance, the EU is nevertheless not illegitimate. It helps the Member States to adapt to a transnational environment in which many decisions have cross-border effects and where pressing problems can only be profoundly addressed if the nation-states pool their political resources. The EU is thus a necessary condition for making democracies democratic—although it neither is democratic only, nor strives to become a democracy.

4.1. Democracy and political equality

A principle of utmost importance to democracy is the political equality of its citizens. To be a citizen of a democracy means having the same political rights as all other citizens. The emphasis on political equality is well established in the literature (cf. Lord 2004: 10). It can mean quite different things, however. Political equality can mean de facto equality, referring to the intensity of citizens' political participation and emphasizing equality in the capacity to engage in politics, in educational achievement, wealth, social standing, and many more aspects relevant for political influence (cf. Dahl 2006). The major difficulty with a sole emphasis on de facto equality is that people persist in being different. Some of these differences are due to factors beyond individual responsibility and should be balanced through community effort. Others, however, reflect individual decisions and should be respected as such. For example, demanding full equality in terms of de facto involvement in politics has a strong paternalistic ring. It sets an objective standard not only for individual rights but also for individuals' choices regarding what they want to do with their time. A more cautious way of conceptualizing political equality is to limit it to formal aspects. Understood in this way, political equality refers to equality in the right to make binding rules and equality in their application. It holds that all citizens should have the same capacity to become involved in the making of laws and that they all should be subject to the law to the same extent, irrespective of wealth, ethnicity, gender, or any other personal attributes. Formal political equality means that citizens enjoy the same right to have their concerns heard and to decide on the rules under which they live.

Formal political equality is of utmost importance for democracy. First of all, it gives direct expression to the moral conviction that we are all born equal and should thus have the same rights and duties, irrespective of where, when, or in what station we are born. Political equality finds its most prominent practical expression in the procedural norm of 'one person, one vote'. The importance of political equality for democracy is also underscored by its importance for the practice of politics and for the policy performance of democratic political institutions. Only if all citizens have an equal right to make their concerns heard and to make them relevant for politics can we indeed assume that public decision-making reflects a practice of self-governance of not only a narrow elite but of the people at large. A similar argument applies to the problem-solving capacity of a democracy. In modern societies, relevant knowledge for dealing with pressing problems is widely dispersed. No single governmental or non-governmental body can convincingly claim to have access to all relevant information and to be able to decide autonomously on the proper solutions to the increasingly complex challenges of modern societies. Political equality gives all citizens, independent of their wealth, race, culture or education, the same rights of intervention and participation in the collection and processing of society's knowledge. It is thus a most important condition for an inclusive process of defining problems and identifying adequate solutions. Political equality safeguards against the domination of a small elite equipped with specialized knowledge. It helps guarantee that the knowledge and the problems of all citizens find their way into politics. Political equality is thus the backbone of democracy, both normatively and functionally.

It is true that political equality is an ideal rather than a reality. Hardly any democratic society today guarantees full equality in political participation or ensures that all are equally capable of making their preferences and concerns heard in the political system. Economic and social advantages persist despite the levelling effects of the welfare state, and individual choices together with fortune contribute further to individual differences. The ideal of political equality is nevertheless of crucial importance to democratic governance. It provides a permanent touchstone for critiques of political practice and it is a most important telos for political reforms. Democracy is in grave danger if the political system neglects the promise of political equality, for the outright rejection of equality is a kind of terminal illness for democratic systems. Democracy, as Robert Dahl puts it unequivocally, 'presupposes that political equality is desirable' (Dahl 2006: 2).

How does the EU fare with regard to political equality? As a starting point for answering this question we will assume that political equality requires a legislative process in which all citizens have the same right of selection of parliamentarians and thus the same influence on the composition of law-making bodies. All democracies are thus tied to the principle of one person, one vote. Federal states diverge somewhat from this principle in that they normally have a second legislative chamber that represents territorial units more or less independently of population. In Germany, for example, all sixteen federal states are represented in the Federal Council. Votes are allocated to smaller states in non-linear proportion to their population such that they receive more votes than they would receive through a straight linear digression. A similar deviation from the principle of political equality can be found in the Senate of the United States. In the Senate, each state is represented by two senators regardless of the state's population. In both cases, the constitutional decision to institutionalize equality among states had very specific reasons, and the goal of making the polity more democratic played no central role. In the German case, the decision to strengthen the *Länder* stemmed from the post-war fear of the Allies that Germany would again become a centralized state dominated by a re-emergent Prussia. The political strengthening of the *Länder* was intended to effect decentralization and thus was supposed to shape the allocation of power, not the promotion of equality. Similarly, the decision of the American founders to balance the House of Representatives with the Senate is less a reflection of democratic ideas but rather scepticism in regard to an unchecked empowerment of the people. Only the House of Representatives was intended to be a popularly elected 'People's House'. The Senate was expected to act as a check against the House and intended to represent the states, even as these retained their sovereignty except for the powers expressly delegated to the national government. Neither the American Senate nor the *Bundesrat* (German Federal Council) fosters political equality, but were intended in fact to limit its practice. Both institutions are expression of a scepticism regarding the ability of the people to govern themselves.

In the EU, political scepticism of the benefits of political equality is even more firmly institutionalized. The European Council, as the EU's most powerful body, decides on the basis of one state, one vote. In these decisions, a citizen of Luxembourg counts as much as 160 German citizens. The Council only slightly relaxes this discrimination by applying either the principle of unanimity, of qualified majority voting, or of double majority voting. Even double majority voting, however, which takes account of both the majority of Member States and of the population, still strongly discriminates against citizens from larger Member States. The European Parliament, as the primary representative body of the citizens of the EU, grants 13.5 per cent of its seats to citizens from its biggest Member State Germany, and 0.8 per cent to Luxembourg's citizens. This allocation still does not reflect correctly their respective actual share of the overall population of the EU and gives a citizen of Luxemburg a voting right equal in strength to that of 16 German citizens. Realizing full political equality would mean overturning this asymmetrical allocation of voting rights and realizing full equality irrespective of nationality. It would mean abolishing the requirement of unanimity in the European Council, ending both qualified majority voting and the double majority requirement in the Council and eliminating digressive proportionality in the European Parliament.

To be sure, just like in the United States or Germany, there are good reasons for the application of the principles of digressive proportionality in the European Parliament and unanimity voting in the European Council. The EU developed in the context of a European history of power politics, of hundreds of years of war, interstate conflict, and of little respect for the legitimate concerns of small states. The fear of being dominated by France or Germany has become an important political legacy in many Member States. Overcoming the tragic history of Europe and establishing an international order in which peace and cooperation drive the conduct of states is a core goal of the EU. Thus, the project of European integration is not primarily motivated by the will to establish democratic governance beyond the state and should not be judged by this standard. It is justified at least as much by the establishment of peace and security among European states. To facilitate international cooperation on the basis of respect for national sovereignty is an important topic for the EU. The argument of this section, therefore, is not that the EU's violation of the principle of individual political equality is necessarily illegitimate. It holds only that individual political equality is incompatible with the idea and practice of supranational integration.

4.2. Democracy and public discursiveness

A second important principle of democracy is that legislative discourses are embedded in a process of free and unconstrained public deliberation in which all citizens can engage without having to possess advanced education or having to be a member of an exclusive political club. To function properly, democracy requires a continual process of constructive debate among competing interests and their claims. In an ideal democratic world, every parliamentary decision is the result of a process of public exposition and justification of claims and alternatives. Under conditions of high social, political, and cultural heterogeneity now characteristic of all modern societies, pure majoritarian decision-making unconstrained by public deliberation easily leads to outcomes that disregard the legitimate concerns of minorities. The work of finding out where the legitimate moral limits to majority power lie and of ensuring that these limits are not crossed can only be done by means of public deliberation. It is only in unconstrained and inclusive public discourses that disparate interests, organized in parties and interest groups, engage one another through the media for the benefit of an observing public audience. It is only by participating in the public discourse actively or passively that a group of individuals makes a demos of politically equal citizens. This crucial role of the public discourse has led many authors to claim that the heart of democracy is not its institutions but the demos itself, or, in modern terminology, the free und unconstrained discourse of citizens conducted in an unrestricted public sphere. As Joseph Weiler puts it, '[i]f there is no demos, there can be no democracy' (Weiler 1999: 337).

In the EU, inclusive public discourses and a free public sphere hardly exist. The EU has only transnational epistemic communities, expert networks, and sporadically emerging publics (Eriksen and Fossum 2002) that disappear as soon as the latest scandal moves from the first to the last page of the newspaper. There is neither a European-wide media that is regularly consumed by more than a narrow elite nor a relevant political movement on the European or national levels working to bridge the gaps that separate the multiple demoi of Europe. Peter and de Vreese (2004) report that television coverage of EU politics takes place only sporadically and is of limited visibility. Newspapers are only slightly more responsive to European integration. Although Sifft *et al.* (2007) observe an intensifying scrutiny of EU politics by newspapers, they nevertheless conclude that most EU politics takes place unnoticed. Gerhards (2000: 294) adds that 'European questions receive the lowest level of media attention in comparison to all other... issue-areas' and Risse and van den Steeg (2003: 3) report that the European public discourse is 'fragile, fragmented and constrained to particular sets of issues'. This defect is all the more serious as European news coverage is strongly biased towards governmental activities and largely overlooks parliaments, party actors, and civil society (Koopmans 2007). Inclusive and effective justificatory public discourses thus face serious obstacles. It is not surprizing that individual identities and public discourses are organized very much into national groups and follow well-trodden national paths. Every national citizenry interprets Europe differently, based on perspectives rooted in its own political culture and swayed by its own political sensibilities. The notion of Europe as a 'community of communications in the making' does not refer to a unified political space but only to a layer of political identity that is established and fragmented along national lines (Risse 2010). Within national discourses, awareness of European political processes may grow without, however, any change in the very national lenses through which Europe is perceived. Empirical work also clearly shows that even these limited processes of Europeanization are confined to western Continental Europe. They do not characterize the United Kingdom, Scandinavia, or Eastern Europe. And even on the Continent, the degree of Europeanization has remained quite stable over time, showing no upward trend. Despite great advances in EU integration, individual identification with Europe is not higher now than it was twenty years ago. In fact, it has even declined slightly.

If the EU viewed the lack of public discursiveness in earnest as a serious threat to its legitimacy, we would expect it to develop a strategy for correcting the problem. Indeed, it would need a grand strategy for reforming the fragmented character of the European public sphere into an encompassing structure of lively and critical debate and policy contestation. No such strategy exists. The EU does not strive to establish an encompassing public discourse but rather seems happily resigned to accept its permanent fragmentation. The Council and the European Council as the two most salient political institutions of the EU have not adopted any communication, resolution, declaration, or legislative act intended to foster the emergence of a European public space. The only two institutions that have somehow addressed the issue are the European Parliament (EP) and the European Commission.

The efforts of both institutions, however, are rather ambivalent. The Parliament approaches the lack of European discursiveness mainly as a public relations problem. The EP diagnoses a 'need to continue efforts to overcome the distance between the EU and its citizens' and refers to the problem as an issue that arises 'if politics fails to be communicated properly' (EP 2010). The way forward suggested by the EP is to ask governments, political parties, universities, public service broadcasters, and EU institutions to explain to the EU's citizens the vital importance of the EU and the need to engage in debates about the EU. It is hard to ignore the scent of paternalism in this approach. It neither analyses thoroughly the reasons for the lack of a European public sphere nor does it ask whether the EP shares any responsibility for the deficit. The EP articulates its understanding of the relationship between governance institutions and citizens clearly enough: institutions instruct and citizens learn. That, however, stands the democratic understanding of public discourse on its head.

The Commission's approach to public discursiveness is equally inspiring. It has been presented most clearly in the White Papers on European governance (European Commission 2001) and on communication (European Commission 2006). According to the White Paper on Governance, '(t)he aim should be to create a transnational "space" where citizens from different countries can discuss what they perceive as being the important challenges for the Union' (ibid., 11). This transnational space, however, is not to serve the primary purpose of discussing the aims and policy orientations of the EU but rather is intended to serve the technical purpose of gathering information about prevailing preferences of citizens for the convenience of the Commission. It 'should help policy makers to stay in touch with European public opinion, and could guide them in identifying European projects which mobilize public support' (ibid.). The instruments intended for implementing the policy speak an even clearer language. The Commission aims at improved consultation with a broad array of governmental and non-governmental stakeholders, easier and broader access of stakeholders to information and, last but not least, improving its webpage. The public discourse that is envisaged by the Commission is supposed to lead to 'a reinforced culture of consultation and dialogue' (ibid., 16) with organized interests, not ordinary citizens. It refrains from thinking in terms of a truly democratic public discourse and instead tasks the European Parliament, the European parties, and Member States with reaching out to ordinary citizens. The Commission thus shares in word only the emphasis on a truly public European sphere. Its approach to implementing this general goal is just like the Parliament's approach, belying its rhetorical ambitions. What the Commission does, in fact, is pursue a technocratic improvement of procedures and to make additional efforts at communicating its policies to citizens. This is not a serious effort to establish a broad European public sphere. Its measures are better understood as aiming at the improvement of governance rather than at honouring democracy (cf. Joerges, Meny, and Weiler 2002). In its White Paper on communication the Commission goes a bit further in moving from an emphasis on information to communication with citizens. It wants to establish communication as a policy in its own right with the ultimate aim of developing a 'European public sphere where the European debate can unfold' (European Commission 2006: 4). The changes that would be needed to give citizens a real 'say' in European politics, however, go far beyond the communicative measures listed and would require major treaty reform, including strengthening the EP's powers as an agenda-setter of policy-making in the EU (Kurpas, Brüggemann, and Meyer 2006). That, however, is off the Commission's and the European Council's political agenda.

4.3. Democracy and problem-solving capacity

Democracy also sets a high standard regarding policy output. Even the most inclusive and discursive procedures fail to deliver legitimacy if they are incapable of producing the outputs demanded by the demos. It is true that no state, democratic or otherwise, has a perfect problem-solving capacity, i.e. is able to fulfill all domestic policy wishes. Many issues like global peace, global respect for human rights, or zero taxation coupled with high public welfare entitlements simply exceed the capacity of any state. Democracies, however, must be expected at least to strive for a maximum of problem-solving capacity and—at the same time—allow its citizens to identify the most serious problems. This right is institutionalized in the agenda-setting and law-making power of the parliament, which guarantees that the people's preferences and concerns are at least as important as governmental interests. It is also an important rationale for a competitive party system. Only by having a number of policy alternatives on the table and by forcing the parties to compete for political support do the people have a guarantee that their preferences will be taken seriously and function as important inputs for policy-making.

In the EU, however, public preferences have little relevance for the political agenda. The EU is non-responsive to nearly all issues unrelated to market regulation, and it is politically predisposed to promote market freedoms and to downplay social justice. By tying themselves to the discipline of European legal provisions, the Member States have subjected themselves to the constitutional bias of the EU towards negative integration and its corresponding pull towards a liberal market order. Fritz Scharpf has famously argued that the EU suffers from a structural incapacity to foster positive integration (Scharpf

1999, 2010a). It promotes the four freedoms of goods, services, capital, and labour but lacks the necessary instruments for positive regulations, for balancing the four freedoms with social regulation, and for responding to demands to restrict market forces. The most important reason for this asymmetry between market-making and market-correcting instruments is that rules of 'negative integration' are vigorously enforced to the detriment of any national restraints on trade and any national distortions of free competition, not only by the European Commission and the European Court of Justice, but also by the national courts in ordinary administrative and civil proceedings. Competition policy and the four freedoms for products, services, capital, and labour have achieved a supranational constitutional status that is hard to challenge by any individual Member State or even by a coalition of Member States. Positive integration, on the other hand, is much more difficult to achieve. Policy interventions in support of social, cultural, and environmental purposes must pass through the bottleneck of the Council and be adopted by qualified majority voting, double majority, or even unanimity. That often leads to conflicts amongst governments represented in the Council. In a large number of policy areas, the costs of institutional adaptation are high, ideological differences significant, and the level of economic development is so divergent that all attempts to re-regulate at the European level are stopped by blocking minorities. Efforts to create market-correcting policies and to re-regulate the market at the European level are thus often obstructed by the very logic of the institutional and normative set-up of the EU.

The effect of this constitutional asymmetry is that all Member States are drawn into a liberal market order, irrespective of prevailing domestic preferences. Greece, Italy, and Spain are now learning the hard way that trying to withstand this process is only feasible for a limited time and at high political and economic costs. We are witnessing a silent political and economic revolution of our domestic political and economic systems that never was explicitly agreed upon in any legislative setting or, even less, in any public discourse. In a frank moment, Jean-Claude Juncker, Luxembourg's prime minister, once described the EU's logic of integration: 'We decide on something, leave it lying around and wait and see what happens. If no one kicks up a fuss, because most people don't understand what has been decided, we continue step by step until there is no turning back' (cited in The Economist, 9/12/2002). It is a strategy of revolutionizing a political order by piecemeal measures, by technical improvements, and harmonization. This strategy can be observed most clearly in the rulings of the ECJ. Since the 1960s, it has adopted a series of decisions that emancipated Community economic regulations from national constitutional standards and developed the four freedoms into mature and persistent components of a supranational ideal of negative and individualistic freedom. Over time, the court's rulings fostered the already latently existing imbalance between positive and negative integration. The national polities of the Member States and their historically established balances between markets and political authority were progressively undermined by transnational and supranational institutional networking, even as no overarching supranational constitutional design has been established so far for compensating for the eventual democratic losses. All this is hard to reconstruct as a justified process. It has not been deliberately decided upon by the Europeans but was advanced by intergovernmental negotiations and the jurisprudence of the ECJ. The EU as we see it today is to a large degree the product of 'integration by stealth' (Majone 2005).

Scharpf's argument is an important critique of the EU's democratic credentials (Scharpf 2010b) because it reveals that a most important area of domestic policy has been insulated from democratic deliberation. The EU is set on a track of promoting a liberal order, irrespective of citizen preferences. The argument also makes clear that the EU is hardly capable of adopting policies that give rise to significant conflicts of interest, demand major institutional adaptation or a change of regulatory ideology. Such policy proposals are unlikely to generate sufficient support in the Council and for this reason are often not even put on the agenda.

This asymmetry of governance capacity is a serious problem because it fosters not only negative integration but also reduces the capacity of Member States to react to the social consequences of liberalization. The on-going process of negative integration has transformed the European economic space such that the welfare states of Europe must transform themselves into liberal, market-oriented states if they are to survive economically (Scharpf 2002). The high competition on the liberalized market puts huge pressure on all domestic industries and forces governments to lower taxes, to repel union demands, and even to adapt the university system to the requirements of intense competition. All national governments in the European Union are forced to compete for mobile capital and firms, to accept lower taxation of capital, and to put more financial burdens on consumption. The four freedoms thus have not only a liberalizing effect but have also clear distributive implications.

An important reason for the limited capacity of the EU to tackle pressing problems can be found in its limited capacity to elicit compliance and its lack of coercive capacities. As has been argued above, the EU is at its core a voluntary order among sovereign Member States. The Member States and the European institutions are well aware that regulations that meet with outright criticism or opposition by individual Member States will be implemented only incompletely or with significant delay. The Commission is therefore very hesitant to put controversial draft legislation on the agenda, and Member States are likewise hesitant to adopt legislation not backed by broad political support. The shyness of the EU's institutions to adopt controversial legislation comes sometimes at a high price, however. Important legislation is postponed or not adopted at all, and much of the legislative workload concentrates on issues of minor importance with limited political salience. The implications of this structural deficit of the EU are grave and become immediately clear if we imagine the consequences that close-to-unanimous decision-making would have for the domestic politics of the Member States. Most of all domestic draft legislation would fail to pass the test of uniting both the government and the opposition and would thus remain dormant. Politics would be voided of much of its substance if only those legislative acts have a chance to be adopted that find no or only very limited opposition. It is here that we come to the heart of the problem-solving capacity of the EU: due to its limited enforcement capabilities the EU is structurally handicapped in dealing with controversial policies and thus remains a political lightweight with a low problem-solving capacity.

Some contemporary authors argue that the importance of the state's monopoly of coercion for eliciting compliance has been overstated and that it can be compensated by 'legitimate' rules (Franck 1990). It is also said that the emphasis on the state's monopoly of coercion overlooks the effectiveness of sophisticated non-coercive governance arrangements (Mitchell 1996, Zürn 2005). High degrees of rule-compliance, it is maintained, can also be realized by a combination of monitoring mechanisms, inclusionary decision-making processes, generally fair rules, and non-coercive sanctions. Although it is true that compliance levels for European regulations are astonishingly high and often no lower than compliance levels for comparable national regulation (Zürn and Neyer 2005), the evidence must not be over-interpreted. A first limitation is that the fact of high compliance tells us nothing about the capacity of an institution to elicit it. As has been argued above, European regulations are adopted with full knowledge of the difficulty of securing compliance and therefore are most often of a convenient, not an inconvenient character. Most often they reflect the existing preferences of most of the Member States. Moreover, the great body of European law regulates trade, is understood as leading to mutually beneficial outcomes, and thus as having no negative effects for any of the parties involved. Only very rarely do conflicts in values or differences in world views make it onto the agenda of trade policy. Another common argument concerning the power of the EU to elicit compliance is that European law has direct effect and that it can be enforced directly by national courts, even against the expressed preference of a national government. This argument, too, has a kernel of truth that is distorted by reification. National courts are indeed required to give European Union law precedence over national law. As part of its '*Solange* II' decision (BVerfGE 73, 339), however, the German federal constitutional court reserved the important right of rejecting the primacy of any European law judged to be in conflict with fundamental rights guaranteed by the German Basic Law. In this way, both the European Union and the European Court of Justice operate under the shadow of the credible threat that European law will be overturned by national constitutional courts if it does not conform to national constitutional frameworks. The direct effect of European law is a conditional capacity, transferred to the EU by a nation-state that can, in principle, revoke it at any time. This stands in fundamental contrast to the power of domestic legislation and represents a critical limit on the autonomy of the European legal system. If the efficacy of European law ultimately depends on resources held by its addressees, it makes no sense to conceive of compliance (or its limits) as residing in the supranational layer of the European Union rather than in its Member States.

4.4. Legitimacy beyond democracy

The preceding sections have shown that the EU falls short structurally with regard to crucial principles of democracy. It neither strives to realize individual political equality, nor does it aim at establishing a European public space. It is content with a problem-solving capacity that is one-sidedly biased towards negative integration and convenient regulations, and takes no significant steps towards overcoming its substantial shortcomings with regard to positive integration and the eliciting of compliance with inconvenient rules. Seen in this light, the EU does not suffer from a democratic deficit; it belongs rather outside the category of democracy. It would be misleading, however, to use these arguments for disputing the EU's legitimacy. The European Union may have normative deficiencies in terms of political equality, discursiveness, and problem-solving capacity, but it also exerts a highly beneficial impact on the quality of Member States' democracies. This beneficial impact works along two major dimensions:

A first dimension refers to the input congruence of decisions: citizens who are affected by a regulation should also be those who decide on its content. There is a gap between those who authorize the rules and those who are subjected to the rules and their effects if the two groups are not identical. Such problems are pandemic under conditions of interdependence. National democracies routinely adopt decisions that affect people beyond their jurisdictions; rarely are such effects seriously reflected upon. If Germany, for example, decides to restrict its migration law, this decision will most likely have repercussions for its neighbours. Asylum seekers headed to Europe might shun Germany and thus increase the burden shouldered by others. The same applies to monetary policy, trade laws, energy policy, etc. In all these areas, national decisions often have external consequences that are insufficiently taken into consideration domestically. Input incongruence thus treats affected citizens differently and discriminates for reasons of nationality. The European Union provides an effective corrective to many of these problems. It provides Member States with an institutional site for monitoring each other's policies and for demanding justifications in cases when a national decision has a negative effect on other Member States. Many of the powers of the EU help it to address problems of input incongruence. Trade law with its constitutive provision of non-discrimination aims to make national legislators aware of the concerns of citizens from other Member States. Competition law aims at limiting domestic subsidies with a view to prohibiting an unfair distortion of competition and the European authority to regulate monetary policy aims at overcoming the formerly dominant position of the *Bundesbank*. In all these areas, European law functions as a mechanism for making 'foreign' concerns an integral aspect of domestic law-making, fostering inclusionary decision-making and thus re-establishing input congruence.

The European Union also has beneficial effects on the representation of weakly organized groups in its Member States. Following Keohane, Macedo, and Moravcsik (2009), the EU shares with other international institutions the potential to 'restrict the power of special interest factions, protect individual rights, and improve the quality of democratic deliberation, while also increasing capacities to achieve important public purposes' (2009: 2). Multilateral institutions are an effective device against the over-representation of well-organized interest groups in many democracies. By delegating policies to an independent agent located 'above' them, nation-states can counter the capture of administrative agencies and foster policies that are more representative of diffuse general interests. The European Commission's role in administering the internal market and its strong role in competition policy can be so justified as a most effective instrument for safeguarding against the influence of national lobbies. The integration of a national political process into a multilateral context enlarges the political audience to whom policies must be justified. The resulting integration of additional concerns, points of view, and experiences often has the additional positive effects in that it fosters learning, allows for an analysis of best practice, and expands the range of information available to national politicians and to the public.

The EU, although not democratic itself, is therefore not necessarily illegitimate. It helps national democracies adapt to interdependence and it is often a positive factor for stimulating reform in the Member States. It can give an impetus for making democracies more democratic and can do so without being democratic itself. Holding the supranational EU to standards of democracy rooted in the nation-state is misleading if and when it makes us overlook the important contribution a non-democratic EU can make to improve democratic governance in the Member States. To talk of a democratic deficit is thus to make use of a misguided analytical language that distorts the normative picture and fails to illuminate some of its most important elements.

Part III
Setting the Standard

5
Justice in International Political Theory

Democracy is not the adequate standard for assessing the legitimacy of the supranational layer of the EU. Democracy, as a way of organizing authority, presupposes normative principles and empirical conditions that are incompatible with the supranational structure of the EU. If we try to legitimate the EU by applying the principles of normative realism, then we must look for an alternative standard. Such an alternative standard should be as normatively compelling as democracy but must not be burdened by empirical and normative assumptions that are inapplicable to the EU. Any new standard should be able to illuminate the normative advantages inherent in a supranational structure without obscuring its disadvantages. It must also be compatible with the institutions and legal structures of supranationalism as they have developed historically and thus abstain from utopian wishful thinking.

The concept of justice is an encouraging starting point for developing such a normatively ambitious and empirically sound standard. Justice is a central concept both of political philosophy and of practical politics. Its centrality in political philosophy is based on the assumption that no attribute of a political system can possibly compensate for a lack of justice. Justice is not just one value among many; it is the first and highest virtue of any political system. It is, in the words of John Rawls 'the first virtue of social institutions' (Rawls 1999a: 3). The concept of justice is, moreover, no less ambitious than the concept of democracy. On the contrary: justice confers to democracy much of its normative accolade. As Parijs (2011: 68–9) argues, democracy is only of value to the extent that it serves the end of justice. Any identifiable democratic deficit within a society need not be bemoaned, provided that such a state of affairs is conducive to justice. Democracy is considered the best-known form of government not only because of its intrinsic qualities as a means for making citizens responsible and active participants in their respective communities but also because we believe that it is more likely to generate just outcomes than any known alternative. If democracy lost this comparative advantage over its competitors, our faith in it would be seriously shaken. To cherish democracy is thus intimately intertwined with our quest for justice. Democracy is the means, but justice is the goal. Serious contemplation of the meaning of democracy, then, must make reference to its relationship to justice. Juxtaposing democracy and justice implies neither that they are in conflict nor that one is normatively superior to the other. The purpose of this discussion is, rather, to develop a reference point that incorporates the essential normative content of the concept of democracy but that does not require democracy's institutional and normative preconditions.

Most political theorists tend to argue that justice can only emerge within democratic structures. From their perspective, only democratic procedures provide adequate means for distinguishing justice from injustice, making any neat analytical separation of the two concepts quite problematic (Nicol 2012). It is argued that justice should not be viewed as the norm that legitimates democracy but rather as the outcome of democratic procedures. It is, so to speak, a dependent variable of democracy. Although the alleged nexus between democracy and justice has some intuitive plausibility, it is a major obstacle for applying justice to international politics. Democracy exists only inside, not between nation-states. If justice can be produced only by democratic procedures, we would have to reject the idea of using justice as a norm for critically assessing international politics altogether. Before accepting this argument and its far-reaching consequences, we should take a closer look at recent efforts to apply the concept of justice to international politics and then decide whether an analytical separation of justice from the concept of democracy is heuristically useful or not. The following sections also serve the purpose of introducing scholars of European integration studies to a debate that has been largely ignored in their literature. The ultimate aim of this chapter is to identify conceptual guidelines for a normatively realistic concept of justice.

5.1. Theories of justice beyond the state

As a philosophical concept, justice is well embedded in international political theory and has served to orientate the normative debate for many decades (cf. Beitz 1973; Walzer 1977). The literature that deals with justice in international politics is organized, for the most part, around the debate between universalism and contextualism (cf. Miller 2002). It deals extensively with questions of identifying the conditions and the scope of legitimate governance beyond the state and is thus of direct relevance to this book.

5.1.1. *Universalism*

'Universalism' is used here for referring to those theories of justice that assume it to be possible to identify general principles of justice that are valid independently of any specific social or cultural context. For universalists, justice is a moral claim that applies everywhere, at all times, and in all conditions (Pogge 2002). In international political theory, universalistic approaches to justice come in two different variants distinguishable by the importance they attach to the state as an addressee and author of legitimate moral claims. A most prominent argument in favour of emphasizing the role of the state was offered by John Rawls. In *The Law of Peoples*, Rawls seeks to identify the content of those principles that all reasonable nations would share irrespective of whether they are large or small, rich or poor, Muslim or Christian. These principles would contain 'a particular political conception of right and justice that applies to the principles and norms of international law and practice' (1999b: 3). This conception of right and justice is that which would be derived from the conditions of the famous veil of ignorance, i.e. under conditions where no people would have any knowledge concerning its size, wealth, or any other attributes that might be relevant for selecting principles of justice. The principles yielded by this process make up the content of the Law of Peoples. They are summarized by Rawls in eight principles regarding the rights and duties of peoples. They must be organized internally in accordance with the principles of freedom and autonomy, their freedom and independence is to be respected by other peoples, they are to be made equal parties to their own agreements, they are to be conferred with the right of self-defence but not of war, they must observe a duty of non-intervention, they must respect treaties and observe specified restrictions on the conduct of war, they must honour human rights and, finally, they have a duty to assist other peoples living under conditions preventing the establishment of a just and decent political and social regime. The eight principles are oriented toward identifying criteria for how peoples are to organize themselves internally and how they should conduct their interactions.

The Rawlsian concept of justice is deliberately state-centred. It sets out to improve the international order, not to overcome it. According to Rawls, morally relevant interaction is conducted mainly among nation-states. Nation-states and not citizens are the proper authors and addressees of demands for justice. By adopting an international concept of global politics, however Rawls distinguishes himself from the great bulk of recent empirical approaches to international relations that describe modern politics as characterized by porous national boundaries, transnational actors, and the existence of a large number of politically relevant horizontal and vertical networks linking governmental representatives, international organizations, and non-governmental actors (cf. Hurrell 2007; Slaughter 2004). The Rawlsian reification of peoples as self-contained units to whom normative qualities can be ascribed makes it very difficult to allow for the possibility that domestic and international political organizations are intertwined. It is established on a state-centred idea of international relations that in fact ignores the today common empirical insight that transnational politics is multi-layered and multi-levelled. Agency does not only apply to states but also to non-state actors. It is even more difficult to apply Rawls' concepts to the EU. The dominance of the executive in international policy-making, the by-passing of national parliaments, the lack of avenues for cross-border participation, and the lack of accountability are problematic issues not broached in his account of global politics.

Most cosmopolitan versions of universalistic theories of justice avoid these problems by focusing on individuals, not states, as the legitimate bearers of claims to justice. Charles Beitz (1999), for example, applies the Rawlsian veil of ignorance not to relations among nation-states (or peoples) but directly to individuals, just as Rawls does in his work on domestic justice. The existence of national borders and national attributions is accorded a low significance for questions of justice because they have a merely derivative significance. According to Beitz, a proper theory of justice that requires individuals to treat a fellow citizen justly must also require them to treat justly any individual whatsoever, irrespective of whether that person happens to live in another country or not. There is no prima facie reason to discriminate between the moral duties that we have towards our family members, our neighbours, or any foreigner anywhere in the world. If we decide that anyone has a legitimate claim to respect and common decency, then we must extend our readiness to apply these principles globally. Cosmopolitan universalism places on us a moral obligation to treat all individuals equally and to make no fundamental distinction between fellow citizens and foreigners.

Cosmopolitan concepts of justice often lead not only to general requirements of fairness but also to quite strong demands for a global redistribution of wealth. For cosmopolitan thinkers, the elimination of hunger and poverty in all the corners of the globe is not an issue of charity; it is a moral imperative, and to ignore it is to affront justice (Pogge 2002). For implementing this moral duty, Thomas Pogge has proposed the introduction of a Global Resources Dividend (Pogge 1998). Under the scheme nations would pay a dividend (tax) on any resources that they use or sell, resulting in a sort of 'tax on consumption' which could be spent on tackling global poverty.

Cosmopolitan ideas also have a strong institutional component. David Held (2010), Richard Falk and Andrew Strauss (2001), and Daniele Archibugi (2009) make the case that individual moral rights can only flourish in a world that is

Justice in International Political Theory

ordered along democratic principles and governed by democratic institutions. Global citizens must have access to a global parliamentary assembly to be able to being able to engage in self-governance and to autonomously and freely decide about the rules under which they are willing to live. Such a parliament would have full rights to set its own political agenda, to levy taxes, and to decide upon spending. It would elect a global government and control the execution of its laws. Global politics would be integrated in a new Global Charter of binding rights and commitments for all political, social, and economic centres of power. Domestic sites of political authority would be subjected to this Charter, as would multinational corporations and non-governmental organizations. It would constitute a global legal order that establishes universal principles and the conditions for their specification. This Charter would also provide for a global division of political and economic power and guide the elaboration of a uniform public and private law.

Although often criticized as visionary and utopian (cf. Dahl 1999, 2001), many of the recommendations sound familiar to students of European politics. The European Parliament has witnessed a long expansion of its authorities and some scholars go so far as to compare its powers and decision-making practices to those of national parliaments (Rittberger 2012; Hix, Noury, and Roland 2007). It has co-decision rights not only in market policy but also in some areas of home affairs and justice; it is consulted in foreign policy and has veto rights over the adoption of international obligations by the EU. The treaties of the EU are often referred to as its 'constitution'. They set up a list of general norms that provide a political framework not only for the European institutions and policies but also for the procedures and content of democracy in its Member States. The treaties and the over 30,000 pages of European law that make up the *acquis communautaire* have become much more than merely a set of rules for the conduct of international affairs in the European Union. They impinge deeply upon the domestic order of the EU's Member States. Individual rights have attained constitutional status in European law, and today any individual can file a suit against its government or any European institution if he or she feels that these rights have been violated. Individual human rights are no longer guaranteed only within the confines of state institutions, and they no longer only depend on the enforcement activities of state authorities. Even issues that were once highly specific to the political culture of the EU's Member States—such as gender equality, penal law, or abortion—are today shaped by European law.

Cosmopolitanism obviously is no longer merely a lofty utopian undertaking uninformed by empirical reality. In the European context, its relevance is hard to dispute. European politics have been transformed from an international order into a transnational legal regime in which citizens are not mere subjects of intergovernmental agreements but are accepted as legitimate bearers of moral rights. Cosmopolitanism also has a great intuitive appeal and, not surprisingly, many today equate universal moral equality with justice. Why, indeed, should moral standards differ from one person to the next and from one kind of relationship to the next? Why should territorial borders be relevant for ethical relationships?

5.1.2. *Contextualism*

This is the point at which the contextualist critique of universalism comes in. Contextualism criticizes universalism for its ignorance of the fact that people always live and orientate themselves within specific historical, cultural, and social contexts (cf. Walzer 1983a). Individuals cannot be meaningfully understood independently from the contexts of their everyday lives. Their desires, motives, and preferences are all deeply shaped by the places and times they live in. Morality, understood as the set of reasonable normative principles held by a community, cannot be adequately understood or criticized if we do not take these factors into account. In a strong version of this argument, we might even be hesitant to accept the very notion of a universal morality and of generally valid principles of justice at all. Morality would then never be properly justifiable except in terms of specific contexts.

Moral contextualism has a long tradition in international political theory. Following Hans Morgenthau (1948), the idea of universal justice misleads us into a wrong-headed belief in a unified global morality, which ultimately serves only to provide the powerful with the crown and sceptre of moral certainty. Instead of following the high road of justice, states should instead try to act prudently. The meaning of justice will always remain contested, and any attempt to establish justice will inevitably lead to conflict, not to any improvement of the world because '(t)here are as many ethical codes claiming universality as there are politically active nations' (1948: 193). Morgenthau argues further that if this were not enough reason to reject the idea of global justice, it should be rejected on pragmatic grounds. When we stake out normative claims in international politics, we introduce elements of irrationality and emotion in decision-making processes that are mastered best by rational calculations of national interest. In a similar vein, the legal theorist Hans Kelsen warns against the ambition to use political means for achieving moral ends because this leads inevitably to the abuse of power. When political leaders turn their backs on the practically possible and sally into the morally desirable, they often enough fall into adventurism, self-righteousness, and fanaticism. In Hans Kelsen's now famous formulation, justice is 'an irrational ideal' (Kelsen 1960: 15–16) and the quest to establish it has brought about some minor goods but much great suffering:

'No other question has been discussed so passionately; no other question has caused so much precious blood and so many bitter tears to be shed; no other question has been the object of so much intensive thinking by the most illustrious thinkers from Plato to Kant; and yet, this question is today as unanswered as it ever was. It seems that it is one of those questions to which the resigned wisdom applies that man cannot find a definitive answer, but can only try to improve the question' (Kelsen 1957: 1).

Contextualism thus rejects universalistic theories as the product of a wrong methodology. They are 'the result of generalizing illegitimately from a limited class of cases—of failing to see that what justice demands in one context may not be what justice demands in a different context' (Miller 2002: 15). Moreover, universalism is criticized for ignoring a manifest characteristic of the human condition: our most important social ties are based on positive discrimination. Most people feel greater love and loyalty for their closest relatives than for strangers, and most could not and would not want to share with all humanity the intimacy they feel toward their partners and friends. A moral duty to stop discriminating would mean imposing a requirement to cool down our feelings of commitment to our loved-ones. Indeed, how many of us are truthfully willing to lend a car, house, or personal wealth to any random stranger? This tendency to discriminate between strangers and friends may be rejected as illegitimate, and some may demand that we overcome it, but in doing so they flee the realm of what can be reasonably expected of normal human beings. We all act in specific social contexts, and in doing so we develop particularistic attachments. To deny this basic condition of humanity is to deny the fact that human beings are social beings and find their happiness in social attachment. Thus there are good reasons, in the mind of contextualists, to discriminate between groups of people on the basis of ascriptions, even on the basis of those they do not wish to have.

Contextualism in international theories of justice comes in two basic forms. A 'communitarian' form is concerned with the conditions under which moral obligations arise and why and when they are compelling for citizens. Communitarian authors like MacIntyre (1995) argue that all this can only be expected to hold in the context of the nation-state. It is the national setting that provides the dense political and cultural interaction that leads to the emergence of a morality integral to public life. In a very similar vein, Miller (2000: 27) holds that 'nations are ethical communities... The duties we owe to our fellow-nationals are different from, and more extensive than, the duties we owe to humans as such'. Outside the boundaries of national community, interaction is sporadic, individualistic, and driven by self-interest rather than by a sense of belonging together. The social foundation of common values beyond the state is comparatively thin and provides no common orientation possessed of compelling normative force. Rival conceptions of morality clash rather than interact (Huntington 1996) and have little chance of being mutually understood or cherished as equally acceptable ideas of the common good. For many communitarians, citizens have a realistic chance of leading a moral life only within the boundaries of their national community. Transnational justice is seen as a contradiction in terms, and patriotism is defended as an important moral principle. The social and cultural accomplishments of national community and the nation-state are valuable, far too valuable to be given up to the haphazard, eroding processes of cultural diversification and globalization.

These arguments are sobering for the project of establishing justice beyond national borders, for international relations are indeed characterized by a pronounced heterogeneity of value orientations and goals. There seems to be no possible basis for the establishment of a political authority that everyone considers just. The idea that a globally-minded public could integrate divergent national value systems into a single discourse on morality ignores the sheer multitude and fleetingness of those national discourses. In Morgenthau's formulation, even in a world of perfect information, no meaningful transnational discourse on moral issues would arise as long as this information is perceived from within different national contexts. People living all around the world might conceivably talk about the same things and eventually might even speak the same language, but due to the plurality of systems in which people are acculturated, their words would hardly be meaningful or useful for outsiders. For the adherents of contextualism, then, the attempt to link international politics with justice is doomed from the start. Politics without the bonds of national community can never meet the preconditions necessary for justice, so the question of who may appropriately demand justice from whom is simply irrelevant for international politics.

A related variant of contextualism can be termed 'institutional contextualism'. It comes to similar conclusions, although from a different path of reasoning. The central argument of institutional contextualism is that the state provides an institutional frame that alone makes demands for justice plausible. In its most basic form, institutional contextualism holds that individuals can only be expected to behave justly if a monopoly of the legitimate use of force exists such as to guarantee identical conditions of freedom for all. In other words: the state is a necessary precondition of justice. We can only be obligated morally to accept outside restrictions on our freedom when we can be certain that others will do the same for us. Anything else is (self-) exploitation and has little to do with the notion of justice. Thomas Nagel (2005) has recently reformulated this argument and applied it to international politics. According to Nagel, states are of fundamental, constitutive importance for realizing justice because they establish a coercive relationship among individuals. They thus put demands on citizens that go far beyond those in international politics:

> 'Sovereign states are not merely instruments for realizing the pre-institutional value of justice among human beings. Instead, their existence is precisely what gives the value of justice its application, by putting the fellow citizen of a sovereign state into a relation that they do not have with the rest of humanity, an institutional relation which must then be evaluated by the special standards of fairness and equality that fill out the content of justice' (Nagel 2005: 4).

Only the organizations of the state can establish equality among citizens, using a monopoly on the use of legitimate force. Thus, only the state can create bonds of citizenship strong enough to support mutual moral obligations: 'Justice is something we owe through our shared institutions only to those with whom we stand in a strong political relation' (Nagel 2005: 5). In contrast to voluntary agreements between two autonomous actors, states create a structure of authority that can force obedience from its members, the citizens, even when its rules oppose their personal interests. Exactly for this reason, states shoulder an especially high moral responsibility, and their actions must be subject to the highest standards possible. In the relationship of all these elements together lies the defining context within which demands for justice can rightly be made (cf. Dworkin 2000: 6). Because there are no institutions above the level of the nation-state able to exercise coercive authority, relations among states cannot possibly serve as a context for demanding justice. Nation-states are, after all, free to make or break contracts as they will, and there is no higher authority able to force them to violate their own interests.

The contextualist critique raises a number of issues that are crucial for assessing the merits of universalism. As an approach, however, it is also confronted with a number of objections. Contextualists are often criticized as relativistic because they assume that there are no context-free points of reference from which questions of justice can be approached. Thus, they assert that no universally applicable moral standards can be formulated. This stands in clear opposition to the intuition that fundamental values such as the abhorrence of torture and the protection of human dignity ought to be afforded the status of universal principle. And indeed, any theory of justice that has as its consequence a categorical negation of all such claims is probably not worth its salt. Nor should a serious theory of justice blatantly disregard the rule of reciprocity, i.e., the famous 'golden rule', which articulates something of a timeless, intercultural consensus about the ultimate meaning of justice. In all world religions and in all known civilizations we find the same basic intuition: only that which places no greater limitation on another's freedom than what we are willing to bear ourselves can be considered just. The

Christian admonition was formulated as 'whatsoever ye would that men should do to you, do ye even so to them: for this is the law and the prophets' (Matthew 7:12). The Talmud speaks a similar language: 'What is hateful to you, do not to your neighbour: that is the whole Torah, while the rest is the commentary thereof; go and learn it' (Babylonian Talmud, Mas. Sabbath, Folio 31a). Comparable passages are found in Buddhism, Islam, and Confucianism. Although it is an important insight that lived contexts are relevant for interpreting ideas of justice, this should not be construed to imply that consensus over values can be reached only within national territories or can only evolve through the processes of nation-building. A rigid application of the insights of contextualism easily overstretches the otherwise correct notion that justice is context-dependent. Its objection to universalism—that relationships of justice are only liveable in concrete political and social contexts and thus inevitably take on temporal, not eternal manifestations— is not a sufficient rebuttal on its own. The golden rule may of course allow for different interpretations, ranging from the simple 'eye for an eye, tooth for a tooth', to the generalization of rules of individual behaviour, to Habermas' sophisticated interpretation of the Kantian categorical imperative (Habermas 1991: 7–8). But at the same time, the existence of a norm of justice that extends across time and cultures is a strong indication that no human civilization is free to define the concept of justice arbitrarily. Justice has a kernel, at least, of universal validity. Thus, different historical and social contexts may generate different approaches to practical ethics and different political systems, but they are all based on common moral ground. In this view, it may be a permanent challenge to adjudicate between different notions of justice, but the task is not impossible. Because all empirical manifestations of justice build on the golden rule, they can all be encompassed by a single rational discourse of mutual accommodation.

A second objection to the claim that concepts of justice are inextricably bound to nations is that this claim rests on an understanding of society based in the tradition of *Gemeinschaft* (understood as a community of shared tradition) rather than *Gesellschaft* (which refers to a community that is bound together by common interests; (cf. Tönnies 1887/2005)). It interprets society one-sidedly as a form of interaction among citizens that is guided not by rational reflection and reasonable deliberations but by historically established feelings of solidarity and belongingness. Such a communitarian understanding of society has little conceptual openness for more instrumental forms of social integration and cannot account for the existence of a transnational community of values (Deutsch *et al.* 1957; Adler and Barnett 1998), the emergence of transnational epistemic communities (Haas 1992), or the growing cross-border interconnectedness of people via interactive media including the so-called web 2.0. It is, in short, based on a theory of society caught in a somehow old-fashioned and romanticized understanding that is hard to reconcile with many real-world phenomena and a more rationalistic approach to society. The argument that the nation state is not merely the most central analytical category for moral claims, but rather their only relevant site, is thus simply not persuasive (Valentini 2011). Rather, we must account for the fact that not only politics and economics but also moral and ethical standards are shaped and affected by the world outside the nation-state. We even might find relevant sites for their development and application in cross-border interactions. Contextualist theories of justice offer little purchase for understanding these processes.

5.2. Justice between universalism and contextualism

Both universalism and contextualism lead to largely untenable conclusions if applied dogmatically. What we need is, rather, a theory of justice that neither exalts a utopian global state nor negates the social connectedness of human beings across borders. We need a theory of justice that avoids the pitfall of setting the nation-state—and the concepts of justice currently associated with it—on a pedestal at a time when the empirical preconditions of their success are undergoing important changes. A theoretically plausible and empirically informed concept of justice must be so constructed as to span the gap between the extreme positions sketched above. It must be open to application in different cultural and political contexts and ought not to discriminate normatively for or against any one of them. It requires an understanding of the just that can be appreciated in both Scandinavia and Greece, by Christians, Muslims, and Hindus, and in both collectivistic and individualistic political cultures. At the same time, it must have sufficient normative gravity as to lay foundations for a vision of the good life and allow us to distinguish between better and worse political arrangements. We should take the contextualists' objection seriously: it is always necessary to interpret justice from within a specific culture, because all peoples have different normative orientations. Yet we ought not to weaken the importance of this observation by turning it into a free ride to highly permissive normative relativism. Common values and norms, as well as the political goals that emerge from them, can exist even in international and multicultural contexts.

Thus it is reasonable to seek a conception of justice that is as free as possible from culturally specific values. Taking account of the fact of global value plurality means that concepts of justice must be formulated such that individuals from different and even incommensurate schools of thought could assent to them (Rawls 1997: 335). This enterprise can no longer focus on building a concept of justice based on specific ideas of the good and the meaningful. The goal must be, rather, to formulate a concept of justice that takes up as much of a neutral position towards all metaphysical truths, ethical convictions, and religious dogmas as possible. It must restrict itself to the role of a mediator between contrary points of view without sacrificing clarity in its guidelines for normative assessment. The concept of justice we are seeking must be able to incorporate those elements that have been identified as just by democratic processes, but it must not be conditioned upon the unrealizable goal of a global democratic state. It must be compatible with the emerging transnational political reality and be applicable to the interaction between individuals, states, and non-state organizations. Further, the mechanisms by which justice is generated must not depend on domestic institutional structures for their theoretical underpinnings; our notion of justice must be conceptually open for functionally similar mechanisms of fostering legitimacy as they exist beyond the borders of the nation-state.

6

Justice and the Right to Justification

Concepts of justice are highly diverse and steeped in tradition. Ever since humanity began reflecting upon the preconditions of an ideal society and the corresponding failings of real life, people have sought the meaning of justice. Not surprisingly, notions of justice today carry a broad range of meanings, from a simple reliance on human intuition or 'common sense' to highly abstract and sophisticated theories. Some tend to equate justice with morality or even a general sense of appropriate behaviour. They claim that justice cannot be defined by means of abstract reflection, but that it necessitates an innate sensitivity to what is right and a naturally felt abhorrence of unjust deeds. Others identify it with the selection of those general principles that reasonable people would choose if freed from their materially based interests through the Rawlsian 'veil of ignorance' (Rawls 1999a). Whilst some schools of thought understand justice as a fair distribution of goods according to need, others emphasize the capability of putting resources to good use or the individual contribution to the production of goods (Sen 2009: 12–15). Justice can refer either to a process of distributing goods or to a certain kind of distributional outcome. It can focus on intentions or on achievements. In short, justice is an intrinsically contested concept in terms of scope, conditions, and content.

In order to derive a concept of justice that can be used properly as an analytical category, it is important to cut a path through these issues and to achieve definitional clarity. In the following chapter, justice is defined as the outcome of a justificatory process in a justified structure of political decision-making. This approach to justice takes its inspiration from the claim that human beings have an inalienable right to justification, i.e., that we are under no obligation to accept limitations on our freedom except those that can be justified by good reasons. Following Rainer Forst, all individuals have a 'fundamental right to justification', which entails 'no political or social relations of control that cannot be adequately justified to each and every affected individual' (Forst 2007: 10). Every use of political power must be justified to all affected individuals, who in turn are expected to accept a well-justified limitation on their liberty. In this understanding of justice, no existing distribution of material goods can claim to represent the just order of things—its mere existence is no evidence of its 'naturalness'. Nor may any rule-making authority neglect the duty to justify itself by persuasive argument. The right to justification invokes not only a right to defend oneself against illegitimate infringements on individual freedom by political authorities; it also implies a right to demand action. The minimal liberal state enjoys no greater *prima facie* legitimacy than the activist welfare state. Both are subject to the necessity of justifying themselves, either in their inaction or in their action.

The idea of a universal right to justification is rooted in an essentially egalitarian concept of liberty. It presumes the principle that all human beings are born free and may be restricted in their liberty only insofar as such limitations can be justified by good reasons. The right to justification protects all citizens equally from unfounded infringements on their liberty and provides a strong defence against arbitrary forms of political authority and control. It implies 'a qualified veto on all norms and practices that cannot be reciprocally and generally justified' (Forst 2007: 370). Everyone thus has the right to be protected against an unjustified violation of his or her liberties and to take appropriate action if a violation does occur.

Justice as justification has an intrinsically procedural and discursive character. It does not refer to a distribution of material or immaterial goods that can be justified on abstract principles. Rather, justice is the outcome of a discourse among political institutions and individuals, where the latter seize their right to justification in conflicts over resource distribution and political influence. Justice as justification is thus a political rather than a philosophical conception of justice and has clear institutional implications. Societies can claim to be just only when they guarantee that all individuals and groups affected by a law are endowed with a fair chance and full abilities to participate in law-making by bringing their concerns and preferences to the table. The search for justice is a political process in which concerns are articulated, arguments are weighed, objections are considered, and justifications are produced. These discourses of justification are of necessity never-ending. Their results are continually called into question because social preferences and attitudes change, technical progress and scientific research bring new knowledge, and moral standards shift. Participants in discourses of justification must therefore always be willing to re-examine the validity of old arguments in light of new developments.

The right to justification is not a recipe for transferring conflict into harmony. Its most essential goals are restricting unjustified infringements on individual liberty and making the use of political power conditional upon the provision of good arguments. It does not overcome asymmetries in power resources but disciplines their use. As a political concept of justice, the right to justification does not attempt to melt different opinions and concerns into a unified idea of what is just and appropriate but rather accepts different opinions as an unavoidable and permanent condition of modernity. Its ambition is not to overcome discord or dissent but rather to establish a constructive political rivalry among different claims, positions and views and thus to create a procedure through which conflict can be channelled into discourse.

Politics is intrinsically controversial, thus a political concept of justice should not make the futile attempt to replace political debate with any purportedly objective truth. The processes of justification discussed here are understood as instruments for legitimating political action; their function is not to persuade political opponents to abandon their interests but rather to motivate them to accept an intended action despite their disinclination to do so. In practice, justifications rarely lead to perfect consensus regarding the legitimacy of the action that is being justified. More often than not, deep-seated differences of opinion remain, even after long political discussions have occurred and good arguments have been formulated and accepted. Such differences can arise for many reasons including different sources of information, different understandings of the basic underlying problems, antagonistic interests, or divergent world-views. Yet even under these conditions, by means of a justificatory discourse agreements can be reached that are qualitatively different from the results of mere negotiation processes.

Eriksen (2009: 51) has introduced the useful category of 'working agreement' for describing outcomes of this sort, referring to agreements based on 'different, but reasonable and mutually acceptable grounds'. In contrast to agreements based on reciprocated conviction, by which all actors consider the same result to be right and appropriate for the same reasons, the reasons underlying a working agreement can be non-reciprocated. One actor might accept a justification out of pure self-interest, another on moral grounds, and yet another for pragmatic reasons. Working agreements are thus a pragmatic compromise around an outcome that we can accept as 'true' or 'right' enough, given the constraints of limited time, short resources, and incompatibility of worldviews. For this reason, working agreements obtain only temporary validity and may be renegotiated and overturned in the future if important new concerns are put on the table or if actors' interests change. Working agreements implicitly acknowledge the fluidity of preferences and knowledge as well as the imperfection of the conditions under which an agreement was reached. An agreement of this type cannot and does not claim to be able to withstand scientific tests of falsifiability, nor does it even represent 'truth' as popularly understood.

Despite their limited claim to an objective truth, working agreements do not appear out of thin air and cannot be changed on a whim. Individual understandings of shared situations are likely to be accepted only as part of a working agreement—or as legitimate challenges to pre-existing working agreements—if they plausibly reflect the set of values and norms shared by a group of communicating actors (Habermas 1973: 218). A working agreement thus never appears randomly nor does it merely reproduce any given asymmetry of power resources. It is an outcome of argument, grounded in the group's views and experiences, and reflects 'a binding structure of common commitments, one that commands respect for the moment' (Eriksen 2009: 51–2).

6.1. What is a justification?

The concept of justice used here puts a strong emphasis on the act of justification through communication. What conditions, then, must speech acts meet in order to be accepted as acts of justification? A justification, according to Rainer Forst, is a morally ambitious speech act that explains the rationale for one's actions or intentions in a manner consistent with the principles of reciprocity and universality. Reciprocity requires that no party involved successfully claims rights or privileges that it denies to others and that the formulation, rationalization, and evaluation of claims are not determined unilaterally. Equally important is the criterion of universality, which requires that the rationale for one's actions be based on arguments that can be accepted by all reasonable individuals affected, irrespective of their policy preferences (Forst 2002, 2007: 224). Note that in Forst's understanding, justification is essentially a moral category. It indicates a type of speech act that demands recognition from others by virtue of its internal structure, i.e. because of its universal and reciprocal validity. Refusing to acknowledge a perfect justification is, from this perspective, an immoral act.

From the perspective of normative realism, such a morally loaded category is difficult to apply. Empirical insight tells us that whilst politics and morality need not be diametrically opposed, neither are they very close cousins. After all, recognition of the moral superiority of a speech act seldom motivates powerful actors to abstain from pursuing their individual interests and to accept alternatives that are less beneficial for them. Philosophers of justice might accept good moral arguments, being those that are reciprocal and universal, as persuasive, but moral argument rarely forces politicians to change their objectives. Successful instances of moral persuasion are not unknown in practical politics; indeed, it would be inappropriate to negate them and many authors have traced the paths some arguments took to obtain

Justice and the Right to Justification

relevance (Kennan 1985; Brown 1992). Indeed, it is commonly emphasized in international relations that '(a)rguing, understood as reason-giving, is all pervasive in international politics: negotiating actors give reasons for their position and demands at almost any time, regardless of whether talks are conducted in public or behind closed doors' (Risse and Kleine 2010: 708). Arguing is nevertheless often epiphenomenal to power and interest. 'Argument (nearly) all the way down' (Crawford 2009) does not necessarily imply that arguments carry more than rhetorical references to morality or that they affect negotiating actors' preferences substantially. The argumentative process is often filled with elements of bargaining and is in most cases more influenced by power asymmetries than a straight truth-seeking process would be.

In order to make the concept of justification compatible with normative realism, it must be divested of some of its moral ballast. For this purpose we can employ a tradition of democratic theory that can be traced back to John Stuart Mill. Following Mill, one of the most important advantages of free political speech lies in the fact that it helps us distinguish between strong and weak arguments. Controversial exchanges tend to sort out weak arguments and improve the stronger ones (Mill, 1861/1991: 42). The prime mover of this process is not a shared morality or a process of justice-seeking but an adversarial culture of communication. Mill does not expect participants in justificatory discourses to engage in an altruistic search for objective truth or the common good. Claimants should be encouraged to clash with each other because this forces them to make their respective arguments as persuasive and water-tight as possible. Justification is therefore not necessarily characterized by cooperative consensus-building. In fact, it is more likely to emerge through the interaction of self-interested and rhetorically sophisticated actors. Justifications do not arise naturally through an introspective process of contemplation but rather from within a structure of interaction. They arise only if agents are compelled to give reasons for adopting certain viewpoints or courses of action (White and Ypi 2011: 385–6). Attempts to disseminate justifications—and to provoke them from others—are most likely to emerge in the context of political contests, as one agent seeks public recognition and attempts to apply pressure on an opponent. Partisanship is thus an important condition of a justificatory discourse. It provides incentives to produce intelligible justifications and to engage in efforts at making them as strong and convincing as possible. A proper interpretation of justification thus does not rule out the space for self-interested political action. In fact, it builds on it.

The kind of communication described with the concept of justification employed in this book is clearly distinct from a 'truth-seeking' mode of communication. Building on Jürgen Habermas' work on the characteristics of truth-seeking, Deitelhoff and Müller (2005), Risse (2000) and others argue that the exchange of claims to valid truth, rightness, and the sincerity of competent speakers in communicative situations all belong to a truth-seeking mode of communication. Actors challenge claims to validity inherent in causal or normative statements and seek consensus about their understanding of a situation as well as justifications for the principles and norms guiding their action. This mode of truth-seeking is goal-orientated, just like strategic interaction, but the underlying logic involves seeking argumentative consensus rather than defending one's fixed preferences (Risse and Kleine 2010). Truth-seeking is thus a mode of interaction that is not only based on the assumption that something approaching 'objective reality' actually exists but also implies that the purpose of communicating is to identify what it means. This is appropriate and useful, of course, for the purpose of scientific inquiry. In this form of communication, arguments are brought for and against a particular statement and the only thing that counts is the quality of the argument itself. The famous 'unforced force of the better argument' (Habermas 1995: 131) compels agreement. In politics, however, the truth-seeking mode of communicative exchange is rare, despite the fact that arguments are often packaged in a claim of universal validity. Indeed, we expect genuine truth-seeking only when topics are of low political salience, when existing interests are weakly structured or when the actors involved in negotiations have no clear political preferences (Haas 1992).

The concept of justification employed here clearly departs from a truth-seeking mode of communication. It assumes that actors are far more self-interested than the concept of truth-seeking allows. Justifications are speech acts that aim at legitimating one's own preferences by providing evidence for their compatibility with the shared goals of the community. Justifications do not require that the individual be predisposed to favour objective truth. They come into play when political action infringes on others' liberties and when this infringement must be explained as being legitimate. They are intended to legitimate an infringement on liberty and to motivate injured parties to accept the infringement willingly, often for the sake of a greater good either for themselves or for the community as a whole. Justifications are therefore highly ambitious speech acts indeed. Their objective is to legitimate the negative effects of one's actions on others by demonstrating their beneficial contribution to a goal that is accepted as being of superior importance. Justifications are typical for political constellations characterized by scarce resources in which material or normative values must be allocated competitively. The political actor who undertakes or proposes an allocation that is suboptimal from the point of view of other parties brings them forward. And they are demanded by those who are disadvantaged or fear disadvantage due to a proposed re-allocation.

6.1.1. *Substantial and procedural preconditions of justifications*

For justifications to be accepted by affected parties as legitimate, a number of demanding substantial and procedural requirements must be met. The substantial requirements include, first of all, that the justification must call upon values and norms shared by both the policy initiator and the addressee of political action. 'Justification depends on certain premises being shared by the agent and the constituency: some degree of common ground, or "frame resonance"... is required if justifications are (1) to be recognized and understood as such, and (2) to be received as convincing' (White and Ypi 2011: 389). A good justification explains an infringement of freedom such that the disadvantaged party voluntarily accepts it as reasonable and appropriate; at the very least, however, the affected party should not be able to reject it without refuting its own normative convictions (i.e. committing a 'performative contradiction'). A simple form of justification is, for example, saying that all motorists must drive on the same side of the road in order to prevent accidents. An affected party cannot challenge the prohibition on any reasonable ground without at the same time rejecting the goal of reducing the overall rate of automobile accidents. Assuming that all motorists prefer fewer accidents to more accidents, a rejection of the rule would amount to a performative contradiction and would be hard to defend publicly. A similarly common example of a justification is the argument that taxes are necessary for the sake of procuring socially desirable goods. Punishments for crime are defended by pointing to a hoped-for deterrent effect with a consequent increase in everyone's security. More complex forms of justification are based in controversial moral or ethical problems and link a particular solution to a specific worldview, justifying the resulting new rules as a logical expression of the worldview. Policies on issues such as abortion, religion, or other deeply ethical matters require these kinds of complex and philosophically sophisticated justifications in order to generate acceptance. Finally, all justifications must present a plausible argument that the policy in question is moderate and entails no more than a necessary minimum of infringement on liberty. We typically reject as arbitrary, unjust, and illegitimate any restrictions on our freedom that are not justified in these ways.

Justifications also have a procedural dimension. The degree to which a policy measure is accepted is often directly dependent on how the concerns of affected parties were addressed. Acceptance-generating justifications are those that sufficiently respond to critical questioning or to objections that the policy sets the wrong goals, makes use of the wrong means, or goes too far in restricting liberties. Proper justifications do not end political discourse but open it. Justifications are an integral part of a continuing communicative process. For this reason, actors often modify and update their justifications.

They incorporate new viewpoints, adjust their lines of argument, and repeatedly re-engage the critical audience. Reason-giving alone is not enough for giving a speech act the credentials of a proper justification. Many argumentative efforts are intended only to legitimate unsuitable, exaggerated, or wholly inappropriate infringements of liberty. Thus, the difference between superficial reason-giving and the more meritorious process of justification is that affected parties have a real chance to respond and to see any of their legitimate concerns incorporated into the proposed policy. The latent power of all participants to alter a proposed policy is of crucial importance for turning mere arguing into a proper process of producing justifications. It provides incentives to the policy-proposing party to take the burden of producing good reasons seriously and it gives the affected parties a motivation to engage in a critical discourse.

Justifications, furthermore, are strongly dependent on independent third parties assessing the validity of arguments and distinguishing between proper justifications and mere subjective explanations of individual motivations. In democracies, the public sphere and the media ideally adopt the role of an independent third party. By publicly exchanging policy suggestions and contesting them, the main participants in public policy discourses address themselves to the public at large more often than to each other. A governing party and its opposition both know very well that they are unlikely to convince each other; they do, however, nevertheless engage in political discourse and the exchange of arguments. A most important reason for this on-going effort is their awareness that they must convince the public of the legitimacy of their policies if they want to stay politically competitive in the long run. Justifications thus have, as opposed to truth-seeking, a triadic rather than a dyadic structure. They are conducted between a policy entrepreneur and a contender, but they also involve an independent third party with the competence to assess the soundness of reasons and to sanction or even prevent policies that lack the buttressing of convincing arguments.

Jon Elster (1998a) offers a persuasive analysis of the importance of a public sphere for a justificatory discourse. The public sphere, he argues, places three constraints on communication. First, speakers who want to sway a public audience, whether it be a specific audience like a jury or an undefined segment of the general public, have a strong incentive to put only those preferences on the table that are not too obviously connected to their personal interests. Public audiences find it harder to accept a proposal that is legitimated only by an appeal to the self-interest of its proponent than one that can claim convincingly to be in the common interest. A second constraint follows from the fact that speakers cannot arbitrarily renounce their public positions and arguments. In order to maintain a modicum of credibility, speakers must keep their actions consistent with their arguments and their arguments consistent with each other. Changing arguments, once they are a matter of public record, often results in a loss of persuasive force if the changes are not themselves well justified. The freedom of argumentative strategizing is thus strictly limited for any speaker who does not wish to be charged with opportunism. A third constraint is that speakers must avoid using a threatening tone in their arguments. The power of the argument must derive solely from qualities inherent to the argument itself.

All these constraints together compel even self-interested and strategic actors to behave *as if* they truly were interested in the public good and *as if* their personal proposal were a step on the path to this goal. Elster speaks here of the 'civilizing force of hypocrisy' (1998a: 111). Actors who in truth seek to maximize their own interests or those of their clients, and who care not for the common good, nevertheless are forced to use the mode of justification in political discourse. Only by so doing can they obtain the additional and often necessary boost of public legitimacy for their position. Even if actors are faking their community orientation, they still wind up creating exactly the argumentative mode of communication that is necessary for making good on the right to justification. Simply put, discourses of justification do not require that participants have altruistic attitudes or that they want to promote the common good. They only assume a common normative basis (the substantial precondition) and a receptive and critical public discourse (the procedural precondition) with the power and the will to sanction unconvincing arguments and policies.

Unfortunately, the public context of speech acts is not always conducive to a justificatory discourse. The practice of democracy is often far removed from deliberative ideals. Governments, for example, know very well that they have privileged access to the media and that journalists pay more attention to official government statements and rationales than to the critical remarks of opponents. Furthermore, powerful lobbies can buy media time and create other communicative spaces whilst diffuse interest groups find it very difficult even to briefly stimulate the public interest. The public sphere is not a space free of power relations (a *herrschaftsfreier Raum*) but is indeed subject to a great number of power asymmetries that create unequal access to audiences. Yet the practice of demanding and giving justifications is not limited to debate in the public sphere. Courts, too, are powerful arenas where citizens can articulate policy-relevant arguments by filing complaints against unlawful or arbitrary governmental actions. The judge serves here as the independent third party who weighs the merits of the arguments and has the capacity to block an administrative act or, in the case of a constitutional court such as in Germany, even to pre-empt legislation before it takes effect. Courts therefore can act as a functional equivalent to the public sphere by imposing a discipline of reason-giving on political actors and thus facilitating a justificatory discourse.

The importance of courts is closely related to the general function of law in fostering justificatory practices. Working agreements become more likely when discourses are encased in a legal structure. The often-noted phenomenon of the legal formalization of international politics and the strong role of the law in the process of European integration are important because the law reduces complexity and provides a firm ground for political interaction. Both issues are fundamental for constructive political discourses. Law reduces complexity by either distinguishing between right and wrong or by offering an arbitration procedure that leads to an authoritative assessment. Law also identifies criteria according to which the merits of an argument are assessed and thus distinguishes between relevant and irrelevant facts. The supportive function of law is one of the main reasons why we are able to get along with each other and why we react in a civilized and respectful manner when confronted with otherness (Habermas 1992: 57). In modern societies, citizens are all too often overburdened with the challenge of understanding different cultures and of coping with otherness and with seemingly incompatible understandings of right and wrong. Although speaking the same language, people with different cultural backgrounds often talk past one another and fail to understand each other properly. The law is an important only medium through which meaningful discourses can be channelled in normatively heterogeneous social contexts and processes of accommodation have a fair chance to take place.

The connection between legally structured discourses and the probability of arriving at working agreements is even clearer in international than in domestic politics. International relations are characterized by a high degree of heterogeneity and a plurality of normative dispositions. The European Union today covers a territory that stretches from Finland to Sicily and from Portugal to Poland. Its Member States have quite different political cultures, traditions of industrial relations, and modes of industrial production. They make use of diametrically different approaches to foreign affairs and sometimes disagree even on fundamental issues of rights. The WTO is even more diverse with its 150 Member States encompassing all great religions and stretching across five continents. An agreement, even a working agreement, uniting all 150 Member States on any important topic would be unlikely indeed without legal support. The huge difference in performance between the stalemated efforts to reform the WTO's constitutional framework and the WTO's highly effective dispute settlement mechanism underscore this point. Negotiations of the WTO treaty are conducted in an international environment of diplomacy and bargaining and have virtually no recourse to international law. They have been deadlocked for years. The dispute settlement mechanism, on the other hand, is integrated within a legal order that is highly structured in terms of its procedural and material provisions. Its success in settling disputes is largely due to the very detailed legal provisions concerning what arguments are valid (reciprocity, the most-favoured nations-principle, the prohibition of discriminating against foreigners, etc.) and where the limits of valid arguments lie.

Very similarly, European politics is most efficient in those areas where laws structure the argumentative discourse among Member States. Treaty law bolsters the administration of the common market and is supported by thousands of directives and decisions of the ECJ. Administrative processes can rely on this legal foundation and are hardly ever deadlocked in the longer run. Member states conduct their deliberations regarding regulations and legally admissible policies under the common roof of the *acquis communautaire*. Intergovernmental discourses, in which legal regulations have little effect on Member States' preferences or actions, often fail to deliver a similarly efficient policy output. The intergovernmental Common Foreign and Security Policy, for example, is notorious for its frustratingly meagre output, its incapacity to produce anything but lowest-common-denominator policies, and declarations that fail to have any significant impact on world politics (Hill 1993; Smith 2006).

These brief examples clearly show that international and European politics is strongly dependent on the function of law to underpin and foster meaningful discourse. Even when discourses are characterized by an exchange of good arguments, they do not necessarily end in agreement, nor do they necessarily lead only to greater mutual understanding. It is just as likely that an exchange of opinion will serve only to make participants realize what separates them. Argumentative interactions taking place between different political cultures—or even between different philosophies of how to regulate trade—have a fair chance of ending in agreement only if participants are willing to subsume their individual claims under a common procedural and material discipline. In politically and culturally heterogeneous contexts, agreement is likely only under the roof of a consensus about which material criteria and procedures apply for differentiating between strong and weak arguments. More than in any national state, political relations beyond the state and outside of normatively integrated communities must be characterized by a high degree of constitutional agreement and legalized procedure for coping with contending claims to justice, if a right to justification is to be implemented that not only gives lip service to the idea but allows it to obtain practical relevance. The process of legalization of international politics and the establishment of institutions with adjudicative functions can be explained as a reaction to this underlying weakness. In international politics, law is the common language and the necessary common standard of rationality for assessing proffered arguments (Johnstone

2003). And it is the only basis on which discursive agreement under conditions of normative plurality is likely.

6.1.2. *Justification and expert communities*

A final word is in order regarding expert communities. Many contributions to the literature on deliberation argue that proper argumentative discourses are more likely when participants share a common life-world—a world of experience in which the same objects are attributed with the same meaning (Risse 2000; Müller 2001). Such shared meanings, so the argument goes, are rare enough in domestic politics and hardly exist at all in international politics. Yet when expert communities working from a common pool of meaning do arise, they are much more likely than political communities to agree on what is to be accepted as 'true'. Due to their common professional background, experts rely on a shared concept of good and bad arguments and often have less difficulty clarifying differences and similarities among multiple relevant arguments and evaluating each argument in the event that differences of opinion do arise (Haas 1992). Environmental specialists from, say, Canada, Egypt, and Denmark are certainly capable of engaging in a constructive, solution-orientated discourse and of ultimately agreeing upon appropriate standards of pesticide use, as long as they have the same understanding of the relevant causal mechanisms regulating the interaction of pesticides and the environment. Very similarly, international commissions have been able to formulate with astonishing ease common ethical standards for corporate behaviour (Ruggie 2002) and extensive catalogues of good governance benchmarks (World Bank 2001). Expert communities are in many cases extraordinarily helpful—and may even be necessary—for finding adequate and justifiable solutions outside the framework of formal negotiations. Experts cloak themselves with the standards and practices of professional rationality and often can come to terms with each other on this basis.

At the same time, arguments regarding the extent and relevance of epistemic communities should not be exaggerated. Epistemic communities only make sense as instruments of decision-making in those cases where they have a clear mandate and where there is unanimity regarding the reasons on which they are to base their decisions and the criteria that are to be applied. Engineers can fix technical problems but are not experts in questions of social responsibility. When technicians begin to formulate solutions to what are ultimately political questions, they rob society of potentially important options. In the European Union, exactly this problem can be observed in the large number of technical agencies that have been established in the past ten years. There now exists a dense network of such agencies dealing with problems ranging from food safety to border security to monetary policy (Rittberger and Wonka 2011). Most of these agencies operate under a very specific mandate and thus within a political space with a pre-defined political rationale. Expert communities exercise an appropriate political role when confined to a politically determined mission that is itself subject to a continual process of political justification. Although the independence of experts is often desirable, it ought not to lead to a situation where experts can insulate both their decision-making processes and their mission assignment from political intervention. Their job must always be limited to the preparation of technical knowledge so as to aid politicians in the formulation of arguments but not to substitute for them.

6.2. Supportive distributive justice

Meaningful justificatory discourses require that participants are equipped with the resources necessary for deliberative interaction and for making sophisticated claims to justice. This requirement links the procedural approach of the right to justification to the literature on distributive justice. Distributive justice takes issue with how the resources of a society are allocated and whether all citizens have adequate access to them. Opinion is anything but unanimous, however, regarding what 'adequate' access actually entails. Relevant contributions emphasize different principles of resource allocation. Whilst some value individual need, others value just desserts, utility, or individual freedom. Most prominent among these suggestions is the idea of equality. The defenders of equality hold that every person should have the same level of material goods and services. This principle is most commonly justified on the grounds that all people are inherently equal, that the dignity of one and all must be respected, and that equality in material goods and services is the best way to guarantee this. Reacting to the critique that an equal distribution of resources can have negative effects on the overall level of provision of goods and thus negatively affect the poorest members of society, John Rawls has modified the principle of equality by introducing the so-called Difference Principle (Rawls 1993). This principle retains the strong emphasis on an equal allocation of goods, but allows for an unequal allocation as long as inequality has the effect that the least advantaged in society are materially better off than they would be under strict equality.

The Rawlsian suggestion to treat any unequal distribution of goods as unjust if it cannot be justified by its beneficial effect for the poorest members of a society is intuitively appealing and serves as an important point of reference in debates about the expansion or contraction of welfare states. It is a concept of justice, however, that addresses itself to the level of production and consumption of material goods and is thus only loosely connected to the right to justification. Both issues are connected, of course. If the basic needs of citizens are not satisfied, if they have no or only limited access to the media and if they lack the necessary education for understanding political processes, then they cannot be expected to challenge sophisticated arguments and to engage in demanding justificatory discourses. Education and expertise are important and often very costly resources. Not having access to them is a major obstacle for deliberative forms of interaction. It is far from clear, however, whether and under what conditions material resources beyond the fulfilment of basic needs translate into an improvement of the discursive capabilities of citizens. Redistributed resources can, and often are, spent by their recipients for things totally unconnected to justifications and reason-giving.

A distributive theory of justice that is intended to complement the concept of justification must nevertheless confront the problem of social inequality and its negative implications for the likelihood of inclusive justificatory discourses. Such an effort can be built on the assumption that an inclusive justificatory discourse will only be likely if all participants are equipped with the necessary material and intellectual resources for making and challenging demanding arguments. At least two sets of problems must be addressed here. The first problem relates to the absolute level of goods needed by participants. This level must be high enough to meet basic physical needs, to allow participants to identify limitations on their own liberty imposed by others, and to voice their concerns in a manner that can be processed by the political system. Participants must, in short, be not only well fed and housed but also educated and free from any major hindrance to political participation. The second problem relates not to access but to capabilities and is even more difficult to overcome. Even if everyone has sufficient resources for participating in the political process, participants may still be unequal in terms of capabilities. Some participants may be able to dominate the discourse due to superior knowledge, ability to process information, or talent in making rhetorically powerful arguments. It is very difficult, however, to determine as a matter of general rule how much difference in deliberative competence is acceptable and at what point deliberative inequality turns into ideological domination (Przeworski 1998). The wealthier the participants are, the more expertise they will be able to gather and the higher will be their ability to make strong arguments. At this juncture, those demanding full economic equality have a point. On the other hand, a capability of identifying grievances and of voicing concerns is obviously not only possessed by the rich but is mastered, too, by the less advantaged members of society. The adequate level of redistribution is therefore hard to assess objectively. As a general rule, however, we might come back to the Rawlsian Difference Principle and apply it more directly to the discursive capabilities of citizens. Unequal distributions of discursive capabilities might then, and only then, be defensible if they improve the epistemic qualities of a discourse with the effect of making the least advantaged better off than before. Because it is extremely hard to prove this, however, the general norm should be that those who are economically better off carry a moral duty to safeguard that those who are less well-off can participate meaningfully in justificatory discourses. And, vice versa, those who are less well-off have a right to have access to the necessary resources for education and information gathering and must be enabled to identify their interests adequately and to produce meaningful justifications for their policies. The resource-rich thus carry a duty to ensure that the condition of their economic advantage does not translate into an unfair discursive dominance and thus distort the whole idea of a justificatory discourse.

This brief discussion has highlighted two important insights into the role of distributive justice in a theory of procedural justice. The first insight holds that distributive measures are an important precondition for levelling the playing field to a degree that all participants have a fair chance to participate. Distributive measures are necessary to ensure that economic disadvantage does not automatically translate into a political gag order. The second insight emphasizes that distributive justice basically functions as a supportive instrument to procedural justice. Procedural justice, understood as the outcome of a justificatory discourse, is the goal; distributive justice is the means of enabling participants to meaningfully engage in justifications. Distributive justice therefore does not primarily address material equality but aims to expand the communicative capacities of discourse participants. It is an approach that focuses distribution on issues of education and access to expertise and the public sphere. It is orientated not at increasing welfare spending for the poor as a good in itself but conditions such transfers on their contribution to society's overall capacity to engage in justificatory discourse.

The supportive function of distributive justice for procedural justice is not only relevant in domestic contexts but also applies to international politics. In international negotiations the problem arises time and again that the complexity of the topics involved simply overwhelms the highly limited human, technical and financial resources of developing countries, their diplomats and political executives (Khor 2001). Many developing countries lack highly educated and well-informed delegates and are thus seldom able to stake out well-grounded policy positions in demanding issue areas. A widely recognized problem of negotiations on greenhouse gas reduction, for example, is that the delegations of many developing countries are small and inexperienced, have little or no access to support from national research institutes, and are unfamiliar with the practices of negotiation (Page 2003: 7).

Busch and Reinhardt (2003) report similarly from the WTO that the legal reforms of the Dispute Settlement Mechanisms have failed to level the playing field in favour of less developed states. Under the new WTO rules, Member States have access to a highly legalized system of settling disputes with shortened time periods, automatic panel establishment, and comparatively easy access to the authorization of retaliatory measures. As opposed to rich Member States, who have employed the new system often to their advantage, developing states have proven unable to make good use of the system and to secure significantly greater concessions. Busch and Reinhardt observe a 'new and growing gap between rich and poor Member States in the performance of the dispute settlement component of the global trade regime' (Busch and Reinhardt 2003: 720). The basic reason for this systemic failure is that it moved the phase of settling most disputes from the early consultation phase to the later formal litigation phase. In litigation, however, concessions seem to be more difficult to realize. Defendants have incentives to gamble that the extra burdens of pursuing the case will deter further action by the plaintiff. It is thus not legal action but informal negotiations in the 'shadow of the law' that are more likely to motivate defending parties to offer concessions. In formal litigation, however, defendants 'tend to dig in their heels' (ibid.) with the consequence that successful resolutions of disputes become less likely. The consequences of this shift differ significantly for developing and developed states. Advanced industrial states generally maintain a large permanent legal and economic staff tasked with WTO and trade law matters, a resource that few developing states have. The move from a 'power-orientated' to a more 'rule-orientated' system contains thus no threat for developed states, but only changes the currency in which the richer states play out their superior resources. For poorer countries, however, legalization often implies additional disadvantages rather than the promise of a levelled playing field. It only too easily means that their traditional source of weakness—namely, the lack of market size and thus retaliatory power—is intensified by a new one: legal incapacity.

Despite the hurdles experienced by less developed states in making use of the legalized structures of justificatory discourses, we need not dismiss the right to justification as utopian. Mechanisms of supportive distributive justice are highly compatible with the practices of international politics and can be identified in many international organizations. One example of such mechanisms is incorporated within the guidelines of the Development Assistance Committee (DAC) of the OECD. These guidelines are an expression of the OECD's goal to support liberal trade policies in all countries. Yet, they are rooted in the insight that the ability of countries to take advantage of the opportunities of a liberal economy depends on their capacity to identify their strategic interests and to formulate them in a national trade policy. In order to increase the chances for developing countries to be integrated into the multilateral trade system in a way that is advantageous for their own development, supportive measures are offered for the formulation of a national trade policy, for setting up effective mechanisms of consultation between the government, businesses, and civil society groups, and for improving internal coordination within the public sector.

In addition to these measures, the Integrated Framework for Trade-Related Technical Assistance (IF)—a joint initiative of the IMF, the International Trade Centre (ITC), the United Nations Conference on Trade and Development (UNCTAD), the United Nations Development Programme (UNDP), the World Bank, and the WTO—provides technical assistance for improving the domestic, administrative, and political structures of participating countries. It encourages the poorest states to put trade issues at the forefront of their development strategies. Another programme guided by the principle of supportive distributive justice is the Joint Integrated Technical Assistance Programme (JITAP). This is a joint effort between the ITC, the UNCTAD, and the WTO which has as its objective an increased presence of eight participating African nations in the multilateral trade system. The essential goals of the JITAP are a better and more widespread domestic understanding of the international trade system, the adaptation of domestic trade structures to relevant international legal guidelines, and the improvement of the performance of domestic exporters on world markets. A number of different activities are undertaken in pursuit of these ends, including the organization of training seminars, the commissioning of studies and country reports, and the development of cross-border structures of communication.

Although most observers welcome such practices, there is, of course, also no lack of fundamental criticism of the limited readiness of international economic institutions to engage in broader measures of redistribution. Thomas Pogge, for example, argues that international distributive justice requires a large-scale redistribution of wealth and direct financial transfers. Existing economic structures, he argues, were created by Europe and the United States and still today cement a structurally exploitative relationship between the first and the third world to the exclusive advantage of the former: 'the affluent countries and their citizens... impose a global economic order under which millions avoidably die each year from poverty-related causes' (Pogge 1994: 220). For him, the causes of the developmental imbalance between poor and rich countries lie not in governance failures of the less affluent nations but in imperialism, colonialism and unfair treatment. Because Europe and the United States still profit from the existing structures of exploitation, it behoves them to support the poor nations of the world, especially in Africa, through a large-scale transfer of wealth.

Neither the analysis underlying the proposal nor the recipe itself is convincing, however. There is no disputing that the most important global economic organizations, including the World Bank, the IMF, and the WTO, were all founded under the leadership of the North, but there is certainly no consensus that these organizations harm developing countries' chances of catching up economically. The WTO, for example, has incorporated the principle of special and differential treatment for its poorest and weakest members (Bernal 2006). This principle recognizes the necessity of showing greater leniency to developing countries in the enforcement of international trade law. Altogether, there are over 150 provisions in WTO law that address the issue of special and differential treatment. Among these are longer deadlines for implementing WTO provisions, technical support as noted above, and privileged market access. These provisions can be interpreted as an acknowledgement of different stages of development among the world's nations and as evidence for the willingness of the richer WTO Member States to take the problems of poorer and weaker trade partners seriously—seriously enough at least to underwrite institutions that promote supportive distributional justice. In addition, it is far from obvious that less developed states would be better off in a world without the IMF, the World Bank, and the WTO. Free trade on the basis of special and differential treatment (WTO), low-interest loans for infrastructure projects (World Bank) and stable currency exchange rates (IMF) are not only in the interest of the North but also of the South. Few nations today ascribe the main underlying causes of underdevelopment and poverty to global economic structures. Instead, there is an emerging consensus that poor education and healthcare systems, widespread corruption, and dysfunctional bureaucracies are at least as harmful to national economic development as the negative effects of the globalized liberal economy (Sen 1999). Calls for a reform of the basic rules of international trade and for financial compensation for historical wrongdoing are made mostly by non-governmental organizations only. Historically affected states such as China, India, Indonesia, or Brazil concentrate their complaints instead on the protectionist policies of the European Union and the USA. They are not prominent critics of free trade and the institutions of the global liberal order as such.

Another objection to demands for large-scale financial transfers is the insight that unlimited inflows of wealth tend to have negative effects on the political systems of the receiving states (Aidt 2009). They easily end up advancing corruption and nepotism, upsetting the balance of power among branches of government to the advantage of the executive. All of what we know about the conditions of successful industrialization, based on the history of successfully developed countries, casts doubt on the belief that external aid promotes sustainable economic development. Almost all known

Justice and the Right to Justification

examples of successful industrial development in countries that modernized after the original wave of European industrialization—including the USA, Germany, and Italy in the 19th century and South Korea, Taiwan, and Singapore in the 20th—accomplished their developmental leap without significant international redistributive measures. In contrast, most of the greatest disappointments in development policy, including most states of sub-Saharan Africa, occurred in the context of comprehensive financial support from the North. The most important conditions for sustainable development are thus likely to be found in internal structural reforms and good governance rather than in external aid (World Bank 2011). Good governance supported by technical assistance, not redistribution as such, is the key to economic development. All of this lends little credence to the analysis that a greater volume of redistribution will lead to greater developmental success. In fact, this cure could be worse than the disease.

In the EU, supportive distributive justice is a far less prominent topic than in the WTO or other international economic institutions. The EU's Member States are economically much more homogeneous than the Member States of the WTO or the IMF. They work under the assumption that all are adequately well equipped to identify their interests, articulate concerns, and develop meaningful justifications. Although the European system of reallocating funds has been reworked on a nearly permanent basis since its inception in the late 1950s and although it has been highly responsive to the concerns of the less developed Member States, it still does not incorporate more than a marginal emphasis on issues of legal, technical, or other forms of assistance. From the time the EU was founded and its system of distributive funds established, poorer Member States have focussed their financial demands on infrastructure projects or on compensation for economic restructuring. None of the distributive funds of the EU today reallocates resources from the richer Member States to the poorer ones for the purpose of increasing their discursive capabilities. The largest fund by far, the European Agricultural Guarantee Fund (EAGF) finances measures intended to regulate agricultural markets, including export refunds and other direct payments to farmers. An infrastructure-orientated European Agricultural Fund for Rural Development (EAFRD) complements it and finances the rural development programmes of the Member States. Basically, both funds are means for subsidizing farmers directly or for supporting domestic subsidization schemes. The low salience attached to issues of supportive distributive justice can be observed also in the fund of greatest direct relevance for less-developed regions, the European Regional Development Fund (ERDF). The principal objective of the ERDF is to promote economic and social cohesion within the European Union through the reduction of imbalances between regions or social groups. Yet its support for administrative infrastructure, legal training, and other forms of

103

technical assistance is far less important compared to the volume of funds channelled into subsidizing roads, airports, or other forms of infrastructure.

Supportive distributive justice figures prominently, however, in the EU's relations with its less developed neighbours to the East and South. In 1989, the EU set up its programme of aid to the countries of Central and Eastern Europe (PHARE). The programme was originally intended to support the process of reform and economic and political transition in Poland and Hungary, but it soon became the financial instrument of the pre-accession strategy for the entire region, leading ultimately to the accession to the EU of the eight associated Central and Eastern European countries (CEECs) following the Essen European Council in December 1994. The two main objectives of PHARE were to help the administrations of the candidate countries to acquire the capacity to implement the Community *acquis* and to familiarize themselves with Community objectives and procedures. PHARE's successor today is the Instrument for Pre-Accession Assistance (IPA). It offers assistance to countries engaged in the process of accession to the European Union (EU) for the period 2007–2013 and has a very similar focus. Its main aim is not to compensate for market pressure but to support institution-building and a broad set of issues of technical and legal assistance. Among them are programmes for fostering administrative and economic reforms, regional and cross-border cooperation, the rule of law, and human rights.

6.3. Transparency

The effectiveness of the right to justification is directly dependent on transparent decision-making procedures. Citizens must have the opportunity to follow legislative decision-making processes and to raise their voice when decisions are to be adopted that have negative effects for them or that are not fully justified in the face of opposition. Transparency is thus of crucial importance for the right to justification. It is a delicate topic in the European multi-level system of governance, however. Among the most important characteristics of the EU's institutional structure are the large number of players involved and the complex processes that precede final decisions. In the EU, neither the Commission, nor the Council, nor the European Parliament can unilaterally pursue their goals without obtaining the approval of the other institutions. It is not just the Member States that have to coordinate their preferences in order to obtain a qualified majority; the need for coordination also applies to European institutions themselves. The Council cannot act without a proposal on the part of the Commission, and it also needs the Commission to manage implementation. The Commission must formulate its legislative proposals in a way that is likely to pass the scrutiny of both the

Council and the Parliament, and it must also secure Member State approval for implementation measures. Furthermore, because the Commission has only limited capacities to enforce European law, it dedicates a great deal of effort to the safeguarding of broad political support for its proposals, consults as many interest groups as possible, and prefers to postpone disputed issues rather than to vote on them.

All these aspects together make European governance a mode of making and implementing decisions that is often informal, opaque, and without clearly traceable lines of responsibility (Papadopoulos 2010: 1034–9). Control on the part of national parliaments is difficult. The length of the delegation chain combined with the magnitude of administrative discretion makes democratic accountability more fiction than fact. European politics is often conducted among networks of policy experts and technical agencies who are deliberately unaccountable to domestic constituencies in order to remain credible to their professional communities. Participating NGOs rarely solve the problem of transparency. They often represent well-organized interests rather than the median voter and are glad if they succeed in making their concerns heard, even if behind closed doors.

Political outcomes of multi-level policy-making are furthermore often the result of a simultaneous process of horizontal compromise between governments and vertical compromise between governments and domestic actors. Under these circumstances, it is often nearly impossible to clearly identify what the interests of governments de facto were and which positions they only maintained as a bargaining move. Governments can easily argue that a particular position adopted or even a negotiation outcome could not be averted, pointing to the extraordinary exigencies of multilevel cooperation. In complex multilevel governance structures like those of the European Union, acts of law can be ratified only if initiated by the European Commission and supported by both a super-majority of Member States and a majority of the members of the European Parliament. In this context, a situation can easily arise in which no one takes responsibility for the result of negotiations. Finger-pointing and buck-passing are inevitable, promoted by an institutional structure that preordains shirking. For similar reasons, the activating dimension of the right of justification, which refers to the right to demand justification for non-action, is weak to non-existent in this context. In front of whose door should political activists shout when no single actor can be identified who had leadership authority and when every policy outcome is the result of complex negotiations?

In light of these constraints, it seems clear that the right of justification can emerge in complex multilevel systems with multiple veto players only when preceded by a comprehensive right of media access. The level of publicity must be high enough to allow the public to follow and criticize the legislative process at any time. The intrinsically public and open nature of the democratic legislative process is a time-honoured principle in place since the very beginnings of democracy. It is ignored only in international politics and finds few supporters even in the European Union. The basic rule that legislative assemblies meet publicly so as to allow citizens to critically monitor the arguments of their representatives existed in the Agora of ancient Greece, was practiced later in the Roman senate and is characteristic of all democratic parliaments in all eras. Only in international politics is this venerable rule disrespected such that the international legislative process occurs without the buzz of a watchful citizenry. The exclusion of the public's critical eye is a tradition rooted in the practice of secret diplomacy, a practice that today is normatively and practically superannuated. It is in blatant contradiction to the right of justification, exactly because it makes it impossible to identify key actors embedded in the interdependent, multi-level governance systems so characteristic of modern international politics. Thus, the establishment of a comprehensive right of media access must be recognized as a necessary precondition for justified structures of justification.

The EU has undertaken in recent years a number of steps to give force to more openness. In its Art. 255 (now Art. 15 TFEU), the Amsterdam Treaty introduced a citizens' right of access to European Parliament, Council, and Commission documents. The implementing regulation 1049/2001 stipulates that 'any citizen of the Union, and any natural or legal person residing or having its registered office in a Member State, has a right of access to documents of the institutions'. Exceptions to the rule must be justified and defended on grounds of public interest, the protection of sensitive personal data, commercial benefits, legal proceedings, or for other important reasons. The Council reacted to the new provision by adopting new rules of procedure in 2006. According to the new rules, all Council deliberations on legislative acts that are to be adopted in accordance with the co-decision procedure (now the so-called 'ordinary legislative procedure') shall be public. Co-decision has become the major type of decision-making in the EU and today covers internal market issues and most areas of home affairs and judicial policy. The rules also provide, for example, that the General Affairs and External Relations Council shall hold a public policy debate on the Council's 18-month programme. They make public all deliberations on the policy priorities of other Council configurations as well as the Commission's presentation—and ensuing debates in the Council—of its five-year programme, its annual work programme, and its annual policy strategy. Although these measures are welcome and contribute to fostering transparency, they do not go far enough. The rules of procedure emphasize that the Council's meetings are generally not public and that all deliberations are covered by the 'obligation of professional secrecy'. They also list some significant exceptions to transparency. Areas that are deemed to be politically sensitive such as foreign and security policy and the harmonization of taxation and migration policy are still deliberated and adopted behind closed doors. The rules of procedure are thus a necessary step in the right direction, but they are not sufficient in and of themselves to guarantee transparency. They still fall short when compared to the standards of the democratic legislative process. Even more problematic is the nearly complete absence of transparency from the European Council and the EU's intergovernmental conferences. Changes to the Treaties and thus to the most important parameters for justificatory discourses are conducted among the heads of state without any interference or critical scrutiny by the media. In all of these areas, the right to justification is still hampered by out-dated practices of intransparency that hark back to the tradition of diplomacy and have little to do with the idea of justice.

6.4. Justified accountability

The structural deficiencies of multi-level governance have stimulated an intense debate in EU studies on how to foster the accountability of the EU (Harlow 2002; Arnull and Wincott 2002). As a concept, accountability is closely related to the right to justification. It emphasizes mechanisms such as peer review, media control, stake-holder participation, and good administrative procedures. Accountability can be understood as a mechanism that obligates an actor to explain and justify their conduct to a forum. It involves 'the provision of information about performance... the possibility of debate, of questions by the forum and answers by the actor, and eventually of judgement of the actor by the forum' (Bovens 2010: 951). Relationships of accountability are between an actor who is asked to give an accounting of past actions and a forum that assesses whether the actor's justification meets applicable criteria. Bovens (2010: 952) distinguishes four defining elements of the relationship between actor and forum. These are 1) the obligation of an actor to report, explain, and justify its conduct to the forum, 2) the option by the forum to question the adequacy of the information and to interrogate the actor, 3) the passing of a judgement on the information given, and 4) the option of positive or negative sanctioning depending on the assessment of the performance of the actor by the forum. All four elements can be institutionalized differently and can vary in the degree to which they are formally institutionalized at all. They can be fully codified or based on informal expectations and social pressure.

Accountability has become a new analytical focus for much of the literature because it provides the means to bolster EU legitimacy without resorting to demands for more extensive parliamentarization (cf. Curtin 2009; Bovens,

Curtin, and 't Hart 2010). It also harmonizes well with EU practices, which makes it attractive for empirically-minded scholars. The major problem of the concept, however, is its analytical and normative indistinctness. Its analytical powers have been criticized as weak and the whole concept has been compared to a 'dustbin filled with good intentions...and vague images of good governance' (Bovens 2007: 449). Indeed, accountability is overburdened by a heavy load of expectations. It is supposed to be able to 'ensur[e] that public officials or public organizations remain on the virtuous path', 'induce reflection and learning', 'identify and address injustices and obligations', 'establish public control', 'prevent and detect corruption and the abuse of public power', 'help creat[e] checks and balances', and foster 'public catharsis' (Bovens 2010: 955).

Certainly, accountability matters to legitimate governance 'because of the presumption that its absence means that those in power have the capacity to act without regard for those who authorize their actions and for those whose lives are affected by those actions' (Barnett and Finnemore 2004: 171). However, the concept of accountability lacks a clear normative underpinning. It is, in the words of Lord and Pollak (2010), an 'unsaturated concept'. It is not outfitted with answers to pressing questions such as who should be accountable to whom, when, and for what reasons. The approach most often used for finding an answer to these questions is principal-agent analysis. It holds that all those who delegate power have the right (and the power) to demand accountability from those actors or institutions to which powers are delegated. Accountability is thus an element of the relationship between a sender and a receiver of political authority. An important strength of principal-agent analysis is its clarity and parsimony. Political relationships can be clearly delineated and responsibilities made easy to pin down. Complex political reality, however, often does not fit neatly into these categories. Principal-agent analysis systematically overlooks that actors who control delegated powers might use them either deliberately or unintentionally against the interests of third parties who have neither delegated nor received authority (Philp 2009). In the principal-agent framework, these actors would have no right to demand or receive accountability for the use of delegated powers. In European politics, such situations are very common. The introduction of the Euro, to name one prominent example, was to a significant degree motivated by the interest of some Member States to set up a counterweight to the German *Bundesbank*. Before the introduction of the Euro, the *Bundesbank* protected the concerns of the German Mark exclusively. Because it was the strongest currency in the EU, however, *Bundesbank* policy had a significant effect on the currencies of other Member States. Whenever the *Bundesbank* decided to raise or lower its interest rates, all other European central banks had to follow even if this meant harming their domestic economic interests. The *Bundesbank*'s decisions thus had a strong effect on third parties who, according to principal-agent analysis, had no moral right to influence them because they had not delegated any powers. There are similar examples in other policy areas, all of which point to the normative limits of principle-agent analysis and its negligence of the external effects of decisions on third parties.

Principal-agent analysis thus leaves a number of pressing questions open and is of little help for explaining the normative thrust of the concept of accountability. Why should only those who possess delegated powers be held accountable when there are many political actors who infringe on other's freedom using non-delegated powers? Are they free to exercise their powers without having to justify their actions? Is there a general rule about situations where it is appropriate to demand and receive justifications? Should these include only principle-agent dyads or should they also include all situations in which individual freedom is limited by the decisions of power holders? None of these questions can be answered without a more elaborate explanation of the normative underpinnings of the concept of accountability. The right to justification can provide this underpinning by connecting accountability to the right to justification. 'Justified accountability' can be explained along the dimensions of who is to be held accountable, to whom we owe accountability, and where to draw the limits of the duty of accountability.

6.4.1. *Who is to be held accountable?*

Justified accountability requires that all political actors who limit individual or collective freedoms or who have the power to enhance it are to be held accountable. Actions that limit liberty must be justified by political actors, including national governments, the Commission, the Council, and all other national, European, and international bodies that produce binding collective rules. These actors have a permanent obligation to explain their actions and to submit to questions regarding their underlying motivations. The right to justification invokes not only a right to defend oneself against the illegitimate infringements on individual liberty by political authorities, it also implies a right to demand action. We have the right not only to insist that others desist from committing unjustified acts, we also have the right to insist that the authorities desist from unjustified inaction when this inaction results in freedoms withheld. The activating component of the right to justification applies to situations where a political authority or an individual possesses the means to eliminate a condition that restricts our freedom but does not do so, intentionally or not. An example is affirmative action policy for the physically disabled, whereby employers are required to give hiring preference to handicapped applicants who are otherwise equally qualified. For cases in which preference is instead given to a non-handicapped applicant, they are obligated to justify that choice. European law, too, codifies the obligation to justify inaction in some cases. For example, Member States not in full and timely compliance with European directives are required to submit on demand a written explanation to the European Commission. Even international law requires the justification of certain kinds of inaction, including the refusal to arrest accused war criminals or the failure to meet treaty-based obligations to reduce greenhouse gas emissions or weapon stockpiles.

6.4.2. Accountable to whom?

Because the right to justification builds upon an individualistic conception of freedom, it is clear that the ultimate addressee of justifications is the affected individual. Its point of departure, both for its passive and active dimensions, is the protection of the individual from infringements of liberty. The right to justification interprets liberty as a fundamental human right: 'The basic principle of the right to justification implies the individual's fundamental right to receive justification, which equates to a qualified veto on all rules and practices that cannot be reciprocally justified' (Forst 2007: 370). Every individual possesses a right to exercise its freedom as long as doing so does not limit anyone else's. Thus, the right to justification is primarily an individual right.

Yet, in the practice of international politics, the right to justification is hard to realize on an individual level. The administrative capacities of European and international institutions would be overwhelmed if all individuals affected by a European regulation directly addressed their concerns to them. No European political institution would be capable of processing thousands or even hundreds of claims simultaneously without neglecting its normal duties. It is a well-established and justified practice, therefore, that governments act as guardians or trustees of the individual right to justification and are given the task, through democratic delegation, to act in the interests of their domestic constituency. Democratic governments can be understood in this sense as the agents of the individual's right to justification. Governments are charged with protecting their constituents' individual right to justification and to exercise it vis-à-vis other societies and governments. Governments are in this way entrusted with a right that is not original to them. As the basic right to justification is inherent only to individuals, its delegation to a government can never mean that citizens lose the freedom to exercise it independently of a government. Additional avenues for raising claims must be offered and citizens be given the opportunity to address European institutions directly if their governments fail to carry out their delegated task. The legitimacy of governments in European politics is thereby made directly dependent on the degree to which they take the individual right to justification seriously and act in the very best interests of those whom they represent.

6.4.3. *Limits to accountability*

Justifications are not only a means for safeguarding our legitimate freedoms but also burdens that we can legitimately impose on others. By demanding others to account for their actions and to produce reasons in their own defence, we oblige others to do something they would otherwise not have done. Justifications therefore have a limiting effect on the freedom of others. It follows from this insight that justifications must be justified themselves, i.e. that there must be limits to the right to justification. A most important issue with regard to the question of when and under what circumstances we are obliged to justify our action is the effect that this action has on other individuals' freedom. We do not always and everywhere have a right to demand justifications from someone. We only have this right if and when someone else limits our freedom or attempts to do so. No one needs to justify to a neighbour, for example, what they do inside the four walls of their home. In a similar manner, France need not justify to Germany or any other Member State of the EU its education, pension, or cultural policy as long as these policies have no significant constraining effect on other countries.

It is also clear that only affected persons and the institutions entrusted with supporting them have a right to request a justification. Our right to demand justifications is directly linked to limitations of our freedom and ends where those limitations stop. We therefore do not have a right to demand justification of someone only because he or she injured the rights of a third person. Only those injured have the right to demand justification and they bear also the burden of proof that such an infringement actually occurred. If Sweden, for example imposes an illegitimate limitation to the import of beef from, say, the United Kingdom, the UK itself must articulate a protest, make the fact of damage plausible, and demand a justification. In European politics, the close nexus between suffering damage and having the right to demand a justification is only modified by the right and the duty of the Commission to articulate its concerns whenever it obtains knowledge of illegitimate limitations on liberty in the form of violations of treaty provisions. The Commission acts here according to the will of the Member States as the 'guardian of the treaties' for the purpose of averting retaliatory measures between the Member States. It thus acts in accord with the competencies entrusted to it by the Member States.

Part IV
Reconstructing the EU

7
Structures of Justification

The last chapter introduced the right to justification as a procedural conception of justice. The right to justification provides not only a normative yardstick for assessing the legitimacy of the EU but can also be used for reconstructing much of the EU's most crucial practices. The EU, so the argument of this chapter proposes, is adequately understood as a normative structure that gives effect to the right to justification. Its institutional order and its legal structure can be reconstructed as embodying a rich reservoir of lessons learned during the history of Europe that have been condensed into a mutually beneficial mode of conflict resolution. These historical lessons constitute a European 'tacit knowledge'. This knowledge is based on the insight that conflicts among states are perpetual in politics and that their resolution requires an efficient and effective legal structure that turns conflicts into constructive cross-border policy-making by transforming international bargaining into transnational justification.

The notion of tacit knowledge may be unfamiliar to many students of European studies. Most of us are used to thinking in terms of legal regulations, formal procedures, and rational cost-benefit calculations. We tend to be highly sceptical of all concepts imported from disciplines like human cognition or business administration. To suggest that we analyse the practice of European politics in terms of the tacit knowledge held by policy-makers or embedded in institutions is to suggest that we 'know' things of which we are unaware. It also means that scientific analysis is capable of making known such unknown knowledge and thus of explaining our own knowledge to us—a difficult proposition for positivists. These claims are far from modest and rightfully meet with scepticism at first take. In organizational studies and in theories of learning, however, references to tacit knowledge are common. They date back to the 1960s (cf. Polanyi 1966) and have an important place in current research (Lam 2000). According to Polanyi, 'we know more than we can tell' (1966: 4). All practice is built on intuitions, hunches, or educated guesses that are informed by a type of knowledge that we are often unaware of.

Such 'tacit knowledge' comes into play, for example, when we use language. We often make use of a large number of grammatical rules that are not known explicitly by us. We nevertheless are well capable of mastering them. Conversely, it is not possible to learn a language just by learning the rules of grammar. Native speakers pick up language by means of 'immersion' at a young age, almost entirely unaware of formal grammar they may be taught later. Likewise, the practice of riding a bike builds on the tacit knowledge that a fall to the left can be prevented by a turn to the left. To turn right, however, you must first countersteer to the left and then allow centrifugal forces to lean you to the right. Few riders are aware of this fact of physics. Fortunately for them, however, knowing the formal laws is not necessary for riding a bicycle. Both examples point to the more general insight that a large part of what we know cannot be easily articulated or communicated. It is a form of knowledge that must be made explicit by scientific analysis before we become aware of it.

Tacit knowledge can reside not only in individuals but also in organizations. Lam (2000) distinguishes between individual tacit knowledge and collective tacit knowledge. Individuals draw on tacit knowledge (so-called embodied knowledge) when using know-how that they never thought about explicitly and may even be unaware of. This is the form of knowledge that we use when riding a bike or using language. Collective tacit knowledge is a form of knowledge that resides in organizational routines and shared norms (Lam 2000: 493). It is based on shared beliefs and understandings within an organization and forms the social environment, consisting of formal and informal rules, habits, and culture. The literature on international organizations is rich in empirical evidence of the relevance of organizational culture and shared beliefs for policy-making (Barnett and Finnemore 1999; Hamlet 2004). The WTO, for example, is built on a diplomatic culture of reciprocity, on the belief in the benefits of free markets and, to a limited extent, acceptance of the rule of law. Practitioners working in international trade issues are quickly socialized into believing that trade law is a type of regulation lying somewhere between power and law. It is applied by an independent dispute settlement body but can be enforced only by an individual signatory party by means of unilateral retaliatory action. Likewise, being a delegate at the UN means adapting to a social environment in which international law is viewed with much scepticism and where national sovereignty still matters a lot. As European practice clearly shows, none of this should be seen as a given that simply reflects 'the way the world is'. Law can be accepted as valid and binding, even if it is formulated and applied beyond the state. Anarchy, to use a famous formulation, 'is what states make of it' (Wendt 1992). It is not part of objective reality but is rather subject to the practices and the tacit collective knowledge embodied in international organizations.

Structures of Justification

The notion of tacit knowledge has not found any explicit mention in the literature on European integration. If one reads between the lines, however, some traces of its insights can be found. According to Rittberger (2003), policy-makers hold certain beliefs about the conditions of legitimate policy making and even about the proper balance between the powers of the different institutions. The empowerment of the European Parliament was not the product of a parliamentary power play, nor did it reflect governmental interests only. It is better explained by the perception of the European political elite (including members of the executive and the legislative) that the expansion of political competences following the Single European Act upset the previous institutional balance and thus weakened European procedural legitimacy. Empowering the EP was perceived to be the appropriate institutional move for re-establishing the democratic legitimacy of the EU. Normative beliefs are thus far from irrelevant for the institutional development of an international organization. Rather, they work to guide actors' preferences when making institutional choices. They 'express a world view that influences behaviour not only directly, by setting standards of appropriateness for behaviour, but also indirectly through selective prefabricated links between values that individuals or collectivities habitually rely upon to address specific problems' (Katzenstein 1993: 267; cf. Rittberger 2003: 208).

Tacit knowledge is obviously of high relevance to understanding the practices of international organizations. If much of what we (tacitly) know is (explicitly) unknown to us but nevertheless important for understanding why we choose what actions and why we decide to maintain or change particular institutions, then science is well advised to invest time and effort in uncovering the contents of tacit knowledge. Unfortunately, the difficulty in working empirically with the concept is obvious. We have no empirical instruments for measuring or even categorizing tacit knowledge, something that cannot be seen and in particular cases may not exist at all. How can we analyse something that we are not aware of? Is it scientifically proper to investigate something that exists (explicitly) only after we have discovered it? Yes and no. Ultimately, it depends on how we approach the challenge. It is surely inappropriate to proceed with a positivistic methodology and to claim that one can measure implicit collective knowledge in an objective way. What is possible, however, is the formulation of an educated guess about the content of tacit knowledge and to make this guess plausible by reconstructing empirical practice in the terms of the educated guess. Everything then depends on the plausibility of the reconstruction and on the question of whether we learn something meaningful about observable practice by 're-understanding' it in the terms of the offered interpretation.

For gaining some firm ground for the interpretative act, we can start by assuming that most policy-makers in the EU are well aware of European

The Justification of Europe

history and of the havoc wrought upon the European continent by unchecked power games. One of the most important lessons of European history is that the European nation-states share a common fate in both good and bad times. Nearly all of them suffered during the great wars in the 17th, 18th, 19th, and 20th centuries, and most of them benefited from periods of peace and prosperity. Working together to ensure prosperity and to avoid conflict, however, is easier said than done. In politics it necessitates at the very least a cooperative mode of interaction. International coordination on the basis of bargaining, i.e. by means of an exchange of threats and promises (cf. Elster 1998b: 6), often fails to deliver the desired outcome. European history is full of such failures. Most prominent are the French humiliation by Germany in 1871 and the French revenge in Versailles in 1918. In both cases, the victorious party used its superior bargaining power to force the other party to accept a peace treaty that ignored legitimate concerns and thus ensured future hostility. It is true that bargaining does not necessarily lead to unfair or unbalanced outcomes. When partners of equal power bargain, and when the exchange of threats and promises reflects this balance, then bargaining often leads to efficient and stable outcomes. If power resources are highly uneven such that one party has no alternative to a proffered agreement, then bargaining often leads to the outcome that that party's concerns are bulldozed. Then, should the balance of power change, the previously outmanoeuvred party has a strong incentive to reverse the outcome, even against the resistance of the other party.

A long-term and sustainable way of 'getting to yes' (Fisher, Ury, and Patton 1991) requires more than a simple aggregation of power resources or a passive trust in the coordinating function of the political market. The parties must go beyond a mere exchange of threats and promises and engage in the search for a commonly acceptable solution. The legitimate concerns of other parties must be taken seriously if stable agreements are to be produced and if politics is to be more than a conflict-prone 19th century balance of power play. Most prominent champions of European integration articulated this agenda in some way. For David Mitrany (1943), it was about transforming international bargaining among the European nation-states into the functional integration of legally bound Member States. Ernst Haas gave voice to the tacit knowledge of a need to overcome bargaining-dominated interaction by demanding an 'accommodation on the basis of deliberately or inadvertently upgrading the common interests' (Haas 1961: 368). Many politicians in the past have echoed this conviction. Even a bona fide Euro-sceptic like Margaret Thatcher emphasized the need to overcome bargaining modes of interaction when she interpreted the EU as a 'family of nations' (Thatcher 1988). It does not severely overtax reality, then, to argue that most policy-makers in the EU are well aware of the importance for the future of the European project of explaining and justifying their preferences to their peers. It is common, if tacit, knowledge in the EU that the true strength of European politics derives neither from the Treaties nor from the dominant threesome of France, Germany, and the UK. The European nation-states form a mutual community of respect, and herein lie the sinews of the European project. A widely held respect for the legitimate interests of other Member States helps to explain why the legal order of the EU and the ECJ's authority are so often accepted without protest. European institutions and legal norms are only imperfectly understood as technical instruments. They must also be understood as instruments for facilitating political discourse among the Member States and for giving effect to the principle of mutual respect. Indeed, this may be their dominant function. The legal order of the EU is not primarily about distinguishing between legal and illegal. It is much more about providing a frame of reference for making arguments, for substantiating claims, and thus for transforming bargaining into meaningful argument. European institutions and the legal order of the EU embody and give expression to the historical lesson that this is a better way of doing politics. They are, so to say, the vessels containing the collective tacit knowledge of European politics.

It would be far too idealistic, however, to interpret European institutions and law exclusively as the result of historical lesson-drawing. Not everyone in Europe shares the same tacit knowledge all of the time. Nor should we forget that the constraints of practical politics impose strict limits on the ability of policy-makers to apply their knowledge, tacit or otherwise. Short-term and narrow interests are often more salient guides of politics. What is reasonable over the long-term often comes at significant immediate costs. Governments are embedded in domestic processes of preference aggregation and are under significant pressure to maximize the sometimes very narrow-minded interests of their domestic constituents. European law and institutions must therefore cope with a structural tension between tacit knowledge and practice. Although governments are aware, if only tacitly, that working together in the European project necessitates pursuing what is in the interest of the Union, they are often hesitant to accept the additional costs of providing justifications to non-constituents and to abstain from actions that maximize the chance of quick benefits. The function of supranational institutions, therefore, is to provide additional incentives for reconciling knowledge and practice, i.e. to bridge the divide between rational action for immediate gain and reasonable long-term goals. Their technical function is to increase the likelihood that political actors will engage in transnational processes of justification despite strong domestic pressure to avoid the costs of justification. They are the means for transforming rational action into reasonable cooperation.

In practice, this technical function of political institutions is burdened by the fact that relations of justification invariably are power relations. Demanding a justification from someone implies restricting their autonomy, limiting their freedom of action, and imposing costs (Keohane 2006). The facilitation of discourses of justification is intimately tied to actual power relations. As these are clearly asymmetrical in international politics, with countries like Trinidad and Tobago on the one side and the USA on the other, it is not surprising that justified international policies are the exception, not the rule. Despite the tacit knowledge of normative interdependence, relations among nations are relations of power. They often produce outcomes tilted in favour of the interests of the powerful and pay little regard to those of the weak. Asymmetries of power exist not only between states, moreover, but also characterize the relationships between governments, parliaments, and citizens. Whilst governments are well represented in international politics, the influence of parliaments and individuals is restricted to domestic political spaces. Given that asymmetrical power structures permeate international politics, these structures indeed seem 'inhospitable to projects for the realization of cosmopolitan or world justice' (Bull 1977: 83). It is here where the European institutional order comes in and proves its uniqueness. The European dualism changes the bias of international institutions from emphasizing order to fostering justice. When asymmetric power relations are embedded in supranational structures, the mode of political interaction is significantly altered. Arguments become as important, or even more important, than power resources. Supranationalism explicates and codifies the tacit knowledge of a need for justificatory political process and thus makes international structures much more 'hospitable' for justice. The following sections illustrate this function of supranational dualism in two crucial dimensions. They provide evidence for its contribution to levelling power asymmetries among the Member States as well as among supranational institutions, governments, and citizens.

7.1. Horizontal justificatory discourses

The Member States are by far the most important political actors in the European Union. They control the constitutional process and the most important political institutions. They provide the EU with much of its administrative staff, set the political agenda of legislative activity, define the scope of political compromise, and have the monopoly on implementing EU legislative output. Analysing horizontal justificatory discourses among the EU's Member States is a fitting starting point for understanding the difficulties and opportunities faced by the EU in giving effect to a right to justification.

7.1.1. Power and interests

The task faced by supranational institutions in fostering justificatory discourses among member states is anything but easy. For understanding why, it is helpful to recall some of the structural elements of international politics and their consequences for political interaction. The first and most important source of obstacles is that states identify their interests and preferences differently than do individuals. Individuals have a certain natural disposition to seek agreement and understanding with other individuals (Habermas 1981). We are not only rational, utility-maximizing actors but also social beings who depend on mutual living arrangements and mutual understanding. We are thus often ready to go to great lengths to reach agreement, even if the only benefit of agreement is the absence of dissent. States are different. Following the mainstream literature, the interest of states is to maximize survival and, if that is guaranteed, to increase relative economic benefits (Waltz 1979). They often perceive each other as competitors rather than as neighbours or partners. That states have a social disposition is rarely suggested (but see Wendt 1999) and difficult to substantiate without personalizing a non-personal entity. Liberals add that the governmental process of identifying preferences is likewise only very marginally affected by a social disposition. Governments normally identify their preferences by means of domestic decision-making processes in which a large number of interests must be satisfied. Lobbies and other domestic constituencies approach governments with their individual political aims and very rarely emphasize or cherish their government's performance in justificatory processes. Because most governments are prodded by the re-election motive, international concerns are second-order and are easily eclipsed in decisions that pit them against domestic concerns. Governments that do not wish to offend public opinion or to be perceived by the public as being preoccupied with second-order problems are well advised to subordinate their international priorities to the domestic agenda. Democratically elected governments who seek electoral success certainly cannot afford to ignore the political wishes of their domestic clientele. Their actions must be guided by policies and positions that enjoy domestic popular support. The interests and preferences of other states are necessarily subordinate.

The domestic bias of national governments has far-reaching consequences for the emergence and survival of justificatory discourses in international affairs. Democratic governments are not the reasonable citizens who populate theories of deliberative democracy. Individuals are free to choose their preferred mode of interaction and represent only themselves. Corporate actors such as governments, in contrast, must in principle prioritize their constituency's demands for political goods. Given these constraints, it seems hard to imagine democratic governments in international politics ever engaging other governments in proper justificatory discourses. In international affairs, democratically elected governments can take other governments and their concerns into consideration only insofar as these are mirrored in the structure of domestic interests.

Given these constraints, it seems quite surprising that arguing is ubiquitous in international relations anyway (cf. Müller 2001; Risse 2000; Johnstone 2003). Governments are often at pains to explain the reasons for their actions and are highly sensitive to any damage to a reputation for fairness. Apparently, the domestic bias of democratically elected governments does not wholly prevent them from developing and using arguments in international discourses. Indeed, the position has been articulated that argumentative processes are actually standard procedure in international diplomacy, not a puzzling exception. International diplomacy, so the argument goes, is suffused with rules and norms and is thus more social and less anarchic than generally assumed (Wendt 1999). Commonly shared norms and informal rules merge to produce a common set of expectations, and these constrain and obligate national actors even when very different cultures are involved (Lumsdaine 1993; Klotz 1995). The customs of international relations—the receptions, the cocktail parties, the language of diplomats, the arcane protocols—all congeal into the great backdrop of ritual. All of this helps to preserve channels of substantial dialogue even during times of intense conflict (Müller 2007: 210). Combined with the norms of international law, this adds up to a 'solid framework for seeking agreement' (Müller 2007: 212). In this context, there is a strong mutual expectation that participants will disdain openly self-serving behaviour and favour instead argumentative modes of interaction.

There are, however, limits on the effectiveness of discourse-based modes of agreement. In modern international politics, and even more so in the European Union, diplomats hobnobbing at cocktail parties do not resolve the most crucial disputes. Problem-solving and political dispute-settlement have become the objects of expert discussions, interest group manipulation, media attention, and national oversight. The structures of bargaining once characterized by diplomacy are today embedded in multi-level systems of bargaining in which delegates are required not only to achieve agreement among themselves but also to make sure their agreements are acceptable back home. Delegates thus negotiate on two levels simultaneously: the international and the domestic level (Putnam 1988). A fundamental problem with justificatory processes in multi-level structures is that solutions that are acceptable at one level may be perfectly unacceptable at another level. The opinion, quite common among

Structures of Justification

international policy-makers, that economic liberalization increases prosperity for all, need not necessarily meet with great agreement among affected domestic actors. Ideas that fly in policy fields de-coupled from domestic issues and domestic publics tend to lose their wings in policy areas that resonate more deeply with ordinary citizens. Thus, the constraining effect of diplomatic norms is hardly likely to emerge in areas on the public's radar screen. The establishment of mutual accommodation through persuasion is in fact predicated on conditions that are quite rare in international politics, including a highly networked life-world and an institutional context that shields policy-making from the public and from influential lobbies. Proper justificatory processes thus emerge only in 'exclusive, insulated forums' (Deitelhoff 2006: 291) and are the power currency of small and middle-sized powers rather than of big powers that have access to traditional power resources.

A second important obstacle to justificatory discourses is the fact that international politics is conducted in an environment that still has a number of structural elements of a self-help system. Governments have in most cases no recourse to an independent authority unconditionally competent to assess the relative merits of arguments and to draw legal or even material consequences in case of illegitimate violations of other states' freedoms. Governments are required to take care of themselves and to undertake the necessary measures for doing so. This self-help character of international politics is pervasive in nearly all policy areas. Even in the policy area with the most densely institutionalized regulatory framework, international trade, governments are required to bring forth concerns about the practices of other states autonomously and to impose, after being authorized by the competent dispute settlement body, unilateral retaliatory measures. To be sure, WTO law installs institutions of justificatory discourse. Governments are obliged to report on domestic legislation and are subject to critical scrutiny by a Trade Policy Review Body (TPRB). Because power relationships are so asymmetrical, however, even open violations on the part of a major power carry no guarantee of legal consequence. A small state's government, especially if dependent on political support from its richer peers, is often well advised to accept the violation of its rights rather than to open legal proceedings and risk facing retaliatory political consequences in terms of limited development aid, political support, or legal counteraction.

The dominance of the most powerful states can also be observed in the WTO's intergovernmental negotiations. Most negotiations are conducted among the major powers in the so-called 'Green-Room procedure', which bars entry to most smaller states. The deals that are brokered there are then presented to the majority of WTO member states only after all important concerns of the larger member states have been addressed and a 'consensus' has been achieved. Proposals handed in by the smaller states have, not surprisingly, a 'habit of dying' (Steinberg 2002: 355). Often, small states abstain from addressing their concerns at all for fear of endangering good relations with the bigger states: 'Small countries like us...cannot take the floor and oppose. We will never do that. There will be a lot of repercussions: 35 per cent of our exports go to the US. Of textiles, 60 per cent goes to the US, so we just have to keep our mouths shut' (anonymous delegate, cited in Kwa 2003: 44).

The self-help character of the international system leads directly to the third obstacle to justificatory discourses, namely the asymmetry of power resources among states. When power is unequally distributed, the concerns of weak states are seldom heard and rarely respected, despite the fact that international law rests on the principle that all states are equal in terms of rights and obligations. The legal principle of absolute equality is constantly compromised by asymmetries of power in real politics. Resource-rich states dominate the processes and the outcomes of international politics in all areas from global trade policy to environmental protection to international security. Small states usually have little choice but to agree to terms set by others. Due to the unequal capacities of nations to translate their particular concerns into obligatory norms in international law, most international treaties and regimes embody the interests of the stronger players. Thus, international legal norms rarely incorporate broad principles of international justice. They are much more likely to give expression to the asymmetric power constellation that existed when they were created (Bull 1977: 88). This is an important reason why the principle of *pacta sunt servanda* (agreements must be kept) is so often violated in international politics. The scepticism articulated by Carr (1983: 174) underlines this point. According to him, insisting that international treaties must be respected is nothing but 'a weapon used by the ruling nations to maintain their supremacy over weaker nations on whom the treaties have been imposed'.

The dominance of large states in international negotiations is not only an international phenomenon but was also clearly evident in the negotiations that led to the founding of the European Economic Community in 1958. Germany and France were able to hash out the fundamentals of the agreement bilaterally without bothering with the claims and interests of smaller Member States (cf. Moravcsik 1998). Germany's main interest in the EEC during the mid-1950s centred on securing access to French markets. With its industrial sector newly revitalized, Germany wanted lower French tariffs or, even better, a complete removal of all tariff and non-tariff trade barriers. France, with its internationally competitive agricultural sector, was interested in lower tariffs on agricultural products but ambivalent towards Germany's push to liberalize the markets for industrial goods. French industry stood to lose market share if domestic markets were fully opened to German firms, and few firms saw export opportunities in Germany. Yet, de Gaulle pursued a strategy of gradual liberalization with the goal of forcing French industry to modernize. French hesitation regarding manufactured goods was matched by Germany's disinclination to liberalize trade in agricultural products. German farms were too small on average to allow economies of scale, and German farmers expected liberalization to initiate a phase of overwhelming competition. The compromise made by Germany and France, which laid the foundation for the European Union, clearly reflects this original interest constellation. In the Treaty of Rome, the two sides agreed to gradually liberalize trade in manufactured goods with the goal of establishing a single market. A single market for agricultural goods was also agreed upon, but with guaranteed minimum prices for producers as a means to allay German farmers' wariness of foreign competitors. This bilateral agreement was essential for the founding phase of the European Union and remained the cornerstone of the European political bargain well into the 1980s.

Today, political processes in the European Union are still deeply influenced by an asymmetric distribution of power resources. This is especially evident in the European Council. Just as realists would predict, 'structural' power factors such as gross domestic product and population are decisive determinants of the relative power of individual states within the European Council (Tallberg 2007). One's political might, not the quality of one's arguments, decides who gets what. The former French foreign minister Hubert Védrine once noted: 'What grants influence in the European Council is first and foremost the actual power of the country. We do, after all, live in the real world. Germany obviously has more power than, say, Malta and Luxembourg. A Member State's actual power is decided by its economy, demography, geography, political system, and diplomatic reach' (quoted in Tallberg 2007: 14). An important mechanism that favours the interests of larger states is the high political price small states can expect to pay if they venture a veto in the European Council. Formally, every Member State is legally entitled to do so. In practice, however, small states are expected to exercise the veto very sparingly and then only in matters that genuinely threaten their most crucial interests (Tallberg 2007: 16). Punching above one's weight can bring significant political costs.

After Eastern enlargement, the power of the larger states seems only to have increased. The European Council has become a more important locus of decision-making with the effect that the relevance of the Commission and the European Parliament has suffered. In the European Council, the big three—Germany, France, and the UK—clearly dominate when they are of one mind. It is extremely difficult for the smaller Member States to undo or block an informal trilateral agreement reached by France, Germany, and the United Kingdom. Similarly, no substantial agreement is possible on any important topic that does not respect the interests of the three most important Member States. Their interests define the boundaries within which negotiations in the European Council are held. Their central role also manifests itself during negotiations held *in plenum*. When talks stall, the Presidency often brings the three large Member States together with a select group of middle-sized states in 'minilateral' negotiations for the purpose of finding a path to compromise (Tallberg 2007: 16).

The larger Member States are also at an advantage over their smaller partners because they have more money, more staff, and more sophisticated technical and scientific expertise. When Germany, France, or Britain formulate a position, they do it only after detailed consultations among relevant ministries, business organizations, research institutes, and other social actors. The sheer wall of knowledge built up by such complex coordination mechanisms tends to daunt other actors, especially those who are still undecided in the later rounds of negotiation. All in all, it is but a small exaggeration to argue that the equality of Member States in the European Council, formally embodied in the principle of unanimity, is a procedural fiction useful only for legitimating the outcomes of the negotiations (Tallberg 2007: 45). These and other current practices in international and European politics seem to illustrate well that international politics is a space of non-justification. It mirrors all the power asymmetries that characteristically divide the community of nations and is highly inhospitable to the right to justification.

7.1.2. Facilitating horizontal justifications

The preceding section has provided ample evidence that justificatory processes are anything but easy to facilitate in international politics. Tacit knowledge of a need to facilitate political integration by respecting common interests does not automatically have traction in practice. The legal order of the EU must confront these issues and establish strong institutional mechanisms if justificatory discourses are to be made robust. A review the EU's institutional order indeed reveals an impressive array of such mechanisms. Over time, the EU has developed a large number of instruments for fostering justificatory discourse, including counterincentives to bargaining. These instruments are in place at all phases of the policy cycle. They aggregate into an effective mesh that filters out openly selfish policies and makes strategies of bare-knuckled bargaining highly unlikely.

The EU's safeguards against openly selfish policy proposals and biased policy initiatives start with the Commission's exclusive right of initiative as regulated in Art. 17 TEU. As the 'Guardian of the Treaties' it is charged with pursuing the interest of the Union as a whole and has exclusive authority to formulate legislative bills. No Member State may introduce any legislative

Structures of Justification

proposal to the EU's institutions. The Commission is free to decide which suggestions it accepts, which it rejects, and which it modifies. No legislative proposal is presented to the Council and the Parliament that has not found the approval of the Commission. The Commission thus serves as a kind of gatekeeper vis-à-vis special interests, even if powerful interests bring them forward. This role is strengthened by the way it is required to handle legislative proposals originating in the European Parliament, a supranational institution that is by definition not particularistic. Whilst the Commission may ignore without comment any suggestion made by an individual Member State or non-governmental actor, it is required either to incorporate suggestions originating in the European Parliament or to provide written justification of its refusal to do so. These rules force the Commission to engage in practices of justification in matters of general concern but not in matters of interest only to particular groups or any individual Member State or group of Member States. Another mechanism intended to help insulate the legislative process from the influence of special and partisan interests is the full control given to the Commission over all stages in the development of legislative proposals, from the very first idea to the fully developed draft legislation prepared for submission to the Council. No legislative proposal leaves the Commission that has not been adopted by the full assembly of Commissioners.

A second important mechanism for filtering out partisan policy proposals is the legal requirement that European legislative acts always include a detailed justificatory section that contains statements made by European institutions during legislative hearings and that summarizes the arguments in favour of the law. According to Art. 296 TFEU, all 'legal acts shall state the reasons on which they are based and shall refer to any proposals, initiatives, recommendations, requests or opinions required by the Treaties'. The list of institutions that are to be consulted differs according to the relevant legal matter. In internal market regulations, it involves the Council, the European Parliament, the Economic and Social Committee and, if the matter has a regional impact, also the Committee of the Regions. Nearly all legal regulations of the European Union begin with summarizing reasons why the new piece of legislation was enacted and what the positions of the different European institutions were. This practice is an important tool for meeting the requirements of justification. It raises the standard of what should be considered a justified legal act and makes it possible to compare new legislation against this standard.

The European Union has committed itself also to the additional goal of respecting a wide array of substantial objectives in its legal acts. Articles 8–13 TFEU stipulate that the EU shall promote gender equality. It shall respect the requirements necessary for promoting employment, guarantee adequate social protection, fight against social exclusion and support education, training, and health protections. Furthermore, the EU is to combat discrimination based on gender, race, ethnic origin, religion or belief, disability, age, or sexual orientation and must promote sustainable development, consumer protection, and animal welfare. This long list of expectations provides the standard against which the EU is required to justify its policies.

The Treaty also explicates the arguments Member States may appropriately use for legitimating exceptions to the discipline of mutual recognition and a liberal market. They may impose barriers to intra-European trade if they can back their action with good reasons as listed in the Treaty in Art. 36 TFEU. Member states must justify themselves 'on grounds of public morality, public policy or public security; the protection of health and life of humans, animals or plants; the protection of national treasures possessing artistic, historic or archaeological value; or the protection of industrial and commercial property'. These self-mandated requirements create a high degree of transparency and traceability in the European legislative process. Although they do not guarantee that European politicians will produce sophisticated justifications, they do at least increase the likelihood that the formulation of legal acts takes all legitimate interests and concerns into consideration and can be justified on that basis. At the same time, the necessity of publicizing the specific rationale for a new law makes it more difficult for special interests to manipulate the legislative process.

The practice of European jurisprudence shows that the procedural discipline imposed on the legislative process is more than a legal fiction; it can be and is enforced in practice. In a decision concerning the applicability of a directive on the admission of cosmetics (C-212/91, 1994, ECR I-171), the ECJ declared the directive to be legally void due to the Commission's violation of procedural rules. According to the Court, the Commission had failed to hear the designated scientific committee in the matter. For this reason, it could not be assumed that all relevant aspects of the matter had been taken into consideration. Since the court was of the opinion that the legislative process was deficient, it annulled the new directive. Similar decisions underlining the legal duty of the European legislative to apply principles of due process can be found in a large number of similar decisions of the ECJ (Craig 2006). They apply, among others, to participation rights of institutional stakeholders, to the principle of subsidiarity, the role of expertise in the legislative process, and to the freedom of information.

It is here that we can see a more general feature of European law. It does not eliminate power asymmetries, but sets up the conditions for disciplining them. EU law tames power asymmetries and makes them compatible with the procedural logic of legal integration. Law is often understood simplistically as entailing only the sum of material norms that proscribe certain actions such as theft, fraud, and jaywalking whilst mandating certain other actions such as paying taxes. This view fails to capture the full essence of the law and leads to a distorting image of the legal process. In fact, EU law hardly ever prohibits any type of political action unequivocally. The regulatory approach chosen by the EU is, rather, characterized by the attempt to define a normative space for a justificatory discourse. EU law functions as an instrument that establishes a broad normative orientation and, simultaneously, defines the arguments that are appropriate for justifying exceptions. This two-track approach, i.e. pre-defining the criteria both of justification and of contestation, is repeated in many policy areas of the EU.

In competition policy, for example, the Treaties of the European Union provide an extensive list of prohibited actions in the interest of fair trade. It gives broad powers to the Commission to prevent 'distorting conditions of competition between Member States' (Art. 32 TFEU). Similarly, Art. 101 TFEU prohibits 'all agreements between undertakings, decisions by associations of undertakings and concerted practices which may affect trade between Member States and which have as their object or effect the prevention, restriction or distortion of competition within the internal market'. EU efforts to prevent market manipulation also encompass any national subsidy 'which distorts or threatens to distort competition by favouring certain undertakings or the production of certain goods...in so far as it affects trade between Member States' (Art. 107 TFEU). This extends also to national tax law. Art. 113 TFEU stipulates that the Council shall 'adopt provisions for the harmonization of legislation concerning turnover taxes, excise duties and other forms of indirect taxation to the extent that such harmonization is necessary to ensure the establishment and the functioning of the internal market and to avoid distortion of competition'. At the same time, however, the Treaty identifies the arguments that can be raised for legitimating exceptions from these rules. Art. 42 TFEU empowers the Council to authorize financial subsidies of enterprises handicapped by structural or natural conditions within the framework of economic development programmes. Art. 101 TFEU allows exceptions if national measures can be shown to improve the production or distribution of goods or promote technical or economic progress. Aid is also deemed acceptable if it has a 'social character' and is granted to individual consumers, or if it is 'to make good the damage caused by natural disasters or exceptional occurrences' (Art. 107 TFEU). The option of promoting development in low-income or high-unemployment regions is also listed. Also allowed are forms of aid that promote 'the execution of an important project of common European interest' that aim at remedying a 'serious disturbance in the economy of a Member State' or that help preserve cultural heritage. Finally, the Commission and the Council are given the option to extend the list by adding any other grounds they deem appropriate.

This coupling of legal provisions with paths to exemption makes clear that European competition law should be understood as defining a political space for regulatory activity rather than a set of prohibitions. It is an invitation to political discourse. It makes free market competition an overarching goal of the EU but—equally importantly—recognizes that Member States are well within their rights to weigh the efficiency gains of competition against other goals. The importance of the procedural aspects of European law should not be underestimated. Their influence on the style of political interaction in the EU emerges from the fact that the exact meaning of an abstract legal norm is never self-evident but rather manifests itself only when applied to a concrete case. The application of legal norms is thus not typically characterized by the comparison of actions against a list of those that are prescribed and proscribed by the law but rather by the balancing of general legal principles and their weighing with legitimate exceptions. When principles conflict—for example, when the individual right of privacy stands in the way of the state's duty to protect citizens from harm—legal guidelines are not self-evident but must be 'found' through prudent application and interpretation. The application of legal principles to a concrete issue is thus an intrinsically argumentative procedure. Legal reasoning is to a large degree about producing and challenging justification and is thus a practice that fosters justificatory discourses. General rules have to be applied to specific cases using the tools of argument before they can become relevant for the evaluation of action.

A most crucial implication of the EU's approach to safeguarding against selfish policies is its non-recognition of an intrinsic legitimacy of governmental preferences. This non-recognition constitutes a major departure from international principles. A fundamental principle of international relations is that the legitimacy of the preferences of democratic states may not be called into question as long as they violate no essential international norms such as peace or human rights. Governmental preferences are normally considered the products of autonomous and sovereign domestic processes that deserve to be respected. In a supranational context, this respect is conditioned upon the agreement of governmental preferences with legal norms that are agreed upon by member states in Treaties. Legal integration transforms sovereign nation-states into legally bound member states. Member state preferences are only considered legitimate if they do not conflict with the legal norms of the supranational community and if they can be defended against legal scrutiny.

The argumentative burden placed on member states has a significant effect on political discourse. It means that arguments, not interests must be fed into the legislative process. The law functions as a filter for preventing positions justified solely on the basis of superior power or based on risible arguments. Only positions that are supported by good, justifying arguments are considered valid. In this way, the influence of power asymmetries on the outcome of legislative processes is reduced, although certainly not completely eliminated. The logic of policy-making by exchanging threats and promises, which is so central to intergovernmental multilateralism, is hemmed in and disciplined by an argumentative mode of communication.

Empirically, the non-recognition of the intrinsic legitimacy of national preferences is manifest in a large number of legal provisions of the European Union and even the WTO. One of the most essential rules of international and European trade policy is that governments must justify any restrictions they impose on market actors. Art. 34 TFEU provides that all restrictions affecting the quantity of imports are forbidden unless they can be justified by the exceptions listed in Art. 36 TFEU. Among these are import restrictions for reasons of public health, insofar as they are not in reality forms of arbitrary discrimination or disguised trade barriers. Similarly, the General Agreement on Tariffs and Trade (GATT) is also based on the contiguity of the principles of non-discrimination (Art. I), reciprocity (especially Art. XXVIII) and liberalization (Art. XXVIIIbis). These principles are simultaneously contextualized and limited by a range of exceptions (especially those listed in Articles XI: 2c, XII, XVI, XXIV and in all of part IV). Thus, neither the European Union nor the WTO forces Member States to accept unrestricted free markets. They are, however, required to ensure that any restrictions they impose on market actors can be justified as a concrete application of European treaty law—or international trade law in the case of the WTO. In this way, the source of the legitimacy of member-state preferences is turned inside out, from being intrinsically self-legitimating to being legitimated only through conformity to an extrinsic legal standard.

The valid reasons for deviating from the norm of non-discrimination are also specified in the European Union and the WTO. In the European Union, the principle of mutual recognition is the norm, as set forth in a communication of the EU Commission from 1979. The communication was made after the ECJ rejected a German import ban on French Cassis de Dijon, on the questionable grounds that it contains less than the minimum amount of alcohol for liqueurs as required under a German law intended to prevent advertising fraud. The Commission responded by announcing that in future it will disallow all Member State measures designed to block imports of goods on the sole ground that they do not meet national product standards. As anchored in the Commission's communication, Member States may not ban the import or sale within its own boundaries of any product that was produced and distributed in accordance with the relevant laws of any other Member State, as long as the product meets 'appropriately and satisfactorily' general standards like those of consumer safety and environmental protection. The principle of mutual recognition has since become the normative cornerstone of market-making policy in the EU (Nicolaïdis 2007). As a principle, it derives much of its normative strength from its intention to create 'the conditions under which reflexive adaptation can take place' rather than 'a fast-forwarded Union' (Menéndez 2011: 6). Mutual recognition accepts the condition that the Member States are 'the co-owners of the same constitutional plot..., and engage in a process of mutual understanding and comprehension' (ibid., 7). The legitimacy of Member States' domestic legal order is taken for granted. They are asked to justify only those specific elements of their order that have external effects on others. European integration facilitated through the principle of mutual recognition implies the substitution of a centralized process of harmonization by a de-centralized process of reflexive adaptation (Schmidt 2007).

In similar fashion, the WTO requires its member states to justify themselves when they deviate from the principle of non-discrimination. In the area of foodstuffs, for example, the WTO Agreement on the Application of Sanitary and Phytosanitary Measures (SPS Agreement) provides that Member States may erect trade barriers only if justifiable as necessary for protecting the health of humans, animals, or flora. This can be understood as an interpretation of the exceptions to the general ban on non-tariff trade barriers allowed in Art. XX GATT. For determining whether unilateral trade barriers are arbitrary, the SPS Agreement requires signatory nations first to refer to international codified standards. Just as under the EU principle of reciprocal recognition, parties to the GATT are fundamentally required to allow the import of all products that conform to internationally agreed-upon standards. The application of more restrictive standards is viewed as acceptable under the SPS Agreement only if they are in proportion to the risk as determined by scientific analysis.

The substantial precautions anchored in European and international trade law are intended to prevent arbitrary and unjustified action by Member States. To legitimate a restrictive trade policy, it is not sufficient to refer to it as the product of domestic decision-making processes. Its justification requires valid, persuasive grounds. In this respect, supranationality in the European Union and the WTO has in fact encouraged the representation of arguments over the representation of power and interest. Another important instrument for fostering the argumentative discipline of Member States can be found in the decision-making procedures of the EU. Most decisions are adopted by qualified majority voting (QMV). By making it necessary to organize supermajorities in order to pass new regulations, qualified majority rule creates a strong incentive for the supporters of a measure to persuade undecided members by force of argument. In principle, of course, coalitions need not be forged through argument; they can also be made by promise of reward and threat of sanction. Thus, qualified majority rule does not

Structures of Justification

guarantee justification-orientated discourses. Yet, not every state can tap the same wealth of resources for offering incentives and making credible threats. Small states usually lack the political and economic resources necessary for success in negotiation games involving bigger players. And for all states, the costs of negotiation-based strategies increase proportionally to the number of states that must be brought into a coalition. This can get quite expensive, even for the big powers, both in terms of material resources needed for positive incentives and the political capital needed for negative incentives. To get two states in the boat, a broker state must make twice the number of promises or threats needed to persuade only one state. Doubling to four the number of partners needed means doubling the costs once again. We see that bargaining under conditions of qualified majority rule can be attractive and effective for coalition-building in situations with a small number of involved states. Yet their attractiveness diminishes rapidly as soon as the number of actors involved increases and in direct proportion to the number of states that have to be persuaded. In contrast, negotiation strategies based on arguments become more attractive as the number of states involved increases, for the cost of an argument does not increase in proportion to the number of its addressees. Qualified majority voting and the necessity of building cross-border political coalitions thus raise the probability that argument-based communication will occur.

The above arguments must not be misinterpreted as implying that bargaining is unimportant for understanding European legislative negotiations. European law works only as a filter that makes openly selfish arguments unlikely and that reduces the set of policy proposals likely to be put on the table to those that can be defended on good grounds. In the practice of politics, this still means that from time to time incompatible but legally equally acceptable proposals enter the floor at the same time. A policy on foodstuff security, for example, may use the more passive mechanism of labelling or the more active mechanisms of positive and negative lists of acceptable ingredients. The argument that all three options should be implemented would hardly be plausible, although each can be defended with good reasons. Likewise, the decision of whether standards for technical products should follow the model developed in state A or state B will not always be made on solely legal grounds. Choosing between two types of plugs is often a technical rather than a legal issue. In all such issues—and many more—bargaining among the Member States remains essential for arriving at a working agreement. In addition, it must be emphasized that neither the law nor political institutions should be misunderstood as actors. They are merely normative orientations that create incentives for actors. Whether the Member States respond to the incentives remains ultimately a matter of sovereign decision and cannot be guaranteed by the EU's institutional order itself.

The Justification of Europe

7.2. Vertical justifications

Horizontal justificatory discourses among the Member States are important for taming international anarchy and for providing a solid foundation for transforming international bargaining into a rule-oriented political discourse. However, they will not make intergovernmental processes more sensitive to individual concerns. On the contrary, the more argumentative the interaction among the governments, and the stronger the requirement of giving legally valid reasons, the higher the risk that non-governmental actors will be bypassed if they cannot provide relevant arguments or co-opted if they do. Intergovernmental legal discipline can easily become an argument for discounting concerns that cannot be couched in the language of Treaty law. For preventing horizontal justificatory discourses from immunizing decision-making from the influence of non-governmental actors, it is of crucial importance to install a vertical layer of justification that connects supranational institutions, Member States' governments, and citizens.

7.2.1. *The dominance of the executive*

Connecting intergovernmental discourses and individual citizens in a more than formalistic way is anything but easy. International relations developed historically between governments. Traditionally, executives are outfitted with authority to formulate and implement international agreements, not parliaments. Governments set the political agenda in foreign affairs, conduct international negotiations, and implement international treaties. The intergovernmental character of negotiations is still a defining feature in most aspects of international relations. Negotiations almost always take place behind closed doors, out of the reach of public scrutiny. The democratic rule that legislative negotiations are fundamentally public matters is hardly ever respected. The dominance of the executive and the corresponding neglect of democratic principles in international negotiations had been justified for many decades on the grounds that the subject matter is politically sensitive, the issues at stake are complex, and ordinary citizens lack interest (Bailey 1948). None of these arguments are persuasive today. If international affairs are politically sensitive, then the public most certainly has a legitimate interest in monitoring and controlling what their governments do in the international arena. Nor is the public's imputed irrationality and ignorance persuasive for the democratically inclined; if these are valid grounds for limiting transparency in decision-making, then democracy itself is called into question. Finally, we can hardly speak of a lack of public interest in international affairs in times of financial globalization, global climate change, and increased global

Structures of Justification

migration. Despite these facts and arguments, the practices of international politics, in terms of citizen–government relationships and citizens' chances of successfully demanding justification from decision-makers, have changed but little during the past 100 years. A number of serious barriers to realizing a right to justification still affect many of the institutions of international politics.

The first essential problem for the realization of transnational justificatory discourses is that national governments retain a monopoly on agenda-setting in international politics. In domestic politics, governments normally operate as the executive arm of the parliament with the task of implementing the preferences of the public as set forth in legislation. In the international arena, however, governments are political gatekeepers that control and decide which issues are brought to the table for discussion and decision. Parliaments can only require their governments to broach a topic in international discussions and direct the attention of other governments onto it. Unlike their role in domestic politics, however, national parliaments have no legal possibility to oblige their own government—much less any other government—to accept or implement any particular agreement or even to consider any specific issue. There are also no effective institutional forums in which the different parliaments could coordinate their agendas, nor do they have any relevant addressees for their demands other than the national executives. National parliaments in European politics are still a fragmented group of domestic actors with severely limited influence on the political process. Thus, governments are often free to prioritize international topics as they wish and to bypass domestic parliamentary scrutiny by pointing to the particular restrictions of the international situation. Not surprisingly, many recent contributions diagnose a serious crisis of national parliaments (Kiiver 2006; Follesdal and Hix 2006).

From a legal perspective, much of this critique looks overzealous. Most national parliaments still reserve the power to reject the ratification of an international agreement. In all dualistic legal systems, international treaties become only enforceable domestic law after parliament has transposed the document into a domestic legal act. The threat of non-transposition in cases where the negotiating government did not respect domestic parliamentarian preferences is a potentially powerful instrument. This, however, is hardly ever used in parliamentary democracies. An important reason is that any refusal on the part of a parliamentary majority to ratify an international treaty would equate to a declaration of no confidence to its own government. In parliamentary systems, governments are elected by the parliamentary majority and express their political preferences and personal choices. Expressing a lack of confidence would amount to an open public embarrassment of the government and likely would provoke high political costs. Failing to ratify a treaty can also lead to the situation that a problem goes unresolved, although it clearly had been regarded as serious enough by the international community to generate a consensus regarding the need for its regulation. Blame for this misfortune and for the ensuing international isolation of the nation would be heaped upon the vetoing parliament and, again, sow distrust of the government. Finally, the role of national parliaments in international politics is hampered also by their informational disadvantages. Executives normally have at their disposal far more extensive expertise for assessing policy proposals. They have, due to their closer contact with domestic interest groups, better knowledge of the preferences of their constituents and are also far better informed about other governments' positions, including the ones they are likely to compromise. Executives also enjoy an informational advantage in the area of technical expertise, which is critical for choosing the best means to implement any given political goal. Because governments, not parliaments, are members of international organizations such as the OECD, the World Bank, or the IMF, they have access to specialized expertise that is unavailable to parliamentarians except under extraordinary circumstances. They are thus better able to assess the 'national interest' and the political feasibility of all available options. A parliament that criticizes or vetoes the results of international negotiations sends the public signal that it nevertheless knows better than the government what could have been achieved despite the fact that it is structurally incapable of obtaining the same quality of information. Taken together, executives are not just the only domestic institution with the ability to shape the international political agenda, they are also in a strong position to influence how parliaments and the public perceive the availability and feasibility of various policy alternatives.

The legislative control of intergovernmental decision-making has been weakened further by the fact that intergovernmental politics often takes place in processes and contexts that are legally non-binding and thus not subject to domestic ratification (Schäfer 2006). Since the 1960s, the OECD has been formulating informal standards for economic, finance, and education policy and reporting the extent to which its member states comply with them. Although the standards are non-binding and member states are not sanctioned for ignoring them, the OECD annual reports have become an important guideline for national economic and financial policy worldwide. Because investors and international rating agencies rely on these reports to make judgements regarding the future prospects of national economies, they have a major impact on national politics.

The Bologna Accords provide an impressive example of how effective non-binding intergovernmental agreements can be. On 19 June 1999 the ministers of education from 29 European countries issued the Bologna declaration, which set forth the goal of merging Europe's separate higher education systems into a mutually compatible European Higher Education

Area by the year 2010. This goal, subsequently referred to as the Bologna process, led to radical reforms in Europe's national higher education systems. In Germany, for example, this meant replacing the traditional five-year *Diplom* and *Magister* degree programmes with three-year bachelor and master degrees supposedly better tailored to the needs of employers. This huge reform implied the setting up of thousands of new curricula guidelines and abolishing an educational system with an illustrious tradition dating to the 19th century. None of this was required by law, nor was it demanded by the *Bundestag*, nor did any competent federal or international educational authority recommend it. It was agreed upon at the international level and implemented by regional governments and university administrators. The *Bundestag* played no role whatsoever.

Inclusive vertical justificatory discourses are also hampered by the absence of a formal opposition in international politics. In domestic politics, governments must present and defend their policies to the opposition in parliament and face public scrutiny for all proposed measures. None of this exists in international politics. Of course, almost every policy or action proposed by a government is met with criticism and counter-proposals from other governments, but these exchanges most often occur behind closed doors and in a diplomatic setting. No public presentation and defence of arguments to a watchful public takes place. Non-governmental organizations such as *Greenpeace* and *Amnesty International* can only partially compensate for the lack of a formal opposition. Due to their lack of democratic legitimation, their inadequate access to information, and their relatively modest resources, they seldom make it into the news if they do not produce dramatic images (think of small rubber boats pestering huge whaling ships) that compensate their limited political relevance.

The fundamental difficulty non-governmental actors face in participating in international rule-making and the resistance of governments to open up the international political process has inspired some observers to explain political internationalization as being driven by a desire of governments to insulate themselves from the domestic democratic process. Following Wolf (1999), political internationalization is giving expression to a *'new raison d'état'*. Governments engage in international cooperation for the very reason of escaping parliamentary scrutiny and regaining political autonomy. Their intent is to escape the obligation to justify themselves domestically and to be able to formulate and implement policies without having to face critical scrutiny. It is difficult, of course, to assess the merits of this argument empirically. Not all governments are driven by the same political logic and not all domestic settings are equally restrictive of governmental policy-making. In addition, it would be remarkable indeed if all international political structures—even only at the European level—had been created for the sole purpose of bypassing domestic scrutiny. The fact cannot be dismissed outright, however, that the international context is indeed highly attractive for governments wanting to escape the right to justification. The transfer of political authority to the international level threatens to effectively dissolve the obligation of decision-makers, created and enforced by the institutions of democracy, to account for their actions. In international politics, governments have a number of ways to avoid this obligation and thus also to devalue the right to justification. Governments are increasingly able to neglect their obligation to justify themselves by bolstering international structures that reduce the relevance of domestic discourses, narrow the autonomy of national parliaments, and influence the public's perceptions of political alternatives. All this is hardly conducive to the right to justification. International relations resemble more of an order of non-justification than of justification, and even in the EU is it far from certain that individual claims to justification will be honoured.

7.2.2. Facilitating vertical justifications

One of the EU's great achievements is the gradual establishment of a number of legal and institutional responses to the growing dominance of national executives. The European Treaties contain multiple material and procedural provisions establishing a dense network of obligatory mechanisms of justification for its Member State governments and the supranational agents being set up by them. Taken together, they provide an effective shield against unjustified governmental policies and limit the capacity of European institutions to conduct policies veiled from public scrutiny. These provisions start with the general rule that all European regulations must comply with the principle of conferral. According to Art. 5 TFEU, 'the Union shall act only within the limits of the competences conferred upon it by the Member States in the Treaties to attain the objectives set out therein'. All authorities not conferred upon the Union in the Treaties remain with the Member States. The Lisbon Treaty also underscores the legal duty of adopting legislation with a strict view to subsidiarity and proportionality. The subsidiarity principle requires the EU to adopt legislation only if the objectives of the proposed action cannot be sufficiently achieved by the Member States themselves but can be achieved at the Union level. It gives expression to a philosophy of self-government that holds that local decisions are, in principle, better than national decisions and that national decisions are better than international ones. Whilst subsidiarity regulates the 'when' of legitimate political intervention, the proportionality principle is oriented at the 'how' of legitimate intervention. It holds that 'the content and form of Union action shall not exceed what is necessary to achieve the objectives of the Treaties' (Art. 5 TEU).

The principle of proportionality is concerned with the quality of an intervention and seeks to minimize the density and intrusiveness of a regulation. Both norms have been given additional bite in the Treaty of Lisbon by adding a 'Protocol on the Application of the Principles of Subsidiarity and Proportionality'. The protocol stipulates that all draft legislative acts must contain a detailed statement making it possible to appraise compliance with the two principles. The statement should contain an assessment of the proposal's financial impact and, in the case of a directive, of its implications when implemented by the Member States. Draft legislation must also include qualitative and, if possible, quantitative indicators that allow assessment of whether the act is necessary at all. These requirements go a long way towards fostering a justificatory practice and help limit the danger of arbitrary intergovernmental or supranational rule-making. The legal assessment of whether they have been adequately applied by the Council, the European Parliament, and the Commission falls under the competence of the ECJ. If asked to do so by a plaintiff, it may judge whether the quality of the justifications given is sound, i.e. 'whether the reasons given are consistent, properly considered and accurately reflected' (Chalmers, Davies, and Monti 2011: 365–6).

The Union's justificatory requirements are also subject to its legal commitment to human rights. In its early years the EU (then EEC) worked under the assumption that it was a technical institution with limited effects on individual liberty. It therefore did not accept a legal obligation to safeguard human rights itself but relied on the Member States' national provisions and procedures. It was only after the ECJ adopted the doctrine of supremacy of EU law in 1964 that it also accepted a responsibility for safeguarding and even actively fostering human rights. A first important source for human rights protection in the EU is the jurisprudence of the ECJ. Although the Treaty itself does not entail any list of fundamental human rights, the ECJ has recognized in its rulings a large number of different rights. Among these are most of the civil rights, economic rights, rights of defence, and the general principles of law found in the national constitutions of the EU's Member States and that also have been embraced by the European Convention for the Protection of Human Rights and Freedoms (Chalmers, Davies, and Monti 2011: 235–6). The Treaty of Lisbon also includes a Charter of Fundamental Rights that is legally binding for all Member States except Poland and the UK, which negotiated an opt-out of ECJ enforcement. The Charter incorporates a wide array of rights and freedoms that goes beyond any other international human rights treaty. It includes not only such basic rights as human dignity, liberty, security, and equality before the law, but also encompasses more profane rights such as the right to job-placement services. Taken together, these rights and provisions have institutionalized another important legal benchmark against which all acts of the Union must be justified.

7.2.2.1. PARLIAMENTS

On a more political level, the most important instrument for fostering justificatory discourses between policy-makers and citizens is the inclusion of the European Parliament and the national parliaments in the political process. All legislative acts of the EU must pass through the bottleneck of scrutiny by the European Parliament before they obtain the force of law. Art. 294 TFEU provides for three separate readings, plus a conciliation procedure should the Council and the Parliament be unable to reach agreement. If the position of the Council and the Commission fails to win a majority of Parliament, or if the institutions cannot agree upon a compromise, the draft legislation dies. The Treaty also gives the Parliament options for initiating new legislation. Art. 225 TFEU gives the Parliament the right to request that the Commission submit any draft bill it considers necessary for implementing the Treaties. Although the Commission is not legally obliged to honour the request, it must provide a written justification to the European Parliament if it does not. The EP can also set up a temporary Committee of Inquiry to investigate alleged Treaty contraventions or maladministration in the implementation of Union law. Such committees are entitled to submit any question to the Commission and to demand a response.

The Treaty of Lisbon also changed the conditions framing the relationship between Member State legislatures and the European executive (including both the Commission and national governments). The new structure is intended to help national parliaments advance from the role of mere 'victims of integration' to that of 'competitive actors' in European politics (O'Brennan and Raunio 2007). To this end, a new procedure was introduced that turns national parliaments into the guardians of subsidiarity in the European Union. It gives national parliaments the competence to assess at an early stage whether a proposed piece of European legislation would lead to an inappropriate centralization of political authority at the supranational level. In this way, national parliaments are supposed to become gatekeepers of the integration process with the task of ensuring that political competencies are allocated according to the principle of subsidiarity. The proposed procedure suffers, however, from several weaknesses that significantly undermine its practicability. After the Commission submits a legislative proposal, national parliaments have but eight weeks to organize a coordinated, written objection signed by at least one-third of all national parliaments. The statement must raise the objection that the draft legislation violates the principle of subsidiarity and explain exactly why. In the unlikely case that the parliaments succeed in meeting this deadline, the Commission is required only to 'consider' it. It is still free to proceed according to its original plans.

It is rather unlikely that the new measure will lead to a major strengthening of national legislatures. The powers given to national Parliaments by the

Structures of Justification

Treaty of Lisbon are clearly insufficient for turning parliaments from national fence-sitters to European policy-makers and will probably be used only under highly exceptional circumstances. The significance of the new rules ought not to be dismissed, however. They give some evidence at least that Member State governments have heard the complaints about executive dominance in the EU, and indeed these complaints have grown ever louder since the Treaty of Maastricht. The rules are a first attempt, at least, to formulate a remedy. They are a reaction, also, to persistently low public interest in the European Parliament, low turnout rates for European Parliament elections, and concerns that national parliaments are losing their traditional legitimating function for democracy. The (admittedly cautious) effort to reactivate national parliaments is significant in its acknowledgement that national parliaments have a central role to play in an integrated Europe. The reforms can and should be understood as an attempt, however weak, at bringing the EU closer to the ideal of a justified political order.

Yet, if the goal is to ensure that European institutions help guarantee a right to justification, the reforms must go much further. At least as important for ensuring the accountability of European institutions would be the ability of Member State parliaments to tie their executives to a binding mandate in all negotiation processes. The Danish *Folketing* provides an example of how to do this, for it gives its European Committee a very high degree of supervisory authority over the government. Before engaging in negotiations leading up to resolutions of the European Union, the Danish government must present its intended goals and positions to the committee and seek parliamentary confirmation. Whenever the government wants to go beyond the parliamentary mandate, it is required to present its policy anew to the committee and obtain a new mandate. The Danish practice of tying its government to a mandate has received both praise and critique in the literature. Whilst it is true that it hampers the ability of the government to help broker deals in European politics, it certainly does tie government policy closely to domestic politics. An alternative form of emphasizing the nexus between domestic and European politics was adopted through a 1992 reform of the German Basic Law. The new Art. 23 stipulates that the German *Bundestag* and the *Bundesrat* are to participate in European Union issues and to this end must be informed by the government 'comprehensively and at the earliest possible time'. The government is required to give the *Bundestag* the opportunity to state its position on legislative acts of the European Union before they take effect and to take these positions 'into account' in negotiations at the European level. In areas that fall within the exclusive legislative competence of the German federal states, the position of the Federal Council is to be treated with 'the greatest possible respect'. Before negotiating at the European level, the government is required to consult it and coordinate its policies. In the daily practices of policy-making, however, the goal of legislative participation is rarely achieved. The *Bundestag* only very rarely articulates a position on European legislative proposals and most of the time remains far removed from the stage of European politics. It remains to be seen whether the reforms of European legislative–executive relations instituted by the Treaty of Lisbon will have an effect on German legislative practice. But it would be unusual indeed for a majority of the German parliament to place the government under tighter controls. Because the majority elects the government in the first place, their fates are intertwined and effective control is unlikely (Duel 2007).

7.2.2.2. NON-PARLIAMENTARY MECHANISMS

Parliamentarism is an important and necessary condition for vertical justificatory discourses among executive actors and citizens. Alone, however, it is probably not sufficient to guarantee their emergence or persistence. Most of the time, most members of parliament are not much better prepared than an ordinary citizen to understand the technically complex issues discussed in the Comission, its comitology committees or the EU's technic agencies. To engage eye-to-eye with other participants in these discussions and to be able to challenge government policies, one needs the kind of specialized knowledge that is usually available only to institutions, not individuals—including individual MPs. Non-governmental organizations (NGOs) are important instruments for pooling the resources of concerned citizens for the purpose of collecting the information necessary for critical inquiries and for articulating relevant political positions. They are thus of direct importance for giving individuals and small groups of citizens a chance to be heard by international bodies. The crucial role of NGOs in helping individuals use their right to justification is an important reason why many international organizations have started to respond positively to demands by NGOs to be included in the international policy-making process. The member states of the WTO, for example, have explicitly articulated their respect for the role of NGOs in increasing public awareness of the WTO and its activities. To this end, NGOs have access to WTO documentation, are regularly invited to attend plenary meetings of the ministerial conference, and are heard in public symposia. Nevertheless, NGOs do not enjoy anything close to unlimited access. They are not directly involved in the work of WTO organs, do not participate directly in member state meetings, and have no means at the international level of gaining access to information above and beyond that which the WTO grants voluntarily. Thus, NGOs do not in fact enjoy a robust right to justification vis-à-vis the WTO. The only way NGOs can directly participate in WTO decision-making is by influencing individual member states. Even in this case, however, the information available to NGOs and the public is limited to that which the member states deem appropriate for them to have.

The integration of non-governmental actors into the policy-making process has been realized to a far larger extent in the European Union than in the WTO (Coen and Richardson 2007). Brussels is populated today by more than 2,500 lobby organizations. These employ roughly 15,000 lobbyists, of which 2,000–2,500 are full-time practitioners (Watson and Shackleton 2008: 93–4). They are a most heterogeneous group encompassing private economic interests that pursue particularistic economic goals as well as public interests with broader non-economic aims. The Commission actively promotes their integration into the policy-making process by inviting many of them to participate in public hearings on legislative activities or consulting them directly if they have expertise that can be of use for the Commission. For structuring its relations with NGOs, the EU has created a system of policy-specific advisory committees that offers selected NGOs the privilege of formal consultation. Unions, consumer protection groups, employers' organizations or scientific experts usually occupy the seats in these committees.

The literature is highly ambivalent in its assessment of the merits of integrating non-governmental actors into the policy-making process. Some authors impart to NGOs an intrinsic legitimacy, linking them to the struggles to overcome poverty, protect human rights, rectify injustice, and prevent environmental degradation. They are viewed as forces for good pushing international politics towards either a deliberative mode of global democracy (Dryzek 2006) or, as discussed in the European context, towards an associative form of European democracy with strong deliberative components (Gerstenberg and Sabel 2002; Finke 2007). Others, however, criticize non-governmental organizations as narrow-minded special interest groups that pursue private interests only. It is argued that they distort the democratic process by exerting an illegitimate influence on policy-makers, that they provide biased information, and sometimes even engage in petty forms of bribery involving dinners, vacations, and other niceties. Lobbyism is also criticized in this literature for its allegedly predominant neoliberal orientation. It is feared that big business will capture (or already has captured) European politics, transforming it into a purely market-driven enterprise attuned exclusively to the needs of capital (Bohle 2006). Empirical evidence in the form of a huge quantitative dominance of business and professional organizations (they represent approximately 76 per cent of EU interest groups, compared to 20 per cent of public interest groups, (cf. Coen 2007: 335)) seems to affirm this fear.

Both approaches to understanding NGOs are overly simplified, however. Non-governmental actors are neither good nor bad, nor are they neoliberal as such. Rather, they simply reflect the diversity of organized society with all its asymmetries of power and expertise, of moral and selfish interests.

Their integration into the policy-making process does not follow a simple pressure-group approach but is more adequately understood as a mutually beneficial process that is beneficial to both sides. European institutions' quest for expertise and know-how meets with interest groups' desire for access to the decision-making process. Both sides therefore often establish a form of *de facto* public-private partnership that is built on mutual trust, reputation, and the awareness of mutual dependence (Watson and Shackleton 2008: 105–8). Lobbyism is not only about a dangerous process of agency capture; it can also support a beneficial process whereby social concerns and non-governmental expertise flow into intergovernmental policy-making. Many authors view the cooperation between political institutions and special interest groups nevertheless with great scepticism. The traditional idea of representation insists that all citizens should have an equal vote and an equal impact on policy-making, independent of the degree to which they are affected by a policy. Interest groups are not seen as fully democratic in the sense that they are not thought to possess the attributes necessary for organizations allowed to exert a special influence on the political process. European politics, however, does not follow all aspects of the traditional model of representation. It combines different modes of representation and puts a strong emphasis on stakeholder participation (cf. Pollak 2007). The normative idea underlying this emphasis builds on a relaxation of the normative assumption that only full political equality of all citizens leads to legitimate policy-making. The Commission's approach distinguishes *de facto* between affected and non-affected parties and accepts the former as having a more immediate and legitimate interest in participation than the latter (MacDonald 2008). Affected parties are thus to be given additional opportunities to make their concerns heard.

A stakeholder-oriented approach to representation is well in line with the insistance that those (negatively) affected by a policy should have a right to hear the justifications of those effects. The integration of special interest groups is justified if and when it gives affected parties the possibility to make their concerns heard and to demand an explanation by policy-makers for their course of action. Non-governmental parties should of course never have a right to impose decisions that are universally binding, nor should they be given a privileged role in their formulation. The inclusion of NGOs serves only as an instrument to open intergovernmental and supranational policy deliberations for critical scrutiny by interested parties. Its purpose is to increase the justificatory discipline imposed on policy-makers. Inclusion gives voice to interested parties even if they formulate what is a minority position in their respective domestic public spheres. The practice of the Commission to give financial support to NGOs representing diffuse interests such as consumers or environmental interests is a helpful instrument for broadening the discourse. It is intended to correct imbalances in the representation of societal interests at the European level, including especially the dominance of business organizations (Greenwood 2006). This practice is a welcome compensation for the organizational advantages enjoyed by businesses groups over groups who represent diffuse social interests. A further important organisational element in the relations with NGOs is full transparency. It is of crucial importance to conduct policy consultations as publicly as possible if modes of representation deviate from the parliamentary principle of political equality of all citizens. The adoption of a code of conduct for interest groups is a helpful step in this direction. The European Public Affairs Consultancies Association (EPACA) code requires non-governmental organizations *inter alia* to declare the interests they represent, to honour confidential information, to not sell for profit to third parties copies of documents obtained from EU institutions, to avoid professional conflicts of interest, and to abstain from giving financial inducements to EU officials, MEPs, or staff. Both instruments—the formalization of lobbying in the form of committee work and the setting up of a code of conduct—facilitate support for individuals and small groups so as to give effect to their right to justification. It is also clear, however, that none of these instruments can guarantee that supranational institutions will accept an obligation to justify their policies. The consultation and temporary inclusion of NGOs into the policy-making process remains a one-sided act of good will on the part of the Commission that is conditioned upon the capacity of NGOs to deliver expertise in return for inclusion. It is thus no exaggeration to describe the access of interest groups to the European institutions as an 'élite pluralism' (Cowles 2001) that lives up to the idea of a right to justification only very imperfectly.

The European Ombudsman is another interesting institutional facet of the EU's institutional order of justification. It is, according to Harlow and Rawlings (2007: 546) 'properly classified as machinery for accountability'. The Ombudsman subjects European institutions to additional scrutiny and is specifically intended to help individual citizens and other legal entities claim their right to justification. Art. 228 TFEU empowers the Ombudsman to receive complaints from any citizen of the Union or any natural or legal person residing or headquartered in a Member State. Complaints are accepted if they concern cases of maladministration by EU institutions, bodies, offices, or agencies. Maladministration as employed in this context is a broad concept. It is not limited to illegal actions but includes a broad array of actions that conflict with the requirement of EU institutions 'to be service-minded and to ensure that members of the public are properly treated and enjoy their rights fully' (European Ombudsman 2011: 15).

The office of the Ombudsman is also entitled to initiate investigations on its own, even if no citizen or company has lodged a complaint. It is thus an institution with the capacity to interpret its own scope of activity creatively and to make maladministration an issue even if no one has raised a specific claim. This capacity is supported by its clear investigative powers. The EU institutions must supply all information and grant any degree of access requested by the office of the Ombudsman. Officials and other employees of EU institutions must also testify at the request of the Ombudsman, although they continue to be bound by relevant aspects of staff regulations, including the duty of professional confidentiality.

The activities of the Ombudsman in the past fifteen years are quite impressive in terms of sheer quantity. It responded to more than 36,000 complainants and completed more than 3,800 inquiries into suspected maladministration. According to its annual report, the main types of alleged maladministration it investigated in 2010 were breaches of duty relating to requests for information (30.4 per cent of inquiries), incorrect application of substantive or procedural rules (20.6 per cent), and unreasonable delays in making decisions (14.1 per cent). The items on the Ombudsman's agenda are thus mostly of minor importance. It has not been involved in general or constitutional issues. The Ombudsman reports on its work by providing an illustrative selection of 'star cases' in its annual reports. Among them are the improvement of public access to clinical studies and corresponding trial protocols on the part of the European Medicines Agency (EMA), and the adoption of a new policy aimed at giving the public much broader access to documents. Other interventions of the Ombudsman led to the granting of access to documents relating to the financing of the EP's acquisition of buildings in Brussels or the provision of a reserved parking space to a physically disabled Commission official.

A comprehensive political or scientific assessment of the effectiveness of the Ombudsman is still lacking. Although the office has authority to pass judgements in any of its selected cases, it has no sanctioning power. Its decisions are not legally binding and do not create legally enforceable rights for a plaintiff or obligations for the institution investigated. The institution is free to follow or ignore the Ombudsman's recommendations. The only instruments available to the Ombudsman for giving its recommendations some bite are direct communications to the European Parliament, the ability to embarrass an agency or official by going public, the assistance provided by counterparts at the national level, and the publicity surrounding the release of the annual reports. It must use publicity-orientated strategies cautiously, however. Because its effectiveness ultimately depends on the voluntary compliance of European institutions to its recommendations for redress, the office of the Ombudsman must nurture 'relations of mutual confidence and esteem' with other European institutions (Magnette 2003: 681). Its normal

Structures of Justification

working style is thus to request the disclosure of off-the-record deliberations if a specific complaint is received and then to settle the matter as quietly as possible.

According to the Ombudsman itself, its strategy of responding to complaints, proposing friendly solutions, and making recommendations nevertheless has 'helped the European institutions to provide redress, to raise the quality of their administration, and—as a result—to come closer to European citizens' (European Ombudsman 2011: 5). It reports that the rate of satisfactory follow-up on its inquires with EU institutions was 81 per cent and that in over 70 per cent of cases it was able to help the plaintiff either by opening an inquiry into the case (12 per cent of cases) or by transferring the case to a more competent office or, similarly, informing plaintiffs where to turn for help (61 per cent). It also reports, however, that the Commission has been sluggish in responding constructively to its critical remarks and that there 'is still important work to be done...in persuading officials that a defensive approach to the Ombudsman represents a missed opportunity for their institution and risks damaging the image of the Union' (European Ombudsman 2011: 33). The ambivalence of these remarks reveals that whilst the Ombudsman's tactic of informal and deliberative problem-solving may be a helpful addition to the EU's more formal and legal mechanisms fostering justificatory practices, it cannot substitute for them.

Another interesting instrument for giving effect to the right to justification is the European Citizens' Initiative (ECI). The ECI was introduced by the Treaty of Lisbon. It gives a conditional right of legislative initiative to European citizens by allowing them to submit a legislative proposal request to the Commission. The instrument came into effect in April 2012, and little can be said about its practical effect on the EU's justificatory practices at this time. It is clear, however, that the Member States were highly cautious regarding its application and established a number of caveats that will most probably limit its political bite. These caveats start with high formal requirements. In order to be binding on the Commission, the initiators must collect one million signatures from EU citizens, distributed across at least one quarter of the EU Member States. The organizers of an ECI must establish an organizational committee composed of citizens resident in at least seven different Member States. Furthermore, the time frame for collecting the signatures is limited to one year. First pilot efforts already clearly show that only well-organized and funded organizations with elaborate pan-European networks have a real chance of meeting these requirements. The process of collecting one million signatures in different Member States is not only very cumbersome but requires either a large number of highly motivated volunteers on the ground or a lot of money to pay for a professionally staffed campaign (Bruno 2011). Administrative procedures must be undertaken in several Member States simultaneously and all relevant documents must be translated into several languages by a team that in all likelihood will never have organized anything on a comparable scale. Furthermore, the highly detailed *acquis communautaire* makes it necessary to acquire sophisticated legal advice for correctly addressing a legislative request so that it does not wither under the scrutiny of the legal services of the Commission or any other European institution. It is also worth noting that the resources necessary for keeping the campaign running must be raised by the organizers themselves and are not reimbursed by the EU.

In addition to the high hurdles for running a successful ECI campaign, its benefits in case of accomplishment are rather uncertain. The ECI does not lead to any legally binding input into the legislative machinery of the EU but only to an 'invitation' that the Commission submit new legislation. Its legal force is similar to a request from the Council of Ministers of the European Parliament, which must be considered by the Commission but can also be rejected. All that the Commission is obliged to do is to state and explain the reasons for its refusal to act in accordance with the ECI. The ECI is thus an agenda-setting rather than a policy-making instrument. An even more problematic aspect of the ECI is that it is restricted to issues of lower importance. It is explicitly restricted to issues that fall under the competence of the Commission and thus excludes proposals for amendments to the Treaty or changes to Treaty provisions. European citizens are thus only invited to participate in the implementation of Treaty law by questioning or proposing secondary legislation that aims at giving effect to the political agenda of the governments of the Member States. They are blocked from influencing the basic rules of the game.

Part V
The EU's Justice Deficit

8

Imperfectly Justified Structures of Justification

Supranational structures of justification reduce power asymmetries, create and maintain justification-based discourses, and tame the anarchy of international politics. Supranationality creates a space for justificatory discourses and transforms international bargaining into transnational deliberation. This function of the supranational layer of European governance is of crucial importance for assessing the legitimacy of the EU. However, the taming of power asymmetries and the establishment of structures of justification do not in themselves lead to greater justice. Structures of justification can further injustice if established on an unjustified normative framework. Legal discourses cement unjust conditions if they merely reproduce norms that reflect the asymmetry of power relationships rather than the outcome of an inclusive and deliberative procedure. International law, however, is well-known for its tendency to codify international power asymmetries and for its limited checks on national interests. It often either only formalizes an already existing state practice or gives expression to the interests of major powers (Mearsheimer 1994; Goldsmith and Posner 2005). It is for this reason that many observers are so deeply sceptical about the capacity of international and European law to produce just outcomes. Following a leading critique, the more efficiently international institutions operate, the less just they are: 'The institutions and mechanisms which sustain international order, even when they are working properly, indeed especially when they are working properly or fulfilling their functions... necessarily violate ordinary notions of justice' (Bull 1977: 87).

The legitimacy of the EU can therefore only be affirmed to the degree that its structures of justification are established in processes that are fundamentally different to these oft-criticized international practices. They must themselves be the product of justificatory processes, of inclusive and discursive constitutional reflections. In his discussion of fully justified structures of justification, Forst specifies the conditions that the process of justification must meet.

'(P)olitical or social structures or laws have to be based on or (at least) be compatible with moral norms applicable to them and must be justifiable within appropriate legal and political structures (and practices) of justification'. Structures of justification must be embedded in a 'fundamentally just basic political and legal structure... in which the members have the means to deliberate and decide in common about the social institutions that apply to them and about the interpretation and concrete realization of their rights'. It is important that 'everyone (can) participat(e) effectively in the practice of justification' (Forst 2010: 731) and that 'dissent should be heard, taken seriously and channelled in such a way that it could lead to a reform of the social structure' (Forst 2010: 733). A just structure of justification must provide for the 'possibility of free and equal participation and adherence to proper procedures of deliberation and decision-making' (Forst 2010: 734). These conditions are obviously highly demanding. Perfectly justified structures of justification must not contradict prevailing norms of morality, they must be embedded in reflexive procedures for adapting to changing normative preferences, and be transparent and open to public participation. Even a perfectly deliberative discourse would be illegitimate if it rested on unfair procedural norms (e.g. the exclusion of important stake holders, withholding of information) or inacceptable material norms (e.g. the violation of basic human rights). To put it in a nutshell, structures of justification are only as good as their normative and procedural context. Thus, only justified structures of justification deserve to be called legitimate. This insight must not be mistaken, however, as a dichotomous test that de-legitimizes all practices that fall short of perfection. Taking into account that justified constitutions only mature gradually, through interpretation and amendment in democratic settings (Dworkin 1986), it is more in line with normative realism to apply them as an ideal type for critically analysing real-world practices with the ultimate aim of drafting improvements.

8.1. Intergovernmental constitution-making

Analysing whether and to what extent European structures of justification are justified starts well with a look at the European mode of constitution making. All treaties and all modifications of the European treaties to date have been undertaken through negotiations between Member States. The dominant role of Member States and the centrality of negotiation as the most important mode of agreement show the extent to which the EU is grounded in the logic of international law. The European Treaties are international agreements that obtain their supranational character only by force of domestic law in the Member States. This is clearly seen in the fact that unanimity is required for treaty modifications, meaning that each and every Member State can single-handedly block change. Since treaty changes must also be ratified through domestic legislative processes, which in some countries require a national referendum, the process of establishing structures of justification is of necessity strongly shaped by negotiations among nation-states. In this context, promises and threats are often as important as the exchange of good arguments and the justification of preferences. It is important to emphasize, however, that EU negotiations are characterized by more than bargaining alone. Negotiations among EU Member States are embedded in social, cultural, and political expectations that greatly limit the ability of powerful states to use the kind of power-play strategies typical of the WTO. All member-state governments are under manifest domestic pressure to secure not only benefits for the domestic constituency but also to work constructively on the project of European integration. Alternative options to broad cooperation, such as a mini-EU composed of France and Germany only, simply do not exist beyond single issue-areas and would be politically unviable in most Member States. A German or French government that caused the fall of the European Union would face enormous difficulties domestically. Intergovernmental negotiations at the European level are coupled with the necessity of respecting domestic social expectations that the European project be supported. This fact is what makes the EU so very different from the WTO. In terms of its social relevance, then, the EU is much more than just another international organization. It is an essential element of the public order in Europe.

These unique qualities of the EU were given expression in the Treaty of Lisbon, if weakly, through a change in the method of negotiating treaty modifications. In future, significant changes in the European Treaties are to be undertaken using the 'convention method' by which the European Council convenes a European convention, whose members include representatives of national parliaments, national governments, the European parliament, and the European Commission. This convention is assigned the task of drafting a consensually accepted reform that is then written up by an intergovernmental conference, as in previous practice, into a modifying treaty that must be ratified by all Member States. The new convention method was intentionally designed to overcome the EU's intergovernmental tradition. Many of its champions hope that the EU's constitutional process will thus be validated by a proper constitutional procedure and that future documents will have a democratic seal of approval that far exceeds that of their intergovernmental predecessors. Public reason-giving and open discussion among all parts of society are expected to supplant—or at least to supplement—intergovernmental negotiations and secret diplomacy.

Past experiences cast serious doubt on whether these hopes are realistic, however. The Convention on the Future of Europe, and its ultimate failure,

The Justification of Europe

illuminates the procedure's shortcomings. When EU Member States agreed in the Laeken Declaration in 2001 to establish the convention, some observers were quick to draw glowing comparisons with the American constitutional convention held in Philadelphia in 1787. It was expected that the assembly would foster a transnational deliberative process among representatives of Europe's citizens. The outcome would free the European project from the dominance of Member State governments and create a new European Union in which a transnational democracy would have a chance to flourish (cf. Eriksen 2009). Few of these hopes were realized. Not only did the citizens of France and the Netherlands refuse to ratify the constitutional treaty, it also became apparent that the Member States never really intended to loosen their grip on the process at all. From the very beginning, the constitutional process was '... marked by a clear contrast between the strong mobilization of political élites and "strong publics" and a very low level of participation of general publics' (Fossum and Menéndez 2005: 34).

Governmental dominance was obvious in all phases of the process. The influence of governmental concerns is most clearly seen in the success of the Member States in setting up a number of safeguards ensuring their control over any recommendations affecting the Treaty of Nice. A first safeguard was the limitation of the convention's function. It was to work only as a preparatory body for an intergovernmental conference, which would remain autonomous in all its decisions, even to the point of rejecting the entire draft. The second safeguard concerned the composition of convention delegates. National representatives (including national parliamentarians) accounted for a full three-fourths of all delegates. Only 16 out of 105 seats were reserved for the European Parliament and the Commission. Although the composition of the convention was intended to open up the process of treaty reform and to break the dominant position of national governments, it did little to change the *de facto* dominance of Member State governments. Even the national parliamentarians (two per Member State) were nominated by their own governments. Thirdly, the mandate of the convention was limited to the answering of questions which the governments had agreed upon in advance. And finally, the Member States gave the chairmanship of the convention to Giscard d'Estaing, who is known as a defender of the concerns of Member States. The Laeken Declaration installed the chairman in a role of crucial importance for the final draft, for the right to 'draw conclusions from the public debate' was left to him alone.

Due to these safeguards, the two original goals of a high degree of transparency and an openness to the influence of public opinion were realized only imperfectly. Many delegates indeed complained that the convention's decision procedures were obfuscating and less than democratic. Luxembourg's Prime Minister Juncker was unabashedly critical, commenting that 'the convention was supposed to be a grand show of democracy, but I have yet to experience a smokier smoke-filled back room' (quoted in *Der Spiegel*, 16 June 2003). Due to these shortcomings, the convention never had a realistic chance of performing as an independent, inclusive, and truly deliberative body.

Magnette and Nicolaides argue that the safeguards imposed by the Laeken Declaration turned out to be fragile because the convention delegates, including the chairman, felt sufficiently self-confident to shun the constraints of their mandate. Instead, so they argue, the delegates affirmed their own autonomy, and their control over the process was never in question (Magnette and Nicolaides 2004: 389). When the first phase of exchanging views had ended and when the drafting of a final text began, however, all convention delegates became increasingly aware that they were negotiating in the shadow of the subsequent intergovernmental conference and the veto power of the Member States. Interaction through argument quickly became marginalized by traditional diplomatic bargaining (Fossum and Menéndez 2005: 36). Defending pre-defined national interests and the building of coalitions among Member States became dominant as soon as concrete issues were put on the table. According to Dinan (2002: 31–2), 'national governments definitely made most of the running. Institutionally, they were best equipped to do so, having the resources of government ministries behind them'. Giscard d'Estaing himself was clearly the one who, ultimately, was the master of the whole process; he also reminded the more disputatious delegates that national governments would ultimately decide the fate of the draft constitutional treaty in the Intergovernmental Conference (ibid.).

As the convention never had a real chance of escaping the influence of Member State governments, it is no surprise that Member States showed little respect for the outcome of its deliberations. Some had hoped that the convention would develop enough normative authority to withstand governmental critique and leave the governments with no choice but to ratify its recommendations. Just the opposite occurred. When it became clear to Spain and Poland that the convention was going to recommend a voting system that would limit their rights without compensation, they did not hesitate to reject the whole draft. The only moment in the entire constitutional process when governmental control ebbed occurred at its very end, when the governments of France and the Netherlands allowed their citizens to decide on the draft by referendum.

8.2. Imperfect democracy

The frustrating experience of the constitutional treaty showed clearly that the convention method provides no guarantee of limited governmental control of the constitution-making process. The integration project has been launched by the Member States and is still under control of the Member States, irrespective of whether it is conducted in the traditional intergovernmental or the new convention method. The crucial role of the Member States in the constitutional process would be hard to defend if they were not themselves democratic entities. The constitution-making process would be little more than an intergovernmental gathering providing the executives with a safe haven for bypassing legislative and public scrutiny without offering any reliable point of accession for the right to justification. Much of the burden of justifying European structures of justification therefore lies on the domestic procedures of the Member States. In fact, domestic democracy and its practices of facilitating deliberative and inclusive procedures do indeed represent the institutional foundation for a European constitutionalization of the right to justification.

In theory, the Member States are indeed well equipped, probably better so, than any other institution to safeguard deliberative and inclusive inputs into the European constitutional process. Democracy offers a sophisticated system for facilitating public deliberation and for contesting policies. Only within national political orders do we find parliamentary processes that protect even poorly organized and financially weak interests and that guarantee the representation of a broad range of social concerns in the political process. Only democratic nation-states have parliaments with high institutional capacities and only here do we find sophisticated public spaces and well-established media systems. Both elements have an important function for giving bite to the right to justification. The parliament, to start with, is the primary institutional site in a democracy for giving voice to the concerns of citizens and for publicly raising demands for justification. Parliament is thus the most crucial institution for guarding democracy. It represents the people and has the capacity to collect the grievances of local constituencies. MPs translate citizen concerns into the language of good argument and into demands for justification. They can force government to give an account of their policies and to respond to the concerns of the citizens. No other democratic institution enjoys a comparable degree of legitimacy in representing those issues.

In modern parliamentarian democracies, the capacity of parliament to fulfil this function is closely related to a well-functioning public sphere and a differentiated media system. Raising concerns and demanding justifications easily becomes ineffective if governments have little incentive to take them seriously. The public sphere provides the most important sounding board against which claims are addressed and governmental responses are critically reflected. This is unlikely to happen, however, unless demands for justification resonate in the media, preventing the government from silencing debate by calling upon its majority in parliament. Only at the nation-state level are the media strong enough to cut through a government's defence mechanisms and connect the communicative spaces of the citizens' life-world and administrative logic. Nothing like this is happening at the European level more than sporadically. European-wide media still do not exist and public interest in following European politics is hampered by its complexity and by the EU institutions' practice of closed-door negotiations. It is also discouraging that no significant progress towards such a sounding board can be observed in recent history.

Unfortunately, the domestic practices of the Member States do not always live up to the high standards required for inclusive and deliberately reflected inputs into the constitutional process. Indeed, substantial deviations are not entirely uncommon. Hungary, for example, adopted a new charter in April of 2011 that the ruling Fidesz party rushed through parliament without proper debate and with little regard to the concerns of the three other parliamentary parties. The Venice Commission of the Council of Europe issued a formal legal opinion on the content of the new constitution and the process of its ratification. The commission criticized the constitution-making process due to a 'lack of transparency, shortcomings in the dialogue between the majority and the opposition, the insufficient opportunities for an adequate public debate and a very tight time frame' (Council of Europe 2011). Under the new constitution, the Hungarian government plans to create so-called 'cardinal laws' in the areas of cultural, religious, ethical, socio-economic, and financial policy. These require a two-thirds majority to pass or overturn, with the result that the laws of the current Fidesz government could be very difficult to reverse in the future. It is plainly clear that the government's policies are intended neither to foster inclusionary and deliberative policy-making nor to respect the right to justification. On the contrary, the new constitution aims at locking in policies with the effect of immunizing them from political contestation.

A similar violation of democratic principles with a corresponding hollowing-out of the right to justification resulted from the aggregation of political power and media control in Italy under its former prime minister, Silvio Berlusconi. He and his family controlled Italy's most important publishing companies, the widely read daily newspaper *Il Giornale* and other magazines. The family also owned all three of Italy's largest private television networks. Such enormous influence on published opinion is extremely difficult to harmonize with a sound appreciation of the media's role in maintaining effective parliamentary rule and the right to justification. Berlusconi's power proved so impenetrable to critical scrutiny that even a 1988 verdict of the Italian constitutional court pronouncing his monopoly as unconstitutional passed by without any effort to break it up. Just the opposite occurred, in fact. By later augmenting his commercial empire with political power,

Berlusconi was able to extend his control to encompass Italian public broadcasting as well.

Both cases are worrisome for those interested in the European institutional order of justification. The existence of well-functioning democratic systems in the Member States is not only relevant for the Member States but has important European ramifications. Domestic political outputs are European inputs, and the policies selected and formulated in the domestic arena provide the most important political input for European constitutional politics. If they are corrupted by biased, unrepresentative or unaccountable procedures, then there is less hope that legitimate forms of European intergovernmental constitution-making can happen. Garbage in, garbage out: corrupt domestic processes translate directly into an illegitimate European political process.

The soundness of domestic democracy is thus correctly defined in the Treaty of Lisbon as an important concern for the EU as a whole. Art. 2 TEU stipulates that the Union is founded on the values of respect for human dignity, freedom, democracy, equality, the rule of law, and respect for human rights, including the rights of minorities. It stipulates that these values are common and binding for all Member States. Art. 7 TEU gives these values political weight. If Member States disregard or violate their duties to comply with democratic principles, their 'rights deriving from the application of the Treaties...including the voting rights of the representative of the government' may be suspended. The provision underscores the important point that flaws in democratic governance at the national level, including problems that limit the right to justification, are not only matters of domestic concern. The close nexus of national governance with European politics and the fact that national governance outputs are important inputs for European politics makes flaws in national democratic institutions in one Member State a concern for the whole of the EU. The EU can only live up to the ideal of the right to justification if its Member States give full force to the right to justification domestically. The EU is therefore right to scrutinize Member States' democratic practices and must not hesitate to suspend voting rights if outright violations occur.

8.3. Strengthening national parliaments

Democracies do not only suffer under unusual circumstances, in the cases of Italy and Hungary. There is a problem inherent to democracy that must be addressed as well: the systemic weakening of parliaments and the corresponding expansion of government power in most states. All parliamentary democracies are built on the basic idea of a principal–agent relationship between parliaments and governments. In this relationship, the parliament

Imperfectly Justified Structures of Justification

legislates and delegates the task of implementation to the government. The government is bound by constitutional law (or established legal practice) to respect the will and the political agenda of parliament. In practice, however, many aspects of this traditional idea of a division of powers between the executive and the parliament have become out-dated. Most legislative initiatives today originate in the ministries and are intended to implement the policies of the government, not the parliament. In most democracies, governments now set the political agenda and carry out the laws. Often, it is not the parliament that controls the government but the government that uses its majority in parliament for controlling the parliament. 'Party government' (Blondel and Cotta 2000) has become the rule and has replaced the idea of a division between legislative and executive power. The strong role of parliament envisaged in many theories of democracy is becoming more a reminiscence of past norms than an accurate description of how modern democracies work. This process is in itself alarming enough. It contributes to a centralization of political power in the hands of the government and weakens the powers of parliament to hold the government to account and to give force to the right to justification. Yet the centralization of power in the Member States is aggravated further by European integration. As already argued in the preceding chapter, European integration empowers national executives by offering them additional opportunities to legislate autonomously, to bypass national legislatures, and to influence the domestic agenda.

The right to justification is highly sensitive to such institutional imperfections. For turning justificatory processes into a cornerstone of democratic practice, national parliaments must be at least as influential politically as governments. National parliaments are the locus in which the sovereignty of a people is exercised, making them the most prominent space for the formulation of popular preferences and inputs into the political process. They are 'the means by which the measures and actions of government are debated and scrutinised on behalf of citizens, and through which the concerns of citizens...may be voiced' (Norton 1996: 1). Only strong parliaments can thus guarantee the right to justification.

The Treaty of Lisbon has recognized the crucial importance of national parliaments. It calls for an expansion of the information and contestation rights of national parliaments. By introducing what is usually called the Early Warning System, it also recognizes them as the guardians of the subsidiarity principle. The growing awareness that national parliaments deserve a more prominent role in European politics was also reflected in the German constitutional court's decision on the Treaty of Lisbon. The German court argued that national parliaments are the most important institutional sites for garnering democratic legitimacy and that they must be given an important role in European policy-making (BVerfGE 123, 126). Its opinion noted that national parliaments, not the European Parliament, are the guarantors of democratic principles. National parliaments thus have a key political function that cannot be replaced by the European Parliament or any other institution. Giving national parliaments a central role in the European institutional system is thus the *conditio sine qua non* of democracy in Europe and a matter of utmost importance to the integration process.

8.3.1. *National parliaments in European constitutional theory*

Whilst many observers join in suggesting that parliamentary rule in the EU should be strengthened, there is hardly any consensus on how to do so in the academic literature. The debate is still nascent. Most observers applaud the Treaty of Lisbon's emphasis on additional parliamentary control mechanisms, as described in the German constitutional court's ruling on the treaty. There seems to be a broad political consensus that national parliaments should play an important role in European politics and be given the legal and administrative capacity for doing so. There is, however, hardly any explicit discussion that directly addresses the question of identifying their adequate place in the European institutional order. Most existing approaches relevant for sketching a European constitutional design still treat national parliaments as being of minor importance only. Supranational approaches, to begin with, start with the suggestion that the European Parliament is the legitimate institution for representing the European demos (cf. Hix 2008, Eriksen 2009). As it is the only directly elected European institution, it is taken to be in a superior position for connecting European citizens to European policy-making. For supranationalists, the EU ought to follow in the footsteps of most federal democracies so that the EP should be made into the first legislative chamber and the Council into the second. Supranationalists also criticize the refusal of the Member States to open the intergovernmental Common Foreign and Security Policy (CFSP), home affairs, and justice policy to full parliamentary participation. Any insistence of the Member States' right to conduct negotiations on an intergovernmental basis is viewed with scepticism and criticized as a limitation of democratic rights. According to the supranational logic, the more competencies the EP acquires, the better European citizens will be represented and the stronger European democracy will be institutionalized. In contrast to the European Parliament, national parliaments play no significant role in supranational conceptions of democracy in Europe (Morgan 2005). Most supranationalists identify European democracy with a concept of federalism in which the legislative competencies of Member State parliaments are limited to issues of minor importance. Following this reasoning, national parliaments should have their legislative and control competencies limited to 'domestic' issues and refrain from getting involved in European affairs. The way forward to a European democracy would be through extending the EP's authority with the ultimate goal of a full parliamentarization within a European federation (Fischer 2010). From an orthodox supranationalist's perspective, any specifically European activity of national parliaments distorts the natural division of competencies between European and national parliaments. The work of parliaments in European affairs is to be conducted by the European Parliament and ought not to be replicated by similar efforts on the part of national parliaments.

Although the supranational conception of European parliamentarism is attractively simple, it is not without deficiencies. The major problem with applying majoritarian concepts of democracy to the EU is that they threaten to distort the EU's delicate balance between individual equality and state equality (see chapter four). Majoritarian procedures presuppose a number of empirical conditions that are not met in the EU and that would be hard to reconcile with its most essential organizational logic. Citizens of small states are deliberately granted a greater say than citizens of the bigger states in order to balance power asymmetries between small and big states. Difference, and not equality of citizens, is thus a core organizing principle of the EU. It constitutes not a deficit in the organizational structure of the EU but gives expression to an emphasis on intergovernmental equality that is alien to the unchecked majoritarian procedures based on individual political equality. The EU thus is not an imperfectly majoritarian institution but deliberately keeps the application of majoritarian procedures under close limitations. It also militates against the broad application of majoritarian procedures in that the European demos is still strongly divided along national lines with no evidence so far that anything close to a European public discourse is likely to emerge. Extending the EP's competencies to those of a regular parliament would threaten to empower an institution with a legislative capacity that is not matched by its public acceptance. It would not reduce the democratic deficit of the EU but would instead threaten to fan the flames of the already existent alienation of European citizens from EU institutions.

An intergovernmental interpretation of EU parliamentarism provides a healthy antidote to the supranationalist position. Intergovernmentalism assumes and accepts that democracy is closely intertwined with the nation-state. According to Scharpf (2009: 181), 'the EU must be seen and legitimated not as a government of citizens, but as a government of governments'. Only the nation-state has the cultural heritage, the constitutional foundation, and the institutional equipment to foster democratic practices. Thus, the Member States are the most important institutional sites for providing legitimacy to the EU, not the European Parliament. The major democratic problems resulting from European integration are the empowerment of national executives, the bypassing of national legislatures, and the new opportunities European integration gives to governments for influencing the domestic agenda (Moravcsik 1994). Europeanization thus has important effects for the quality of domestic democracy and threatens to distort the balance of power between the executive and the legislative. Most intergovernmentalists would therefore subscribe to the position that all political competencies on the European level are—and must be—enumerated and strictly limited to those areas where the nation-state is functionally deficient and where democratic societies are willing to pool political resources with other Member States.

The implications for the role of national parliaments in the EU are straightforward. There are no grounds for accepting the claim that a supranational parliament's competences should be as broad as those of the Member States. The contribution of national parliaments to democratic legitimacy is elemental, whereas the EP's contribution to the legitimacy of the European Union is merely additional. From an orthodox intergovernmentalist's perspective, there must be strict limitations on law made above the Member State. Law proper (as opposed to mere regulations, directives, or decisions) is tied to democracy, and democracy is tied to the nation-state. National parliaments may thus delegate norm-setting competencies to intergovernmental bodies or supranational agencies, but they must at the same time institutionalize appropriate control mechanisms for ensuring that those norms do not contradict national constitutional provisions and that the agents do not misuse their discretionary powers. The German Federal Constitutional Court's rulings go a long way towards affirming this understanding of the proper role of national parliaments in Europe. Its approval of the Treaty of Lisbon was specifically conditioned on the strengthening of the *Bundestag*, whilst the expansion of the competencies of the EP was understood to be largely irrelevant to the goal of furthering democracy (BVerfGE 123, 267).

This brief overview underscores the difficulty in finding an adequate place for national parliaments in the European institutional order. Although most observers agree that national parliaments must be better integrated in the European multi-level system, there is as yet no convincing plan to turn them from passive observers into active participants. European integration is thus faced with some pressing questions. What is to be done about national parliaments? What is their adequate place in the European multi-level polity, and how can they be empowered and motivated to occupy that role?

8.3.2. *The control function of national parliaments*

Most analysts hope to find an answer to these questions by strengthening the control capacities of national parliaments over policy-making in Brussels. The Amsterdam Treaty appended a 'Protocol on the Role of National Parliaments in Europe', intending to 'encourage greater involvement of national Parliaments in the activities of the European Union and to enhance their ability to express their views on draft legislative acts of the European Union as well as on other matters which may be of particular interest to them'. For implementing that goal, all Commission consultation documents, draft legislative acts, and minutes of Council meetings are to be forwarded automatically to national parliaments. Moreover, national parliaments are given an eight-week review period between the publication of draft legislation and the date when it is placed on a provisional agenda for the Council. This review period is anchored in the protocol, also appended to the Treaty of Lisbon, which introduces new measures for the application of the principles of subsidiarity and proportionality. According to the protocol, the Commission must review a legislative proposal if a reasoned opinion by a third or a fourth of all parliaments (depending on the policy issue) claims that the proposal would violate the subsidiarity principle.

Both protocols offer helpful procedural avenues for giving effect to the right to justification. They provide national parliaments with additional information, granting them eight weeks of reflection before draft legislation is handed over to the Council, and give them the right to either ask the Commission to reconsider its proposal or to produce additional reasons for justifying it. The protocols are to be welcomed, for they demonstrate a new-found respect for national parliaments. It is rather unlikely, however, that they will have much practical effect. Even if half or more of all national parliaments voice reservations about draft legislation, the Commission need only respond by justifying 'why it considers that the proposal complies with the principle of subsidiarity', Art. 5(3) TEU. After having produced its reasons, it can proceed as planned. There is no legal possibility to block the Commission aside from going to the ECJ and thus forcing a basically political decision into the sphere of legal reasoning. It is also difficult to imagine how a quarter or, indeed, even a third of all national parliaments could possibly formulate a joint, reasoned opinion in eight weeks. Very exceptional circumstances would be necessary for spurring national parliaments to overcome the costs of coordination. In addition, the Commission can always use clever timing so that the eight week deliberation period occurs when many parliaments are out of session.

Efforts to strengthen national parliaments' control capacity are not limited to the EU level but can be observed at the domestic level too. All national parliaments of the Member States have set up European Affairs Committees and equipped them with the necessary legal resources for scrutinizing their government's policies (see Auel and Raunio 2011). The Danish *Folketing* has served for many Member States as a role model. As noted in chapter seven, it controls governmental policy-making by tying it to a mandate given in advance of intergovernmental negotiations (Laursen 2005). Before entering negotiations, the responsible minister must present his or her position in person to the European Affairs Committee of the *Folketing* and garner majority support. The members of the committee have the right to propose amendments. The minister has no right to enter into any negotiations in Brussels without first acquiring a committee-approved negotiation mandate. Likewise, if developments in negotiations in Brussels seem to call for a change in the national position, the minister must present such changes to the committee and plead for its approval. Danish provisions are also very sensitive to any transfer of political authority to supranational institutions. According to Art. 20 of the Danish constitution, the delegation of competencies requires a five-sixths majority in the *Folketing* or a simple majority plus an approving referendum. In practice, all European treaties since the accession of Denmark to the EU have had to pass through this bottleneck.

The Danish procedures are often praised in the literature as a model case of effective governmental control by the parliament. Much of the effectiveness, however, is adequately explained not by the procedures themselves but by the political context in which they operate. Denmark has a long tradition of minority government and of parliamentary majorities with a strong interest in closely scrutinizing their government. Danish opposition parties were always eager to use the European Affairs Committee for actively influencing governmental policies. The Danish case thus highlights not only the potential importance of national parliaments for keeping European politics under democratic control but also shows that success seems to be dependent on factors that are beyond the control of the parliament itself. The importance of context is clearly shown by experiences in other Member States with equally powerful European Affairs Committees. Austria provides a telling case (cf. Pollak and Slominski 2003, 2011). It is often noted that the Austrian Parliament has the strongest constitutional provisions for parliamentary participation in European policy-making. It has the right to receive every type of information concerning all projects within the framework of the European Union and is entitled to adopt opinions that bind the Austrian government in all negotiations and voting in the EU. In practice, however, the Austrian parliament hardly ever uses its powers of control. Only opposition parties seem to use the institutional competencies at their disposal for gaining information on the government's EU politics. A first important reason for the very limited parliamentary activism is that parliamentarians are often simply overburdened by the information load and the complexity of multilevel EU governance. According to Pollak and Slominski (2003), parliamentarians often do not understand the relevance of European politics for domestic issues or are incapable of processing the information adequately. A second reason might be even more important. The majority of MEPs in a parliamentary system are of the same party as the government. They thus have few incentives to scrutinize their government's activities: 'The result would be similar to a defeat of a governmental bill, namely a public and therefore humiliating opposition to the government by its own parliamentary majority, something the majority will usually have no incentive to risk, because it may undermine their own political credibility' (Auel 2007: 492). National parliaments are thus only too often voluntary victims of the integration process. Most parliamentary systems are practicing an intense cooperation between the parliamentary majority and the elected government. 'Party government' (Blondel and Cotta 2000) thus has become an important feature of many modern democracies with the effect that the government controls Parliament, rather than the other way round. Given these conditions, strengthening the control capacities of national parliaments might simply be the wrong strategy if the goal is to tie European politics closer to European citizens and to prepare the ground for an effective justificatory discourse. A third reason is that the members of many national parliaments are remarkably uncritical of governmental decision-making when it comes to European affairs. In some Member States, European politics is still considered a part of foreign policy and thus is deemed the prerogative of the executive. In other Member States, the progress of European integration is treated as a good in itself and beyond political opposition. One now famous and illustrative incident involved Hans-Christian Ströbele, a member of the *Bundestag* for the Greens. During hearings of the German Federal Constitutional Court on the European arrest warrant, he was asked why the *Bundestag* had simply accepted the draft legislation and failed to question it properly. Ströbele, a man known for political integrity and seriousness, answered that in this case he felt himself morally 'unfree' due to the legislation's positive contribution to deepening integration (cited in *Der Spiegel*, 23 June 2010). Indeed, the European Affairs Committee of the *Bundestag* reacted to the bill presented by the government with a mixture of ignorance, lack of interest, and subaltern deference. The media spoke, quite appropriately, of the parliament as a 'black hole'. Its failure to critically evaluate the government's bill was criticized as a 'total collapse of parliamentary control'. The more general lesson to be learned from these events is that even the best procedures and institutions are worthless if not accompanied by a critical and self-confident opposition. Justification is not a product of institutional procedures alone; someone must stand up and demand it. In the *Bundestag*, however, there exists no such culture of watchfulness in regard to the European integration process. The tight control exercised by the *Folketing* over the Danish executive is thus by no means representative of parliamentary practice even if the necessary procedures are in place.

8.3.3. The communication function

Fortunately, control is not everything. An alternative option for increasing the role of national parliaments in the EU is to strengthen their communication function. The *Folketing*, for example, has opened an EU information office accessible to citizens and civil society organizations (CSOs). It provides resources on European issues to interested citizens. A recent comparative study on consultation processes in the EU reports that even the European Affairs Committee consults the CSOs' representatives on all proposals of interest (Legg 2010). The openness of the Danish European Affairs Committee to the public results in 'a kind of common ownership of the EAC' (Legg 2010: 20) by citizens, parliament, and the government. Danish practices of EU debate are much praised in the literature, although some observers criticize that the practice of mandating hampers the negotiation power of the Danish government and would probably lead to a complete blockage of policy-making in the EU if extended to all Member States.

Danish procedures for opening European politics to public scrutiny have also had the positive effect of raising the salience of European affairs in Danish domestic politics (Münch 2001: 126). European politics in Denmark has become an essential part of domestic politics. It has moved out of the sphere of bureaucratic interaction and has become a part of the public discourse. Although this awareness may, from time to time, encourage greater public criticism of the EU, it is attractive from the perspective of the right to justification. Critical inquiries and public contestation force a government to explain its case, to respond to critiques, and to justify its course of action. Policies become public and outcomes have a higher probability of reflecting the variety of citizens' concerns.

Theorists such as John Stuart Mill have long highlighted the so-called communication function of parliaments. According to Mill, one of the most central functions of a parliament is to provide a space for debating politics and for communicating with citizens. The parliament is not only the agent of the citizens and the principal of the government but constitutes a political space in its own right. It is a forum in which preferences and concerns can be voiced and where differences can be clarified. It is to parliament that the government must justify its policies. The communication function of parliament and its role as a transmitter between government activities and citizen awareness has somehow lost salience in domestic politics since Mill's time. Today, newspapers and other media closely watch all domestic governmental activities. Some observers have already hailed the advent of a 'media democracy' in which newspaper and television programmes take on many of the functions that formerly were in the hands of parliamentarians. In European affairs, however, things look quite different. Peter and de Vreese (2004) report that television coverage of EU politics takes place only sporadically and is of limited visibility. Newspapers are only slightly better adapted to European integration. Although Sifft *et al.* (2007) observe that scrutiny of EU politics by newspapers is intensifying, they also conclude that EU politics go mostly unnoticed. Risse and van den Steeg (2003:3) report that the European public discourse is 'fragile, fragmented and constrained to particular sets of issues'. This defect is all the more serious when we consider that European news coverage is strongly biased towards governmental activities and by and large overlooks parliaments, party actors, and civil society (Koopmans 2007). Inclusive and effective justificatory public discourses thus face serious obstacles from the media itself.

A more promising way to revitalize the communicative function of national parliaments might be to awaken the EU's sleeping beauty, the 'Conférence des organes parlementaires spécialisés dans les affaires de l'Union' (COSAC). COSAC was founded in 1989 for the purpose of strengthening the role of national parliaments in community matters by bringing together their Committees on European Affairs. Its most important task today is to promote the exchange of information and best practice between national parliaments and the European Parliament. COSAC also has the right to submit non-binding contributions to the European Parliament, the Council, and the Commission. COSAC thus serves as an informative platform that organizes the discourse among the European Affairs Committees of the national parliaments.

Although it is true that COSAC has had no significant effect on European policy-making or on the development of the European constitutional order so far (cf. O'Brennan and Raunio 2007; Raunio 2009), it is nevertheless an institution with huge potential for giving effect to the right to justification. It emphasizes parliamentary deliberation and de-emphasizes intergovernmental bargaining. COSAC brings together national parliaments and moves European politics closer to its citizens. It can help to pool resources on the European level without further adding to the dominance of Member State executives in the political process. COSAC, however, should not be involved in routine decision-making. That task is already well conducted by the European Parliament and there is no need to duplicate its work. More urgently needed is a permanent constitutional body that overcomes the defects inherent in the treaty-changing provisions of the Lisbon Treaty. The ambivalence of the treaty in emphasizing a stronger role for national parliaments in the policy-making process, while being silent on their constitutional role in adopting the treaties, is hopelessly outdated today. COSAC should take up the task of better integrating national parliaments in the European Union. It should be transformed into an Interparliamentary Constitutional Assembly (IPCA) with a monopoly on proposing treaty reforms. It should have the authority to review all practices and competencies of the EU, to propose amendments to the Treaties or any other aspect of EU law. The new IPCA would ensure that the EU's constitutional development is not a product of intergovernmental bargaining alone. Via its members, it would be in permanent close contact with national parliaments and, through them, with the democratic sovereign of each of the Member States. If COSAC were transformed into an IPCA, the European Affairs Committees of the national parliaments would no longer only observe and occasionally criticize governmental politics. They would instead become central actors in the European institutional order. National parliaments would reclaim the key role which was prescribed by national constitutions and demanded by the German Constitutional Court but which nevertheless has been so difficult to realize under current conditions of domestic parliamentarism. It would serve as an important corrective to the role taken on by the European Court of Justice. Turning COSAC into an IPCA would be an important institutional reform for helping to justify European structures of justification. These structures would no longer be unduly shielded from critical scrutiny by the requirement of intergovernmental unanimity but would become subject to permanent critique and eventual reform. The IPCA could propose a harmonization of corporate taxation, the introduction of a European tax for financing infrastructure, the phasing out of outdated structural funds, a balancing of the four freedoms with the social protection of workers, and many other projects that are today blocked by the opposition of single governments. The IPCA would thus have the potential to move the EU a significant step closer towards a justified structure of justification.

9

The EU's Imperial Foreign Policy

The EU is part of a broader set of international economic, political, and ecological systems, and its decisions often affect other states' policy autonomy. It has become an important global player responsible for a large proportion of global trade and is an important force for fostering democracy and human rights. Even ignoring trade among its own Member States, the EU is the leading exporter of goods in the global market. All Member States together have a larger GDP than the United States, are second in global oil consumption, and enjoy the dubious distinction of being the planet's largest debtor (CIA World Factbook). The EU has deployed troops in a number of military interventions in the last ten years, sends representatives to most international organizations, and has participated in a large number of international conferences. The euro is the world's second most important international reserve and trade currency, bolstering the EU's already substantial economic influence around the world. The EU and its Member States together are also the world's largest provider of development aid. The growing importance of the EU for international affairs and global governance underlines the need to question not only the EU's internal order of justification but also to reflect on its normative qualities as an actor in global politics.

9.1. Normative versus realist power

Early efforts at categorizing the foreign policy of the EU have entertained the notion of a 'civil power', suggesting that the EU works under self-imposed limitation to use only economic and other non-coercive means of projecting power (Duchene 1972). Since then, much of the debate has revolved around the question of whether the EU has its own particular foreign policy profile, one that is perhaps structurally different from almost all nation-states, and whether its actions in international arenas meet its own high normative standards for politics within the EU. These debates on the EU's international performance are driven in large part by the controversy between idealism and realism. For some years now, researchers have propagated the idea that the EU should be seen as a 'normative power' (Manners 2002, 2011) or even as a 'cosmopolitan polity' (Eriksen 2007) that conducts foreign policy not by projecting power but by serving as a role model for the world. In Manners' words: 'the concept of normative power is an attempt to suggest that not only is the EU constructed on a normative basis, but importantly that this predisposes it to act in a normative way in world politics' (Manners 2002: 252). Following this line of reasoning, the EU is radically different from all other major powers. Its built-in predisposition to limit itself in the pursuit of its own interests would make it the only global power driven by values and principles, not by interests (Lucarelli and Manners 2006). The EU is said to act by offering market access in exchange for the domestic application of principles of good governance and human rights. It refrains from issuing military threats or intervening directly. Furthermore, the EU is thought to derive its influence from its attractiveness as a new form of political organization that emphasizes legal integration, common rules, and human rights. It does not exert influence directly by employing its power resources for changing the course of action of other states but trusts in its function as a role model. The connotation inherent in the notion of a normative power is so positive that some observers have even suggested that the EU is a 'force for good' (Sjursen 2006), i.e. an international actor that only pursues the global interest.

The idealists' position has not remained unchallenged, however. By the early 1980s, observers were calling attention to the oxymoronic qualities of the term 'normative power' (Bull 1982). More recent studies emphasize that the EU's bargaining strategy within the WTO seeks relative rather than absolute gains and that a closer look at its performance provides little evidence for thinking that the EU has a built-in bias towards favouring outcomes that are good for everyone (Zimmermann 2007; Dür and Zimmermann 2007). In areas where its competencies make it comparable to nation-states, as in trade policy, its policy performance is as 'realistic' as that of any other major power. In a similar vein, Steinberg (2006) shows that the EU's negotiating strategies in the WTO resemble classical power politics and seldom defer to the concerns of developing countries. The EU would thus seem to be at least as much a 'realist power' (Hyde-Price 2006) as a normative one.

For a normatively inspired analysis, however, both approaches to understanding the EU's policy performance are incomplete, if not outright misleading. First of all, they both suffer from a misunderstanding of the EU's policy-making process. Both approaches analyse EU foreign policy as if it were the product of a central actor or as if it reflected a centrally administered master plan. Both overlook the fact that EU foreign policy is the product of a large number of *ad hoc* decisions, is conducted in policy-specific coalitions among the Member States, and lacks the 'actorness' (Groenleer and van Schaik 2007) required for assigning a specific identity to its behaviour. In practice, the European Common Foreign and Security Policy (CFSP) hardly lives up to its name. EU Member States are allowed to act outside the EU framework, and frequently do so, either alone or within other multinational frameworks such as the UN, the Organisation for Security and Cooperation in Europe (OSCE), the Council of Europe or NATO. In addition, formal or informal coalitions of the willing, contact groups of the major EU powers including the UK, France, and Germany, or bilateral initiatives are often the forums in which European foreign and security policies are formulated. Even when the EU organizes a unified policy, competencies are often divided among the High Representative, the Commission with its external relations service, and the Council. There is still no single telephone number a foreign power could dial in order to talk to an actor in charge of strategically planning and implementing the EU's conduct in international affairs. The very idea of a European interest in world affairs that goes beyond a vague reference to peace, security, freedom, and democracy (European Council 2003) is simply alien to the EU. Its policy guidelines are often nebulous by necessity and lack a clear programme for implementation.

A second shortcoming of both approaches to dealing with the EU's foreign affairs profile is that they apply an understanding of foreign policy that is analytically restricted to the deliberate projection of power (or norms) onto third parties and that overlooks the fact that unintended effects of domestic policy are sometimes just as important as the intended effects of deliberate foreign policy. Indeed, European foreign policy has 'developed essentially as a by-product of its internal dynamics' (Zielonka 2008: 478). For example, the Common Agricultural Policy (CAP) and the domestic regulation of greenhouse gases were never intended to be instruments for influencing third parties. They are, however, policies that concern many nation-states in the world and have significant effects on them. These and many other policies are therefore quite 'foreign' in effect although not in intent. A concept of foreign policy that exclusively focuses on the intentions of a policy-making actor is too narrow and ignores important real conditions prevalent in the 21st century. Due to growing interdependence and cross-border linkages between states, many policies in areas formally unrelated to the CFSP have significant effects on third parties beyond the EU's borders and must be taken into account when analysing the EU's role in global politics. Only a concept of foreign policy that focuses on the effects of the EU's actions is adequate for analysing an increasingly interconnected world in which domestic and foreign policies merge together. The very distinction has become blurred, making it senseless to think of 'foreign policy' as something limited to the formal portfolio of ministers and commissioners.

A final shortcoming of both approaches is that they are normatively under-specified. It is far from clear whether the concepts of normative power and realist power refer to anything normatively sound or problematic. If Europe is a normative power, this implies not only that EU policy-making is biased to favour human rights, the abolition of the death penalty, and democratization. It also entails an unwillingness or inability to apply hard power when necessary, as for example in the case of genocide or other serious threats to global peace. The idealistic approach also suffers from a normative hubris in that it simply assumes that the European experience is normatively superior, a model for the rest of the world, without reflecting whether the rest of the world in fact admires anything European.

The concept of 'realist power' is normatively no less ambiguous. Its normative deficit lies in its complete lack of any meaningful notion of due process, universal values, or global public goods. It one-sidedly emphasizes the prevalence of national interests over all other concerns and thus implicitly rejects the idea that policy-making under conditions of interdependence must pay some measure of respect to the concerns of affected third parties. On the other hand, realism does caution against assuming that our normative preferences are universally valid. The interventions in Iraq and Afghanistan have made it clear that moral imperative and political practice ought not to be conflated and that prudence in distinguishing the good from the possible is a necessary quality in policy-making (Hyde-Price 2006).

A more appropriate EU foreign policy analysis avoids all three shortcomings. Analysis should be empirically based, building on an understanding of policy-making as conducted in multi-level structures of arguing and bargaining. It should avoid legal formalism and be broad enough analytically to include also domestic policies that have significant effects on foreign policy. It should, finally, be established on sound normative categories. The right to justification is a promising starting point for developing such an understanding. It focuses on the effects of the EU's actions, independently of their regulatory intention. Secondly, it can easily embrace all policies that have external effects. It encompasses migration, market, and energy policy to the degree that the decisions adopted in those policy areas have external effects beyond the borders of the EU. Foreign policy is then not only about intentionally projecting power onto others but is defined as the entirety of the EU's external effects, independent of whether they are the product of deliberate decision-making or unintentionally caused by policies with primarily domestic intention. Third, the right to justification is normatively sophisticated enough to clearly distinguish between justified and non-justified policies. Justified policies are those policies that grant affected parties a relevant role in the process of decision-making ('ownership') and that accept independent third parties with authoritative decision-making capacity as arbitrators in case of conflicting claims about the appropriateness of policies. Unjustified policies are policies that were formulated and implemented without the input of affected parties or that refused to accept the competence of independent parties for assessing the merits of arguments in defence of alternatives.

9.2. Europe as an empire

The right to justification harmonizes well with the recent work interpreting the EU as an imperial power. Calling the EU an empire seems unusual to many scholars, as it evokes negative associations with Europe's history of imperialism and warfare. If taken as an analytical category, however, the concept of empire can help us reflect constructively on the distinctiveness of EU policymaking. Beck and Grande prominently use the empire metaphor for describing a polity with distinctive internal and external mechanisms for producing political order. It is 'not based on national demarcation and conquest...but on overcoming national borders, voluntariness, consensus, law, transnational interdependence, and the political added value accruing from cooperation' (Beck and Grande 2011: 24). It is a type of polity that overcomes the nation-state's historical heritage of closing up against the outside, viewing the external as something to be mistrusted. For an empire, borders between territories are no longer demarcation lines that clearly distinguish between 'us' and 'them' but are understood as shifting frontiers to be managed. They open up opportunities and allow for the structuring and re-structuring of the conditions of exchange. Empires also differ significantly from nation-states with regard to their internal ordering mechanisms. They are established on 'asymmetrical forms and rights of membership among their various territories and the associated groups of subjects' (Beck and Grande 2011: 27). These asymmetrical relations are not relations of dominance and subordination; rather, they allow Member States to choose autonomously the degree to which and in which area they prefer to be integrated. Because the EU reproduces all these characteristics to a large degree, it is interpreted by Beck and Grande as a 'cosmopolitan empire' not only novel in character but also worthy of praise for the following reasons. The EU, they write, '*annuls* fixed borders and makes them variable', is 'multinational, multi-ethnic [and] multi-religious', is integrated through 'voluntary agreement', is the product of 'a conscious *negation of force*', 'respects differences' and 'is based on the mutual respect of its members' (Beck and Grande 2011: 34–41). The EU, in short, is a non-imperial empire that deserves much praise and political support for its overcoming of the genetic deficits of the nation-state.

Jan Zielonka pioneered EU foreign policy analysis using the concept of empire, writing that the EU's foreign policy is imperial because 'it tries to assert political and economic control over various peripheral actors through formal annexations or various forms of economic and political domination' (2008: 475). Interestingly, however, it does so by novel and anti-imperialistic means. 'Its territorial acquisitions take place by invitation rather than conquest. Legitimizing strategies of the Union do not follow the usual imperial motto of 'might is right'.... The periphery is often able, gradually, to gain access to the decision-making mechanisms of the European metropolis. Its sovereignty is not denied, but merely constrained by the policy of EU conditional help and accession' (Zielonka 2008: 475). Zielonka is quick to add that the EU sometimes also uses its economic power, bribes countries, or even uses open coercion. The roses planted by the EU can sometimes become quite thorny. A closer analysis informed by the right to justification clearly shows that the European empire is Janus-faced when dealing with the rest of the world.

9.2.1. Benevolent imperialism

For assessing the foreign policy of the European empire, it is helpful to distinguish between two kinds of imperialism, based on their tendency either to promote or undermine the right to justification. Benevolent imperialism, to start with, is a form of foreign policy that most EU policy-makers would probably describe as normatively and empirically appropriate for the EU. It involves deliberately exporting a mode of governance that relies on the voluntary adoption and implementation of European norms on the part of recipient states and that directly or indirectly fosters the right to justification. It is driven by a self-confident pride among EU policy-makers in the achievements of the European integration project and by their conviction that the rest of the world has important lessons to learn from Europe. The then president of the Commission, Romano Prodi, made this distinctively clear in 2001 when declaring that 'Europe needs to project its model of society into the wider world. We are not simply here to defend our own interests: we have a unique historic experience to offer...' (cited in Pardo 2007: 141).

The EU's aspiration to work for the betterment of the globe and to use its foreign policy to export its domestic model of governance is plainly codified in the Treaty. According to Art. 21 TEU, the Union's foreign policies shall be guided by the principles of 'democracy, the rule of law, the universality and indivisibility of human rights and fundamental freedoms, respect for human dignity, the principles of equality and solidarity, and respect for the principles of the United Nations Charter and international law'. Although the EU's foreign policies are also explicitly conceived as instruments for fostering its interests, the EU nevertheless claims to subordinate its foreign policy to universal values. The catalogue of its foreign policy goals repeats this claim and lists among its central values the consolidation and support of democracy, the rule of law, human rights, the principles of international law, peace, the prevention of conflicts, international security, environmental protection, the sustainable management of global natural resources, disaster relief, multilateral cooperation, good global governance, and sustainable development in developing countries with the primary aim of eradicating poverty.

Policies that give expression to benevolent imperialism can be observed in at least four important areas. A most obvious first example is the EU's enlargement policy after 1989. As a European policy, it is subject to Art. 49 TEU and guided by the so-called Copenhagen criteria, which make domestic democracy, the rule of law, human rights, and respect for the concerns of minorities necessary preconditions of membership in the EU. Candidate states must meet these criteria if they want to become eligible for membership. The Copenhagen criteria are often used as an example of how democratization can be promoted from the outside, or, to use the terminology of the relevant literature, as an example of how to conduct 'external governance' (Schimmelfennig and Lavenex 2009, Schimmelfennig 2008). By using positive support mechanisms such as technical assistance and financial support, and by offering the option of becoming a full member of the EU, eight Central and Eastern European countries (CEECs) completed in a very short period of time what amounted to a fundamental transformation of their political and economic systems and turned from socialist states to market-based democracies with protections of individual rights and freedoms fully equal to the highest EU standards. These transformations helped overcome the forty-year-old political division of Europe and have undoubtedly contributed to peace and stability throughout the continent. They have been met with unambiguous praise in the literature and are often described as the biggest success in European external policy ever (Bale 2008, chapter 11). The transformation process was indeed strongly influenced and fostered by the EU. The Commission not only instructed applicant states about what they should do— in terms of legislation or administrative reform—but also sent its envoys to specific ministries and governmental agencies to guide and monitor the required changes. Fostering enlargement was a clear case of benevolent imperialism in which the EU offered its norms and practices to third parties and made them attractive by tying their adoption to the promise of gaining market access and the other privileges of full membership. It was a policy that served not only the EU's interests but also those of its Eastern European partners.

An even clearer example of benevolent imperialism was the EU's policy towards the Balkan states after the dissolution of Yugoslavia. After the devastating war, Kosovo and Bosnia and Herzegovina especially were close to collapse. Not only was their military security threatened by Serbia, but their internal legal and administrative systems were in complete disarray. Members of the judiciary were often poorly educated and even the most basic legal standards were systematically violated. Governmental administrations lacked both the necessary hardware and the bureaucratic staff for rebuilding the civil service and for ensuring the correct execution of political and judicial processes. Since then, the EU created what amounts to semi-protectorates in both countries, governed by European officials under the formal auspices of the UN. The EU and its Member States have donated billions of euros in technical assistance and put peacekeepers and police forces on the ground. Many of the laws enacted and many of the institutions existing today in these countries were drafted or created by EU experts and operate under EU supervision. Still today, EU officials frequently intervene in the details of economic and fiscal policy (cf. Zielonka 2008: 476). Like an enlargement policy, the EU's policy in the Balkans is mainly about exporting its norms, but it makes their implementation on the part of Kosovo and Bosnia and Herzegovina voluntary. Voluntary consent by local authorities is rewarded by technical and financial assistance intended to help recipients comply.

The Commission has explained the underlying motivation of its policy toward neighbouring states in a programmatic paper on its so-called European Neighbourhood Policy (ENP). The paper argues that the EU policy is not an expression merely of the EU's own interests, but is an outgrowth of the sense of duty felt by the EU, 'not only towards its citizens and those of the new Member States, but also towards its present and future neighbours' (European Commission 2003: 3). The Commission writes that it is motivated 'to promote [...]regional and sub-regional cooperation and integration' with a view toward 'fostering political stability, economic development and the reduction of poverty and social divisions' (ibid.). In this benevolently but clearly articulated sense, EU policies towards individual states are part of a broader effort to structure the European continent. The Commission's goal is no less than imperial: 'to develop a zone of prosperity and a friendly neighbourhood—a "ring of friends"—with whom the EU enjoys close, peaceful and co-operative relations' (ibid., 4). The Commission makes clear that it intends to use positive incentives rather than sanctions to achieve its goals. The prime instrument is the offer of market access and visa-free regimes for the mobility of persons in exchange for the adoption of European values, standards, and procedures. 'In return for concrete progress demonstrating shared values and effective implementation of political, economic and institutional reforms...the EU's neighbourhood should benefit from the prospect of closer economic integration with the EU' (ibid.). It is telling that the EU not only focuses on promoting the economic interests of well-organized domestic interest groups but that it follows a very broad strategy designed to touch on nearly every area of public administration and organization. It is a policy that aims at state-building and market-making rather than at interest-projection, although these motives are often hard to distinguish in practice. The broad approach of the ENP finds expression in a large set of instruments. The EU's policies support measures for democracy promotion and human rights, entail measures to establish a well-functioning legal system, and even intervene in technical areas such as promoting social inclusion, education, health, training, housing, and a large variety of technical standards for industrial products, services, transport, energy and telecommunications networks, environmental and consumer protection, health, labour and minimum quality requirements.

The EU's policy of benign imperialism also applies to international agreements with countries in more distant parts of the world. The broad approach taken by the EU is most obvious in the systematic practice of including a human rights clause in all bilateral trade and cooperation agreements with third countries. This clause currently applies to more than 120 countries with which the EU maintains bilateral agreements (Nwobike 2005: 1383). In the Cotonou Agreement, which covers trade relations between the EU and a large number of African, Caribbean, and Pacific countries, the benign imperialism of the EU finds clear expression in its incorporation of human rights references. The agreement views the ACP–EU cooperation as not only providing market access but as following the broader agenda of sustainable development and respect for and promotion of human rights. The signatories to the agreement must agree that respect for all fundamental human rights and freedoms, including respect for basic social rights, democracy, the rule of law, and transparent and accountable governance are an integral part of sustainable development. Breaches of any of those essential elements may result in the suspension of the benefits accruing under the agreement. The most important instrument used by the EU for fostering compliance with the provisions of the agreement is direct financial support provided by the European Development Fund (EDF). The EU has in the past used the EDF not only for positively supporting policies related to human rights but also for suspending its financial assistance to selected ACP countries in cases of open violations. In the case of Haiti, it reacted to reports by a mission of the Organization of American States (OAS) of widespread irregularities and fraud in the general elections in 2000 by suspending direct budgetary aid and withholding future aid from the EDF. Similarly, the EU reacted to the deterioration of the political situation in Zimbabwe in 2001 by a suspension of funds due under the EDF and a travel ban on politicians and officials of the ruling ZANU-PF (cf. Nwobike 2005: 1392).

Benign imperialism has many positive effects for the recipient countries. It gives effect to democratic rule and respect for human rights and thus contributes to the right to justification. It is a form of foreign policy, however, that is not subject to normative assessment by an independent third party and thus does not fulfil the criteria of a properly justified policy. Benign imperialism is driven by the EU's normative principles and as such is practiced without the possibility of discussing alternatives and with precious little space for negotiation. It is fundamentally a take-it-or-leave-it proposition in which one side determines the rules of the game.

9.2.2. Reckless imperialism

Not all of the EU's foreign actions are benign. Reckless and benevolent imperialism are close cousins. Reckless imperialism is a mode of external action that either intentionally super-ordinates European interests over contradictory but equally legitimate concerns or that produces effects for third parties who had no influence over the European practices that produced them. It is a form of imperialism that clearly undermines the right to justification. An example of reckless imperialism is the EU's role in transforming the GATT into the WTO. The WTO did not emerge as the result of benevolent offers to GATT signatories, but was rather the product of open pressure on less powerful states to sign up to an agreement that one-sidedly favours industrialized nations. The European Union and the United States pursued a strategy in the Uruguay Rounds of replacing the old GATT agreement, a product of diplomacy, with a much more formal and codified structure that would encompass a revised version of the existing treaty (the General Agreement on Tariffs and Trade, GATT) and expand it with an equally binding General Agreement on Trade in Services (GATS), an agreement on Trade Related Intellectual Property Rights (TRIPS), and an agreement to protect investment flows (Trade Related Investment Measures, TRIM). Many developing countries distanced themselves from the American and European position, seeing no advantage in signing the GATS, TRIPS or TRIM agreements.

To counter the opposition of developing countries, the USA and the EU worked out and employed a tactic, later dubbed 'the power play', over the course of 1990. The tactic involved bundling the GATS, TRIPS, and TRIM agreements together with additional agreements allowing the sanctioning of illegal dumping and subsidy practices and integrating all of them into what would become the WTO. Developing countries were not afforded the choice of either staying in the old GATT, with its diplomatic mechanisms of conflict resolution, or joining the new WTO with its comprehensive regulatory framework. The tactic was to offer developing countries a package deal that they could scarcely afford to refuse due to the discontinuation of the GATT. And it worked. After the European Union and the USA signed the WTO agreement in 1994, they threatened to revoke their membership of the GATT. As a consequence, all the GATT Member States who wished to retain the privileges associated with the most favoured nation status granted by that treaty, including tariff-free access to American and European markets, were forced to join the WTO and thus to accept conditions specified in the unloved GATS, TRIPS, and TRIM antidumping and subsidy-regulation agreements. The WTO was thus the spawn of a power-dominated negotiation process between North and South in which developing countries were pressed into a choice between accepting without reservation the position of the industrialized countries or losing access to markets in Europe and the United States. Developing countries were forced into a deal where they 'got little and gave up a lot' (Steinberg 2002: 366).

A similarly blunt case of an unjustified foreign policy is the use of export subsidies for agricultural goods. Under the Common Agricultural Policy, the European Union sets minimum price levels for certain farm products in order to encourage farmers to continue food production. These minimum price levels in many cases are higher than the world price level for the same products. When farmed products are to be exported to third countries, it is necessary to bridge the price between the EU price level and the world market price level. Although subsidizing exports seems at first glance to be beneficial for importers because it lowers the price they have to pay for imports, it sometimes has devastating effects on third world countries. The widespread use of subsidies on the part of the EU (and other OECD countries) has rendered more efficient and cheaper production elsewhere unprofitable and has entrenched a few developed countries into the role of world food suppliers. By subsidising food production and then exporting it, developed countries introduce a dynamic into the world trade system that erodes the competitiveness of the agricultural sectors in developing countries. Farmers in developing countries are structurally disadvantaged, forced to undervalue their products in order to sell them at all on the global market. This strips developing countries of long-term capacity to earn the export income necessary for financing imports of productive capital. In this way, export subsidies often disrupt and impede economic development in less-developed countries (Peters 2006). It is a system that costs some of the poorest countries billions of dollars in lost trade every year. The EU props up a system that in effect denies African countries the chance to grow out of poverty. The proffered justifications for export subsidies vary depending upon the product and industry, but proponents frequently invoke notions of self-sufficiency or national security. There exists no global forum, however, where these reasons can be evaluated and where their merits can be assessed authoritatively. Subsidizing agricultural exports is thus an openly unjustified policy that should be ended, the sooner the better. The Commission has announced that it plans to end its practices in 2013. It is to be hoped that it will carry out these plans and extend its newly expanded consciousness to address the fact that nearly all European farm products are subsidized and thus directly serve to prevent developing countries from constructively integrating themselves into a global division of labour suited to their needs.

Biofuels provide another intriguing instance of serious side-effects of EU policy impacting on third parties who had no voice in policy-making. Following growing concerns over global warming caused by the use of fossil fuels for transportation, the EU started a large-scale programme to subsidize the use of biofuel. These policy interventions significantly increased demand for certain agricultural products such as feedstock and led to an increasing scarcity of farmland. Demand for farm-grown fuels has propelled global crop prices to record highs, increasing the number of people globally who are forced to live on the edge of starvation for economic reasons (Grunwald 2008). It is feared that the use of land for growing fuel leads to the destruction of forests, wetlands, and grasslands that store enormous amounts of carbon. Although the effects of the efforts of the EU to substitute gas and oil with biofuel potentially affect the whole globe, there is no procedure in place that would force the EU to justify itself to a global audience or to react to concerns from outside the EU. Subsidizing biofuels therefore is as unjustified as any other policy that makes no account of affected parties and arrogates to itself the right of unilateral action.

A final example of an unjustified EU policy is its practice of concluding fishing agreements with African countries without taking responsibility for the adverse ecological and social effects these agreements produce (cf. Ilnyckyj 2007). To meet growing internal demand for fish and to maintain jobs in its commercial fishing fleet, the EU has signed agreements with many African and Indian Ocean countries that now permit hundreds of European ships to work in foreign waters. According to *Greenpeace*, almost a quarter of all fish taken by the European fishing fleet is caught outside EU waters, most of which are coming from the once rich West African fishing grounds. What makes this practice particularly harmful is that European fishermen use highly subsidized, commercial fleets to compete with poor, local artisan fishermen who almost never have access to official aid programmes and cannot compete with the EU's modern ships. For many African countries, selling access rights and fish landings to the highest bidder makes economic sense. It is often an important source of income for the national budget and an important source of foreign exchange badly needed to service and reduce national debt. At the same time, however, selling those rights to foreign companies can have significant long-term costs through the loss of income for local fishermen, environmental damage, and the depletion of native fish stocks. The long-term erosion of sustainability can outweigh short-term financial gains (cf. Kaczynski and Fluharty 2002). The effect of European fishery policy is thus to export its overfishing problem to Africa without accepting full responsibility for the social and ecological damage this entails. After having emptied its own seas—about two-thirds of stocks in European waters are overfished—the EU is now repeating this environmental sin abroad.

Responding to the growing criticism, the EU started some years ago to negotiate a new generation of fishing agreements that include measures to avoid over-fishing, that give national fleets prioritized access, and that require greater local involvement in fish processing in order to increase the value of the exported product. European Union officials can now claim that the EU's practices are not as bad as many critics assert. The EU argues that it is being misused as a scapegoat for Africa's management failures and the misdeeds of other foreign fleets. They argue that African officials oversell fishing rights, inflate potential catches, and allow pirate vessels and local boats free rein in breeding grounds. While much of this is true, it must be added, however, that many administrations of African states are practically incapable of domestically implementing the environmental and economic safeguards included in the treaties. The so-called 'cash for access' agreements negotiated between the EU and West African coastal states are thus fundamentally unsustainable in practice. Large scale fishing vessels often operate illegally in fishing zones exclusively reserved for small-scale fisheries, and use prohibited gear, including nets with finer mesh sizes, which are not permitted. Few African countries have the means to enforce treaty stipulations. Doing so would entail the constant monitoring of quotas, rest-period compliance (for fish stock replenishment), and equipment use. Given the lack of coastal state enforcement capacity, the EU must assist in funding and undertaking enforcement if the bilateral agreements are to be sustainable. States with limited access to technologies like aerial and satellite surveillance will not be able to maintain environmental standards without aid. The EU's practices thus downplay environmental and moral concerns in favour of short-term economic and political considerations and harm the long-term prospects for the economic development of West African states. They have serious adverse consequences, including malnutrition and increased pressure on terrestrial resources. The absence of effective mechanisms to ensure sustainability, coupled with the lack of efforts to create them, makes the EU's practices unjust and works to the detriment of many West African nations.

The right to justification is not only helpful for identifying policies that are unjustified but can also be used for identifying unjustified non-policies. The global tax regime is a case in point. States enjoy the autonomy to set tax rates for the employment of productive capital. The OECD has limited this freedom only at the margins by adopting a set of codes that prohibit certain unfair practices such as tax advantages to certain forms of capital or double taxation. The OECD codes, however, do not include any provision regarding the absolute level of taxation to be applied and are silent on the problem that taxes are often lowered for the purpose of luring capital away from other states. The *de facto* non-existence of a global tax regime that limits international competition for capital has set in motion a race to the bottom that puts downward pressure on overall taxation. It also means that '[m]obile factors of production have the opportunity to "shop around" to minimize their tax burden' (Dietsch and Rixen 2011:1), thereby undermining the *de facto* tax sovereignty of states. Nominal corporate tax rates in the OECD countries have decreased from an average of around 50 per cent in 1975 to an average of below 30 per cent in 2005 (Dietsch and Rixen 2011: 7–8). In response to the increasing difficulty of taxing highly mobile capital, many states were forced to broaden the tax base and to impose additional financial burdens on less mobile forms of capital, on labour, and on consumption. As a consequence, inequalities of income and wealth both within countries and across borders have risen. It is hardly possible to describe this process in the terms of a justified policy. The redistributive effects are not the product of domestic or international political processes but are forced upon affected societies by the external competitive pressures of an unregulated market. It is here where global economic policy lacks a competent institution that is either in charge of proposing common standards for capital taxation or is responsible for its redistributive domestic effects. In the absence of such a body, global capital taxation policy is an unjustified and thus unjust policy. It is true that the EU cannot be made responsible alone for the lack of such an institution. It can be demanded, however, that the EU makes a contribution to its establishment. The EU's silence—its continuing failure to suggest an institution for harmonizing international taxation rates—qualifies as an unjustified non-policy.

9.3. Towards global responsibility

In international politics, proper justificatory processes are still a rare exception to the general rule that decisions are reached by bargaining, and characterized by a brazen neglect of costs that accrue to third parties. The international system is by and large an order of non-justification in which most states insist on exercising their sovereign right to autonomously choose their own course of action. The EU is not much different. Although many of its policies follow the spirit of benevolent imperialism and can be defended with good reasons, hardly any EU external policy is justified in the sense discussed in this book. It is true that the EU, like most nation-states, seeks to protect its reputation in the international system and thus usually provides reasons and explanations for its policies to third parties. Its websites are full of explanations of the soundness of its policies, and it is quite likely that most EU politicians are convinced that these statements are more than just rhetoric. Very few of the EU's policies, however, meet the standards demanded by a universal right to justification. The reasons and explanations given by the EU for its external policies are rarely submitted to an independent third party with the authority to nullify unjustified actions. The EU's credentials as a justified political order thus differ starkly along the divide of internal and external affairs. In domestic affairs, the EU may well be on the right path towards giving force to the right to justification, but it is far from this goal in its relations with the rest of the world. What looks like a well-organized system of organizing accountability in internal affairs, looks from the outside like an inward-looking empire with little concern for external effects. A proper and encompassing justification of the EU can only be formulated if the double standard dividing its internal and external relations is overcome and if much more effort is invested in establishing institutions that allow affected non-EU parties to make their concerns a relevant factor in EU decision-making. A normatively sound understanding of policy-making in an increasingly interdependent world cannot stop at the legal borders of the EU polity but must accept a responsibility for external effects, wherever they occur. Doing so would improve the EU's global standing as a normative power and lend much more credibility to the claim that it strives to contribute to global wealth and the provision of public goods.

It is true that the prescriptions of the right to justification are often difficult to honour in practical policy-making. Any attempt to implement the moral imperative of allowing all parties affected by a binding policy to influence its formulation would generate serious real-world issues. How can artisan fishermen from West Africa participate in negotiations leading to new contracts with the EU? Who should represent African nations if one cannot trust their governments to adequately promote the people's interests and to implement the outcome properly? Taking into account that EU policy-making is heavily shaped by well-organized interest groups, we must be hesitant to rely on the ability of EU leaders to pick and apply the right moral standards. What would the procedure look like that would correct, at least, the most egregious effects of a policy? Similar problems arise for biofuels, global taxation, and European agricultural subsidies. In all of these cases, it is much easier to point to the problems European policies generate, including the failure of EU institutions to consider the interests of affected third parties, than it is to devise an adequate procedure for correcting problems and generating participation. A discussion of the possible options with a consideration of their relative advantages for designing innovative participatory arrangements would fill an additional volume, but the fact that the task is daunting must not be misused as an excuse for remaining silent on institutional reform. At the very minimum, we should demand that Europe take on the burden of explicitly investigating and reflecting on the external effects of its domestic policies for third parties. Draft legislation, which now must be justified by a discussion of issues of subsidiarity and proportionality and by listing the contributions of the different European institutions, should in future also be obliged to assess external effects. This would provide the basis for a critical assessment of whether the EU takes its claim to be a 'non-imperial empire' (Barroso 2007) seriously. It is true that no such provision would guarantee that the EU actually takes the concerns and grievances of affected parties so seriously as to qualify itself as a genuine 'force for good' or as a 'cosmopolitan polity'. What it can do, however, is to provide the critical public with the EU's official and explicit reasons for each specific policy, including reflection on external effects. In this way, it can invite contestation of its policies and prepare the grounds for the most important precondition of a universal right to justification: the unconstrained but legally structured public discourse.

Part VI
Conclusion

10

Conclusion

10.1. The EU's promise

The European Union is a dualistic polity that is not gradually replacing its Member States but is rather supplementing their functions. Its modus of operation is not the transfer of competencies but the joint exercise of pooled competencies on the normative basis of the principle of mutual recognition. The EU comprises a set of institutions and rules that are clearly delineated in terms of both function and scope. They provide the Member States with an additional layer of governance for internalizing the external effects of policy and thus contribute to the justification of Member States' democracies. Although the EU has developed from a technical regime in Coal and Steel to a polity with a set of competencies far broader than any other international organization, its authority is still strictly limited. It is misleading therefore to suggest that we will witness an automatic process of ever-greater union by means of uncontrolled spill-over effects. Supranational politics is not about overcoming the nation-state but about internalizing external effects. It is not likely to lead to an ever-closer union but will remain restricted to those policy areas where interdependence is obvious. That the EU is structurally different from nation-states is also underscored by its character as a fundamentally non-coercive polity that rests on voluntary cooperation, albeit disciplined by supranational law. Supranationalism cannot guarantee compliance with its rules but must put strong emphasis on accommodating the diversity of its Member States' interests, cultures, and traditions. The principle of mutual recognition is thus a normative cornerstone of the EU's approach to policy-making and is likely to stay so as long as the EU remains a supranational polity. The need to balance individual political equality with international equality and the structural limitations on applying majoritarian decision-making procedures are further implications of its non-coercive character. They are also important reasons why both the concepts of 'state' and 'democracy' are essentially useless for understanding and justifying the EU's practices.

Although the argument of this book seems to put primary emphasis on justice and to downplay democracy, it is ultimately oriented towards explaining the relationship between national democracy and transnational justice or, in other words, between the Member States' and the supranational layer of governance. Legitimacy in the multi-level system of the EU can only be properly understood if it encompasses the domestic and the international level. The normative promise of national democracy to foster self-governance will only survive Europeanization if an organizational layer that fosters transnational justice supplements it. Only if interdependent national democracies cooperate via a supranational level of justificatory discourse can we expect them to systematically concede that the external effects of their decisions are relevant for domestic decision-making (cf. Joerges and Neyer, 1997). Democracy entails that the rulers and the parties affected by rules are identical. If this standard is to be respected, i.e., if we are not ready to accept the effects of other nation-states' decisions without having had the chance to make our concerns heard in 'their' decision-making processes, and if we are not willing to make other citizenries subject to our decisions, then we have to work out a system of collective multi-level governance in which national democracies open themselves to the concerns of foreigners. Otherwise, the external effects of the internal practices of our democracy will impose illegitimate costs on foreigners, and, when foreign democracies make their policy choices, on us. Under conditions of interdependence, therefore, transnational justice and national democracy mutually support and necessitate each other.

The main message of this book is cautiously optimistic. The EU provides an adequate cure to many of the problems that modern democracies are facing in a globalizing world. Legal integration internalizes external effects and democratizes democracies by transforming strategic international bargaining into a justificatory transnational discourse. Under these conditions, the systematic production of justified cross-border policies becomes possible. The EU promotes the cause of justice by providing an effective remedy to horizontal and vertical power asymmetries, as well as to the arbitrariness of untamed anarchy. The constitutionalization of justificatory requirements changes the mode of representation from preferences and power to arguments and reasons and thus transforms intergovernmental bargaining into transnational deliberations. It provides safeguards against the impact of vertical power asymmetries on the justificatory discourse and exerts a compliance-pull by increasing the costs of non-compliance to powerful and weak states. All together, this is no mean accomplishment and deserves much praise.

It can well be understood as opening up chances for more justice in international politics.

10.2. Taking the promise seriously

It must be added, however, that the practices of the EU are far from perfect. Justificatory discourses are only imperfectly realized in many of its policies, namely in the Common Foreign and Security Policy, in asylum and migration policy, and in monetary and financial policy. In all these areas, Member States insist on their national sovereignty and do not allow for justificatory practices. Policy-making is shielded from public scrutiny and the European Court of Justice has only very limited or no competence to assess the merits of arguments in these fields. It is also openly clear that the constitutional development of the EU is only loosely connected to parliamentary participation and that the individual right to justification is finding little access here. A much stronger role for national parliaments and the transformation of COSAC into a constitution-building institution is needed.

Much of the growing political frustration of EU citizens would be alleviated if national parliaments took centre stage in EU politics. It is also of the utmost importance to publicly address the impossibility of facilitating supranational democracy and to be open about the functional limitations of supranationality. European politics is still deeply embedded in a culture of integration by stealth, closely connected to a belief in the merits of technocratic governance and a deep mistrust in the capacity of ordinary citizens to understand politics. EU policy-makers often explain policies publicly, but they hardly ever address institutional and procedural reasons for their limited and often disappointing substance. Much public frustration thus originates from overly optimistic expectations of the EU's problem-solving capacity and is due to a lack of knowledge about the difficulties of conducting effective and efficient policies in a fundamentally non-hierarchical polity. It is high time to explain the EU's structures to its citizens and to down-size the often far too ambitious rhetoric of EU policy-makers. The supranational layer of the EU is not democratic and will probably never become democratic. All efforts to foster governance without proper government and to equip the EU with parliamentary participation without giving it full agenda-setting powers will not suffice to establish a polity comparable to the democratic nation-state.

It is against this background that a public debate in Europe should be conducted for deciding on the future of Europe. This debate should not only be about voting rights, new directives, or other particularities of the EU. It should be about its most basic structures and be centred on the issue of whether European citizens are ready to risk their Member State democracies for transforming the EU into a full-blown, state-like entity, equipped with a monopoly of coercion and full legislative powers given to the European Parliament. The argument of this book is not a normative argument that rejects this option. It is a reconstructive argument that interprets existing structures. Thus, taking this step would be fully compatible with the arguments produced in the preceding chapters, if demanded by the citizens of Europe.

For living up to its promise, the EU must also invest much more effort in reforming its external actions. The dominant obsession of many EU policy-makers with the EU's 'actorness' and policy coherence is normatively insufficient and should be replaced by an emphasis on policy effects for third parties. The EU's foreign policies mostly reflect domestic concerns and pay only lip service to the right to justification. The EU, therefore, might be on the right track in terms of its overall domestic structure, but it is still very much a traditional imperial power in its interaction with third parties. Overcoming this deficit necessitates conducting systematic assessments of the impact of both international and domestic policies on third parties. It also implies working towards a stronger application of the right to justification in international organizations. The EU is a major power in the WTO and responsible for many of its regulations and their effect on developing countries. Yet it has not accepted any duty to justify its policies towards other states or independent third parties beyond the settlement of disputes regarding the implementation of WTO norms. That is a practice that is in sharp contrast to the right (and duty) to justification.

10.3. Affirming normative realism

The methodology used for making the argument of this book is built on the assumption that a politically relevant normative theory needs to do more than simply describe the difference between the real and the ideal. It should start from an empirically informed understanding of its object and base its arguments on a balance between empirical assessments and normative claims. The theory developed here is a realistic theory of justice in this sense. It does not concern itself with normatively pure models of politics for communities of saints, but looks rather for the best in an existing organization and installs this as the standard for a normative critique of the way this institution works. Normative realism takes the promise of institutions at face value and holds them to account for their failures to deliver corresponding procedures and policies. This is, of course, not the stuff of revolution but of reform. Normative realism bends normative vision to political pragmatism. It is not likely to fall prey to blind idealism, nor can

Conclusion

pointing to the incompatibility of theory and reality negate its prescriptions. Grounded analytically and empirically in real institutions and events, its relevance for political practice is guaranteed. Normative realism is an approach that draws inspiration from normative intuitions and empirical phenomena alike without, however, allowing one of the two to dominate the other. Normative realism aims at drawing a balance between the 'is' and the 'ought', i.e. it takes both norms and facts as equally important elements of reality. A realistic conception of justice is a reconstructive conception that expands the borders of what we consider possible without losing touch with reality. The choice for the normative realist therefore is not between normative and empirical theories but between theories with a different mix of normative and empirical claims. Positive theories must take normative dispositions seriously and normative theories need a proper assessment of the empirical facts.

Is that an affirmative and structurally conservative way of reflecting about the EU? Should we not uphold the classical distinction between the world of norms on the one hand and the world of facts on the other hand in order to safeguard normative purity? A first argument for countering this claim is to point to its problematic implications. Upholding the unrealistic normative standard of democracy for a layer of governance that aims at supporting but not substituting Member State democracy makes it extremely difficult to describe even the most laudable and uncontested EU policy as being justified. Tying the legitimacy of the EU inseparably to democracy closes the analytical door to reflecting constructively about the conditions of legitimate governance beyond the state. It is an argument that forces us to either demand establishing the European federal state or—if that is deemed to be too utopian—to recommend downgrading the EU irrespective of the merits of its policies and the public support they achieve. It is utterly unhelpful for all those who accept that the credibility of the democratic nation-state's promise to realize self-governance has run into serious problems and that it is in need of support by an additional layer of inter- or supranational governance. Not realism, but idealism is thus a *de facto* recipe for political conservatism and the most likely outcome of constitutional nationalism.

Pragmatic arguments do not convince everyone. An alternative defence is to note that all theories, be they normative or explanatory, have limited applicability. They are established on abstract categories and simplifications that are valid to the degree that they match empirical conditions. International relations theory, for example, is built on the assumption of international anarchy and perpetual conflict. Democratic theory applies to governance in state-like structures and presupposes a monopoly of coercion, a shared political culture, a nation-wide media etc. None of this applies to the EU. It is neither a state nor an international regime but is established on a combination of elements from both political realms. It combines the hierarchical legal structure of the state with the anarchical political structure of the international system. The EU is a supranational entity and supports a political class of its own. Taking this *sui generis* character seriously implies accepting its dual character as a starting point of analysis just like we are accustomed to accepting the anarchical character of the international system or the coercive character of the state as preconditions of meaningful analysis. That is exactly what normative realism does. There is nothing conservative or affirmative about it. It is an intellectual move that takes the difference between political science and philosophy seriously in claiming political relevance by contributing knowledge to refining our understanding of the political world and the means for improving it. That, however, can only be done convincingly if facts are somehow fed into normative analysis. By keeping in touch with reality, normative realism is politically relevant and can make a legitimate claim to have an impact on politics. That is quite the opposite of conservatism and uncritical affirmation.

10.4. Beyond normative realism

The argument developed in this book fits well with the EU's supranational structure but is hard to apply to international politics. A normatively realistic analysis of the international system must start from the empirical insight that the international order is an order of non-justification. Almost all states insist on their sovereign rights to autonomously choose their policies. It is true that foreign policies are often publicly explained, that states produce reasons for their courses of action, and that foreign policies sometimes have beneficial effects on their addressees. Almost no foreign policy in the international system, however, meets the criteria of the right to justification. Third parties affected by processes occurring without the boundaries of their own jurisdiction are hardly ever invited to meaningfully participate in domestic decision-making, and the international system knows no institutional provisions for making foreign policies systematically subject to legal scrutiny. Applying the right to justification to international politics thus is a form of analysis that goes beyond normative realism. The international system lacks the empirical preconditions that allow its reconstruction as an (imperfectly justified) order of justification. It is a form of politics that can be critically analysed but not affirmed or even reconstructed by applying the right to justification. The right to justification can well be used, however, for inspiring normative reflections on how the international system could be reformed to give force to the right to justification. Such a normative reflection follows the methodological lines of many cosmopolitan institutional thinkers. Authors such as Held, Falk, Beitz, and Archibugi try to identify the institutional preconditions of a legitimate global polity by applying a normative standard that is only loosely related to its empirical context. It is an approach that is normatively idealistic rather than realistic and of philosophical rather than political relevance.

Reflecting, nevertheless, along the lines of normative idealism, we might first think of a global constitutional assembly that concludes a kind of global document for codifying the right of all contracting parties to demand justifications from other contracting parties if they undertake actions that have a constraining effect on their own liberties. The global document would also entail a generalized duty to provide explanatory reasons on demand. It would, thirdly, include a list of those policy areas to which the right to justification applies or does not apply. The new political order would not be without limits. Its material competencies would encompass only those areas where external effects of individual states' actions are significant and where national policies are handicapped by other states' policies. Trade policy, environmental policy, migration policy, monetary policy, and security policy would become parts of its competency, whereas education, health, and cultural policy would not. The allocation and depth of competencies would have to be organized by a constitutional body that follows along the lines of an interparliamentary constitutional assembly as outlined in chapter eight. A basic requirement of the new order of justification would also be to accept the jurisdiction of a reformed International Court of Justice (ICJ) in all cases where a complaining party does not accept the reasons provided by a defending party as sufficient. The reformed ICJ would be an institution far stronger than the recent ICJ. It would no longer be limited in its jurisdiction to cases where both parties (including the defending party) accept its competence, but follow the WTO practices in reversing the consensus principles. All cases would fall under its jurisdiction, provided that at least one party assents. A global prosecutor would support the ICJ with the competence to monitor state compliance with adopted legal obligations. The prosecutor would have the right to bring charges to the court autonomously, even if no state raises an objection to any other state's practices. The ICJ would thus be developed into a full-blown body of generalized legal overview in joint practices of the international community. It would have the competence to assess the reasons produced by states when acting on legal obligations and guarantee that unjustified policies do not go unnoticed and unchallenged.

The international order of justification would also need a legislative assembly with full agenda-setting and law-making authority, constrained only by the material and procedural limitations codified in the global document and modified by the global interparliamentary constitutional assembly. The legislative body would have the primary competence to specify the provisions of the global document and to apply it to political challenges as they arise. This body would not be established according to the principle of 'one person, one vote' but rather follow the practices of the EU in applying the principle of digressive proportionality, thus giving smaller states a safeguard that they have at least some say without, however, allowing an exploitation of the bigger states. It would have to realize a careful balance between larger and smaller states that makes deliberative processes of consensus-seeking likely without prohibiting effective policy-making. Just as in the EU, all contracting parties would have the right to bring a suit to the ICJ in cases in which the legislative assembly violates the principles of subsidiarity and proportionality, and ask for nullification. The global legislative body would have to be built on domestic democratic or at least inclusive procedures that guarantee that member states' delegates to the global interparliamentary assembly represent their societies rather than their governments. A domestic democratic order (or any other justifiable political order that gives effect to the right to justification) would be a prerequisite for membership in the global legislative body.

An international order of justification would also provide for non-governmental stakeholder input, possibly in a second legislative chamber with the right to halt legislation until all legitimate concerns have been heard and debated. This proposal is greatly in accordance with the suggestion that multiple transnational publics, organized around specific topics or international institutions, can promote new political practices of cross-border deliberation and thus contribute to a legitimate form of post-national governance (Dryzek 2006). According to Dryzek, civil society organizations can counter the established power position of international organizations by criticizing and opposing their policies. They demand justifications for policies, challenge institutionalized political practices, and demand an inclusion of otherwise unheard concerns. Similarly, James Bohmann stresses the beneficial effect of 'contestation through global networks' and praises this as 'the central feature of democracy beyond the state' (Bohmann 2005: 294). Bohmann describes the development of a wholly new transnational structure of public discourse characterized by numerous parallel demoi, each specific to its own policy field. According to Bohmann, a new political space would arise that could sustain a global democracy. Although it might be questioned whether the discursive structure envisaged by Dryzek and Bohmann qualifies as democracy, the proposal as such has much in common with the general line of reasoning outlined in this book. Civil society organizations would be invited to criticize and contest the rules established by the global interparliamentary assembly. Contestation through global networks would be accepted as an integral element of a global political discourse and as an important means for fostering justificatory practices.

An international order of justification would neither need a global monopoly of coercion nor should it have one. It would remain a voluntary order that can be exited by any party at any time. Only members that accept its legal discipline, however, would be entitled to enjoy the benefits of its liberal trade order and thus have access to the markets of the EU, the United States, and China. Non-compliance with any of the global legal provisions, be they in human rights or trade law, would be brought to court by the global prosecutor, identified as a violation of treaty obligations by the ICJ, and lead to rectification or a discontinuation of benefits. To make the system more attractive to developing countries, the WTO would have to undergo significant change. It has to develop from its current status as an institution catering basically to the interests of industrialized states toward an institution that is far more sensitive to developing states. It would have to be equipped with a significant redistributive element that supports developing countries in catching up with the more developed states. Even more importantly, the new WTO would end all developed countries' practices of subsidizing agricultural production and make free trade in agricultural products an essential part of its order. If enjoying the benefits of the reformed WTO were made conditional on general compliance with the right to justification in both its international and domestic dimension, it could be expected that it would exert a compliance pull comparable to the common market of the EU. The EU, the United States, and China would also have a strong incentive to comply with the legal discipline of this new global regime. It would stabilize the existing international order, provide market-based political integration with a new source of legitimacy, and promote democracy all over the world. If this new order were anywhere near as attractive to outside countries as the EU is for its southern and eastern neighbours, then the world of international relations might be significantly altered and global anarchy be tamed without having to establish a global state. But this, of course, is (only) normative idealism.

Bibliography

Abbott, K. W., R. O. Keohane, A. Moravcsik, A. -M. Slaughter, and D. Snidal (2000). 'The Concept of Legalization', *International Organization*, 54(3): 401–19.

Adler, E., and M. Barnett (1998). *Security Communities*, Cambridge: Cambridge University Press.

Aidt, T. (2009). 'Corruption, Institutions and Economic Development', *Oxford Review of Economic Policy*, 25(2): 271–91.

Alter, K. J. (2001). *Establishing the Supremacy of European Law: The Making of an International Rule of Law in Europe*, Oxford: Oxford University Press.

Andersen, B. (1991). *Imagined Communities: Reflections on the Origin and Spread of Nationalism*. London: Verso Books, revised edition.

Archibugi, D. (2009). *The Global Commonwealth of Citizens: Toward a Cosmopolitan Democracy*, Princeton: Princeton University Press.

Arnull, A., and D. Wincott (2002). *Accountability and Legitimacy in the European Union*, Oxford: Oxford University Press.

Auel, K. (2007). 'Democratic Accountability and National Parliaments: Redefining the Impact of Parliamentary Scrutiny in EU Affairs', *European Law Journal*, 13(4): 487–504.

Auel, K., and T. Raunio (2011). 'Introduction: National Parliaments, Electorates and EU Affairs', Paper presented at the Humboldt-Viadrina School of Governance—Workshop on National Parliaments in the European Union, Berlin, April 2011.

Avbelj, M. (2011). 'Supremacy or Primacy of EU law—(Why) Does it Matter?', *European Law Journal*, 17(6): 744–63.

Bailey, T. A. (1948). *The Man in the Street. The Impact of Public Opinion on American Foreign Policy*, New York: Peter Smith Publications Incorporation.

Bale, T. (2008). *European Politics. A Comparative Introduction*, Houndmills/Basingstoke: Palgrave Macmillan.

Barber, B. (2005). 'Global Democracy From Below', in D. Held et al. (eds.), *Debating Globalization*, Cambridge: Polity Press.

Barnett, M., and M. Finnemore (1999). 'The Politics, Power, and Pathologies of International Organizations', *International Organization*, 53(4): 699–732.

Barnett, M., and M. Finnemore (2004). *Rules for the World: International Organizations in Global Politics*, Ithaca/N.Y.: Cornell University Press.

Barroso (2007). Cited in EUObserver 11.7.2007. http://euobserver.com/18/24458,%20last%20accessed%2014/5/2012.

Bibliography

Beck, U., and E. Grande (2011). 'Empire Europe: Statehood and Political Authority in the Process of Regional Integration', in: J. Neyer, A. Wiener (eds.), *Political Theory of the European Union*, Oxford: Oxford University Press.

Beitz, C. (1973). *Political Theory and International Relations*, Princeton: Princeton University Press.

Beitz, C. (1999). 'Social and Cosmopolitan Liberalism', *International Affairs*, 75(3): 515–29.

Bergström, C. F. (2005). *Comitology. Delegation of Powers in the European Union and the Committee System*, Oxford: Oxford University Press.

Bernal, R. L. (2006). 'Special and differential treatment for small developing economies', in: R. Grynberg (ed.), *WTO at the Margins. Small States and the Multilateral Trading System*, Cambridge: Cambridge University Press.

Blondel, J., and M. Cotta (eds.) (2000). *The Nature of Party Government. A Comparative European Perspective*, Basingstoke: Palgrave.

Bohle, D. (2006). 'Neoliberal Hegemony, Transnational Capital and the Terms of the EU's Eastward Expansion', *Capital & Class*, 30(1): 57–86.

Bohman, J. (2005). 'From Demos to Demoi: Democracy beyond Borders', *Ratio Juris*, 18 (3): 293–314.

Börzel, T., T. Hofmann, D. Panke, and C. Sprungk (2010). Obstinate and Inefficient. Why Member States Do Not Comply with European Law', *Comparative Political Studies*, 43(11): 1363–90.

Bovens, M. (2007). 'Analysing and Assessing Accountability: A Conceptual Framework', *European Law Journal*, 13(4): 447–68.

Bovens, M. (2010). 'Two Concepts of Accountability: Accountability as a Virtue and as a Mechanism', *West European Politics*, 33(5): 946–67.

Bovens, M., D. Curtin, and P. t'Hart (2010). *The Real World of EU Accountability. What Deficit?* Oxford: Oxford University Press.

Brown, C. (1992). *International Relations Theory: New Normative Approaches*, New York: Columbia University Press.

Brunkhorst, H. (2007). 'Unbezähmbare Öffentlichkeit—Europa zwischen transnationaler Klassenherrschaft und egalitärer Konstitutionalisierung', *Leviathan*, 35(1): 12–29.

Bruno, E. (2011). *The European Citizens' Initiative (ECI): Entrusting Civil Society Participation Versus Enhancing the Democratic Legitimacy of the EU Institutions?* Masterthesis, Bruges: College of Europe/Bruges Campus/Politics and Administrative Studies.

Bull, H. (1977). *The Anarchical Society. A Study of Order in World Politics,* Basingstoke: Macmillan.

Bull, H. (1982). 'Civilian Power Europe: A Contradiction in Terms?', *Journal of Common Market Studies*, 21(2): 149–70.

Burgess, M. (2000). *Federalism and the European Union: the Building of Europe, 1950–2000*, New York: Routledge.

Burley, A. -M., and W. Mattli (1993). 'Europe before the Court: A Political Theory of Legal Integration', *International Organization*, 47(1): 41–76.

Busch, M. L., and E. Reinhardt (2003). 'Developing Countries and General Agreement on Tariffs and Trade/World Trade Organization Dispute Settlement', *Journal of World Trade*, 37(4): 719–35.

Bibliography

Cappelletti, M., M. Seccombe, and J. H. H. Weiler (1985). *Integration through Law: Europe and the American Federal Experience, Vol. 1: Methods, Tools and Institutions. A Series under the General Editorship of M. Cappelletti*, Berlin/New York: De Gruyter.

Carr, E. H. (1983). *The Twenty Years Crisis: 1919–1939*, London: Macmillan.

Cass, Deborah (2005). *The Constitutionalization of the World Trade Organization*, Oxford: Oxford University Press.

Chalmers, D., G. Davies, and G. Monti (2011). *European Union Law* [Second Edition], Cambridge: Cambridge University Press.

Coen, D. (2007). 'Empirical and Theoretical Studies in EU Lobbying', *Journal of European Public Policy*, 14(3): 333–45.

Coen, D., and J. Richardson (2007). *Lobbying in the European Union: Institutions, Actors and Issues*, Oxford/New York: Oxford University Press.

Council of Europe (2011). 'Opinion on the New Constitution of Hungary, adopted by the Venice Commission at its 87th Plenary Session (Venice, 17–18 June 2011)', Venice: Opinion no. 621/2011, CDL-AD(2011)016.

Cowles, M. G. (2001). 'The Transatlantic Business Dialogue and Domestic Business-Government Relations', in: M. G. Cowles, J. A. Caporaso, and T. Risse (eds.), *Transforming Europe. Europeanization and Domestic Change*, New York: Cornell University Press.

Craig, P. (2006). *EU Administrative Law*, Oxford: Oxford University Press.

Crawford, N. C. (2009). 'Homo Politicus and Argument (Nearly) All the Way Down: Persuasion in Politics', *Perspectives on Politics*, 7(1): 103–24.

Crum, B., and J. E. Fossum (2009). 'The Multilevel Parliamentary Field: a framework for theorizing representative democracy in the EU', *European Political Science Review*, 1 (2): 249–72.

Curtin, D. (2009). *Executive Power of the European Union. Law, Practices, and the Living Constitution*, Oxford: Oxford University Press.

Curtin, D., and M. Egeberg (2008). 'Tradition and Innovation: Europe's Accumulated Executive Order', *West European Politics*, 31(4): 639–61.

Dahl, R. (1999). 'Can International Organizations be Democratic? A Sceptic's View', in: I. Shapiro, and C. Hacker-Cordon (eds.), *Democracy's Edges*, Cambridge: Cambridge University Press.

Dahl, R. (2001). 'Is Post-National Democracy Possible?', in: Sergio Fabbrini (ed.), *Nation, Federalism, and Democracy*, Trento: Editrice Compositori.

Dahl, R. (2006). *On Political Equality*, New Haven/London: Yale University Press.

Daniels, N. (2011). 'Reflective Equilibrium', in: *Stanford Encyclopedia of Philosophy*, available at: http://plato.stanford.edu/archives/spr2011/entries/reflective-equilibrium/,%20last%20accessed:%2017/10/2011.

De la Porte, C., and P. Nanz (2004). 'The OMC—a Deliberative-Democratic Mode of Governance? The Cases of Employment and Pensions', *Journal of European Public Policy*, 11(2): 267–88.

De Neve, J. -E. (2007). 'The European Onion? How Differentiated Integration is Re-Shaping the EU', *Journal of European Integration*, 29(4): 503–21.

Deitelhoff, N. (2006). *Überzeugung in der Politik. Grundzüge einer Diskurstheorie internationalen Regierens*, Frankfurt am Main: Suhrkamp.

Deitelhoff, N., and H. Müller (2005). 'Theoretical Paradise—Empirically Lost? Arguing with Habermas', *Review of International Studies*, 31(1): 167–79.

Deutsch, K. W., Sidney A. Burrell, Robert A. Kann, et al. (1957). *Political Community and the North Atlantic Area; International Organization in the Light of Historical Experience*, Princeton: Princeton University Press.

Dietsch, P., and T. Rixen (2011). 'Tax Competition and Global Background Justice', Paper presented to the European Consortium for Political Research, Reykjavik, August 2011.

Dinan, D. (2002). 'Governance and Institutions: The Convention and the Intergovernmental Conference', *Journal of Common Market Studies*, 42(1): 27–42.

Dryzek, J. S., (2006). *Global Deliberative Politics*, Cambridge: Polity Press.

Duchene, F. (1972). 'Europe's Role in World Peace', in: R. Mayne (ed.), *Europe Tomorrow: Sixteen Europeans Look Ahead*, London: Fontana.

Dür, A., and H. Zimmermann (2007). 'Introduction: The EU in International Trade Negotiations', *Journal of Common Market Studies*, 45(4): 771–87.

Dworkin, R. (1986). *Law's Empire*, Cambridge/Mass.: Harvard University Press.

Dworkin, R. (2000). *Sovereign Virtue: The Theory and Practice of Equality* [Second Edition], Cambridge/Mass.: Harvard University Press.

Egeberg, M., and J. Trondal (2011). 'EU-Level Agencies: New Executive Centre Formation or Vehicles for National Control?' *Journal of European Public Policy*, 18(6): 868–87.

Ehlermann, C. (2005). 'WTO Decision-Making Procedures, "Member-Driven" Rule-Making and WTO Consensus-Practices: Are They Adequate? Are WTO Decision-Making Procedures Adequate for Making, Revising and Implementing Worldwide and "Plurilateral" Rules?', Online Publication, Frankfurt/Berlin: WilmerHale, in Ernst-Ulrich Petersmann (ed), *Developing countries in the Doha Round: WTO decision-making procedures and negotiations on trade in agriculture and services*, Florence, Robert Schuman Centre, European University Institute.

Elgström, O., and C. Jönsson (eds.) (2009). *European Union Negotiations: Processes, Networks and Institutions*, London: Routledge.

Elster, J. (1998a). 'Deliberation and Constitution Making', in: J. Elster (ed.), *Deliberative Democracy*, Cambridge: Cambridge University Press.

Elster, J. (1998b). 'Introduction', in: J. Elster (ed.), *Deliberative Democracy*, Cambridge: Cambridge University Press.

Eriksen, E. O. (2007). 'The EU—A Cosmopolitan Polity?', *Journal of European Public Policy*, 13(2): 252–69.

Eriksen, E. O. (2009). *The Unfinished Democratization of Europe*, Oxford: Oxford University Press.

Eriksen, E. O., and J. E. Fossum (2002). 'Democracy through Strong Publics in the European Union?', *Journal of Common Market Studies*, 40(3): 401–24.

European Commission (2001). 'European Governance. A White Paper', Brussels: COM (2001) 428 final.

European Commission (2003). 'Wider Europe—Neighbourhood: A new Framework for relations with our Eastern and Southern Neighbours', COM (2003) 104 final.

European Commission (2006). 'White Paper on a European Communication Policy', Brussels: COM (2006) 35 final.

Bibliography

European Commission (2010). '27th Annual Report on Monitoring the Application of EU Law (2009)', Brussels: COM (2010) 538 final.

European Commission (2011). '28th Annual Report on Monitoring the Application of EU Law (2010)', Brussels: COM (2011) 588 final.

European Council (2003). 'A Secure Europe in a Better World—European Security Strategy', Brussels.

European Ombudsman (2011). 'Annual Report 2010', Strasbourg.

European Parliament (2010). 'European Parliament resolution of 7 September 2010 on journalism and new media—creating a public sphere in Europe', Brussels: 2010/2015(INI).

Falk, R., and A. Strauss (2001). 'Toward Global Parliament', *Foreign Affairs*, 80(1): 212–20.

Featherstone, K. (1994). 'Jean Monnet and the "Democratic Deficit" in the European Union', *Journal of Common Market Studies*, 32(2): 149–70.

Finke, B. (2007). 'Civil society participation in EU Governance', *Living Reviews in European Governance*, 2(2).

Fischer, J. (2010). 'Die Vereinigten Staaten von Europa', in: Bertelsmann Stiftung (ed.), *Europa wagen*, Gütersloh: Bertelsmann.

Fisher, R., W. Ury, and B. Patton (1991). *Getting to Yes: Negotiating Agreement Without Giving In* [Second Edition], New York: Penguin Books.

Follesdal, A., and S. Hix (2006). 'Why There is a Democratic Deficit in the EU: A Response to Majone and Moravcsik', *Journal of Common Market Studies*, 44(3): 533–62.

Forst, R. (2002). 'Zu einer kritischen Theorie transnationaler Gerechtigkeit', in: R. Schmücker, and U. Steinvorth (eds.), *Gerechtigkeit und Politik. Philosophische Perspektiven. Deutsche Zeitschrift für Philosophie, Sonderheft 3*, Berlin: Akademie-Verlag.

Forst, R. (2007). *Das Recht auf Rechtfertigung. Elemente einer konstruktivistischen Theorie der Gerechtigkeit*, Frankfurt am Main: Suhrkamp.

Forst, R. (2010). 'The Justification of Human Rights and the Basic Right to Justification: A Reflexive Approach', *Ethics*, 120(4): 711–40.

Forst, R. (2011). *The Right to Justification: Elements of a Constructivist Theory of Justice*, New York: Columbia University Press.

Fossum, J. E., and A. J. Menéndez (2005). 'The Constitution's Gift? A Deliberative Democratic Analysis of Constitution-Making in the European Union', *ARENA-Working Paper*, 5(13).

Franck, T. M. (1990). *The Power of Legitimacy Among Nations*, New York: Oxford University Press.

Genschel, P., and B. Zangl (2007). 'Die Zerfaserung von Staatlichkeit und die Zentralität des Staates', *Aus Politik und Zeitgeschichte*, 20–1: 10–16.

Gerhards, J. (2000). 'Europäisierung von Ökonomie und Politik und die Trägheit der Entstehung einer europäischen Öffentlichkeit, in: M. Bach (ed.), *Die Europäisierung nationaler Gesellschaften, Sonderheft 40 der Kölner Zeitschrift für Soziologie und Sozialpsychologie*, Wiesbaden/Opladen: Westdeutscher Verlag.

Gerstenberg, O., and C. F. Sabel (2002). 'Directly-Deliberative Polyarchy: An Institutional Ideal for Europe?', in: C. Joerges, and R. Dehousse (eds.), *Good Governance in Europe's Integrated Market*, Oxford/New York: Oxford University Press.

Goldsmith, J. L., and E. A. Posner (2005). *The Limits of International Law*, Oxford: Oxford University Press.

Greenwood, J. (2006). *Interest Representation in the European Union* [Second Edition], Houndmills/Basingstoke: Palgrave Macmillan.

Groenleer, M. L., and L. G. van Schaik (2007). 'United We Stand? The European Union's International Actorness in the Cases of the International Criminal Court and the Kyoto Protocol', *Journal of Common Market Studies*, 45(5): 969–98.

Grunwald, M. (2008). 'The Clean Energy Scam', *Time Magazine U.S.*, 27/3/2008.

Haas, E. B. (1958). *The Uniting of Europe, Political, Social and Economical forces 1950–1957*, London: Stevens.

Haas, E. B. (1961). 'International Integration: The European and the Universal Process', *International Organization*, 15(3): 366–92.

Haas, E. B. (1964). *Beyond the Nation State*, Stanford: Stanford University Press.

Haas, E. B. (1968). *The Uniting of Europe, Political, Social and Economical Forces 1950–1957* [Reprint], Stanford: Stanford University Press.

Haas, P. M. (1992). 'Introduction: Epistemic Communities and International Policy Coordination', *International Organization*, 46(1): 1–35.

Habermas, J. (1973). 'Wahrheitstheorien', in: H. Fahrenbach (ed.), *Wirklichkeit und Reflexion. Walter Schulz zum 60. Geburtstag*, Pfullingen: Neske.

Habermas, J. (1981). *Theorie des kommunikativen Handelns*, Frankfurt am Main: Suhrkamp.

Habermas, J. (1983). 'Interpretive Social Science vs. Hermeneuticism', in: N. Haan, R. N. Bellah, P. Rabinow, and W. M. Sullivan (eds.), *Social Science as Moral Inquiry*, New York: Columbia University Press.

Habermas, J. (1991). 'Vom pragmatischen, ethischen und moralischen Gebrauch der praktischen Vernunft', in: J. Habermas, *Erläuterungen zur Diskursethik*, Frankfurt am Main: Suhrkamp.

Habermas, J. (1992). *Faktizität und Geltung. Beiträge zur Diskurstheorie des Rechtes und des demokratischen Rechtsstaats*, Frankfurt am Main: Suhrkamp.

Habermas, J. (1995). *Vorstudien und Ergänzungen zur Theorie des kommunikativen Handelns*, Frankfurt am Main: Suhrkamp.

Habermas, J. (2001). *The Postnational Constellation: Political Essays*, Cambridge: MIT Press.

Habermas, J. (2011). *Zur Verfassung Europas. Ein Essay*, Berlin: Suhrkamp.

Habermas, J. [C. Cronin, P. De Greiff (eds.)] (2000). *The Inclusion of the Other. Studies in Political Theory* [Third Edition], Cambridge: MIT Press.

Hamlet, L. (2004). 'Assessing the Impact of Organizational Culture on International Organizations', Paper presented at the 2004 Annual Meeting of the International Studies Association, Montreal, March 2004.

Harlow, C. (2002). *Accountability in the European Union*. Oxford: Oxford University Press.

Harlow, C., and R. Rawlings (2007). 'Promoting Accountability in Multilevel Governance: A Network Approach', *European Law Journal*, 13(4): 542–62.

Hathaway, O. A. (2004). 'Between Power and Principle: A Political Theory of International Law', *University of Chicago Law Review*, 72(2): 469–536.

Hayes-Renshaw, F., and H. Wallace (1995). 'Executive Power in the European Union: the Functions and Limits of the Council of Ministers', *Journal of European Public Policy*, 2(4): 559–82.

Heisenberg, D. (2005). 'The Institution of "Consensus" in the European Union: Formal versus Informal Decision-Making in the Council', *European Journal of Political Research*, 44(1): 65–90.

Held, D. (2010). *Cosmopolitanism. Ideals and Realities*, Cambridge: Polity Press.

Hill, C. (1993). 'The Capability-Expectations Gap, or Conceptualizing Europe's International Role', *Journal of Common Market Studies*, 31(3): 305–28.

Hix, S. (2008). *What's Wrong with the European Union and How to Fix it*, Cambridge: Polity Press.

Hix, S., A. Noury, and G. Roland (2007). *Democratic Politics in the European Parliament*, Cambridge: Cambridge University Press.

Holzhacker, R. (2007). 'Democratic Legitimacy and the European Union', *Journal of European Integration*, 29(3): 257–69.

Hooghe, L., and G. Marks (2001). *Multi-Level Governance and European Integration*, Oxford: Rowman and Littlefield.

Hudec, R. E. (1999). 'The New WTO Dispute Settlement System Procedure: An Overview of the First Three Years', *Minnesota Journal of Global Trade*, 8(1): 1–53.

Huntington, S. P. (1996). *The Clash of Civilizations and the Remaking of World Order*, New York/London/Toronto/Sydney: Simon & Schuster.

Hurrell, A. (2007). *On Global Order. Power, Values, and the Constitution of International Society*, Oxford: Oxford University Press.

Hyde-Price, A. (2006). 'Normative' power Europe: a realist critique', *Journal of European Public Policy*, 13(2): 217–34.

Ilnyckyj, M. (2007). 'The Legality and Sustainability of European Union Fisheries Policy in West Africa', *MIT International Review*, 1(1): 32–41.

Ipsen, H. P. (1987). 'Europäische Verfassung—nationale Verfassung', *Europarecht*, 22(2): 195–213.

Joerges, C. (2006). 'Deliberative Political Processes Revisited: What have We Learnt about the Legitimacy of Supranational Decision-Making', *Journal of Common Market Studies*, 44(4): 779–802.

Joerges, C. (2007). 'Democracy and European Integration: A Legacy of Tensions, a Re-conceptualisation and Recent True Conflicts', *EUI Law Working Papers*, 2007(25).

Joerges, C., and J. Neyer (1997). 'Transforming Strategic Interaction into Deliberative Problem-Solving: European Comitology in the Foodstuff Sector', *Journal of European Public Policy*, 4(4): 609–25.

Joerges, C., Y. Meny, and J. H. H. Weiler (2002). *Mountain or Molehill? A Critical Appraisal of the Commission White Paper on Governance*, Florence/New York: European University Institute-Robert Schumann Centre/NYU School of Law-Jean Monnet Center.

Johnstone, I. (2003). 'Security Council Deliberations: The Power of the Better Argument', *European Journal of International Law*, 14(3): 437–80.

Kaczynski, V. M., and D. L. Fluharty (2002). 'European Policies in West Africa: Who Benefits from Fisheries Agreements?', *Marine Policy*, 26(2): 75–93.

Bibliography

Kahler, M. (2004). 'Defining Accountability Up: The Global Economic Multilaterals', *Government and Opposition*, 39(2): 132–58.
Kant, I. [W. Weischedel (ed.)] (1982). *Die Metaphysik der Sitten. Werkausgabe Band VIII* [Fifth Edition], Frankfurt am Main: Suhrkamp.
Katzenstein, P. J. (1993). 'Coping with Terrorism: Norms and Internal Security in Germany and Japan', in: J. Goldstein, and R. O. Keohane (eds.), *Ideas and Foreign Policy*, Ithaca: Cornell University Press.
Kelsen, H. (1957). *What is Justice: Justice, Law, and Politics in the Mirror of Science. Collected Essays*, Berkeley: University of California Press.
Kelsen H. (1960). *Reine Rechtslehre*, Wien: Springer.
Kennan, G. F. (1985). 'Morality and Foreign Policy', *Foreign Policy*, 64(2): 205–18.
Keohane, R. O. (2006). 'Accountability in World Politics', *Scandinavian Political Studies*, 29(2): 75–87.
Keohane, R. O., S. Macedo, and A. Moravcsik (2009). 'Democracy-Enhancing Multilateralism', *International Organization*, 63(1): 1–31.
Khor, M. (2001). *Rethinking Globalisation. Critical Issues and Policy Choices*, Black Point/Winnipeg: Fernwood Publishing.
Kielmannsegg, G. (2003). 'Integration und Demokratie', in: B. Kohler-Koch, and M. Jachtenfuchs (eds.), *Europäische Integration* [Second Edition], Opladen: Leske + Budrich.
Kiiver, P. (2006). *The National Parliaments in the European Union: A Critical View on EU Constitution-Building*, The Hague: Kluwer Law International.
King, G., R. O. Keohane, and S. Verba (1994). *Designing Social Inquiry: Scientific Inference in Qualitative Research*, Princeton: Princeton University Press.
Kissling, C., and J. Steffek (2008). 'CSOs and the Democratization of International Governance: Prospects and Problems', in: C. Kissling, P. Nanz, and J. Steffek (eds.), *Civil Society Participation in European and Global Governance: A Cure for the Democratic Deficit?* Basingstoke: Palgrave Macmillan.
Klotz, A. (1995). *Norms in International Relations. The Struggle against Apartheid*, Ithaca/New York: Cornell University Press.
Koopmans, R. (2007). 'Who Inhabits the European Public Sphere? Winners and Losers, Supporters and Opponents in Europeanised Political Debates', *European Journal of Political Research*, 64(2): 183–210.
Kurpas, S., M. Brüggemann, and C. Meyer (2006). 'The Commission White Paper on Communication. Mapping a Way to a European Public Sphere', *Centre for European Policy Studies (CEPS) Policy Brief*, 06(101).
Kwa, A. (2003). *Power Politics in the WTO, Focus on the Global South*, Bangkok: Chulalogkorn University.
Lam, A. (2000). 'Tacit Knowledge, Organizational Learning and Societal Institutions: An Integrated Framework', *Organization Studies*, 21(3): 487–513.
Laursen, F. (2005). 'The Role of National Parliamentary Committees in European Scrutiny: Reflections based on the Danish Case', *Journal of Legislative Studies*, 11(3/4): 412–27.
Lavenex, S. (2011). 'Concentric Circles of Flexible 'European' Integration: A Typology of EU External Governance Relations', *Comparative European Politics*, 9(4/5): 372–93.

Bibliography

Legg, J. (2010). 'Effective Consultation with Citizens in the EU', *Volonteurope Reports On*, 2.

Lepsius, M. R. (2000). 'Die Europäische Union als Herrschaftsverband eigener Prägung', *Harvard Jean Monnet Working Paper*, 00(12).

Lewis, J. (2005). 'The Janus Face of Brussels: Socialization and Everyday Decision-Making in the European Union', *International Organization*, 59(4): 937–71.

Lord, C. (2004). *A Democratic Audit of the European Union*, London: Palgrave Macmillan.

Lord, C. (2007). 'Democratic Control of the Council of Ministers', *Oesterreichische Zeitschrift für Politikwissenschaft*, 36(2): 125–38.

Lord, C., and J. Pollak (2010). 'Representation and Accountability: Communicating Tubes?', *West European Politics*, 33(5): 968–88.

Lucarelli, S., and I. Manners (eds.) (2006). *Values and Principles in European Union Foreign Policy*. London/New York: Routledge.

Lukas, M. (1995). 'The Role of Private Parties in the Enforcement of the Uruguay Round Agreements', *Journal of World Trade*, 29(5): 181–206.

Lumsdaine, D. H. (1993). *Moral Vision in International Politics: The Foreign Aid Regime, 1949–1989*, Princeton: Princeton University Press.

MacDonald, T. (2008). *Global Stakeholder Democracy*, Oxford: Oxford University Press.

MacIntyre, A. (1995). 'Is Patriotism a Virtue?', in: R. Beiner (ed.), *Theorizing Citizenship*, New York: State University of New York Press.

Magnette, P. (2003). 'Between Parliamentary Control and the Rule of Law: the Political Role of the Ombudsman in the European Union', *Journal of European Public Policy*, 10(5): 677–94.

Magnette, P., and K. Nicolaides (2004). 'The European Convention: Bargaining in the Shadow of Rhetoric', *West European Politics*; 27(3): 381–404.

Mair, P., and J. Thomassen (2010). 'Political Representation and Government in the European Union', *Journal of European Public Policy*, 17(1): 20–35.

Majone, G. (1998). 'Europe's "Democratic Deficit": The Question of Standards', *European Law Journal*, 4(1): 5–28.

Majone, G. (2005). *Dilemmas of European Integration: The Ambiguities and Pitfalls of Integration by Stealth*, Oxford: Oxford University Press.

Majone, G. (2010). 'Transaction-Cost Efficiency and the Democratic Deficit', *Journal of European Public Policy*, 17(2): 150–75.

Manners, I. (2002). 'Normative Power Europe: A Contradiction in Terms', *Journal of Common Market Studies*, 40(2): 235–58.

Manners, I. (2011). 'Un-National Normative Justification for European Union Foreign Policy', in: J. Neyer, and A. Wiener (eds.), *Political Theory of the European Union*, Oxford: Oxford University Press.

Mattila, M. (2009). 'Roll Call Analysis on Voting in the European Council of Ministers After the 2004 Enlargment', *European Journal of Political Research*, 48(6): 840–57.

Mearsheimer, J. J. (1994). 'The False Promise of International Institutions', *International Security*, 19(3): 5–49.

Menéndez, A. J. (2011). 'United They Diverge? From Conflicts of Law to Constitutional Theory? On Christian Joerges' Theory', *ARENA Working Paper*, 11(2).

Bibliography

Mill, J. S. (1861/1991). *Considerations on Representative Government*, New York: Prometheus Books.

Miller, D. (2000). *Citizenship and National Identity*, Cambridge: Polity Press.

Miller, D. (2002). 'Two Ways to Think about Justice', *Politics, Philosophy, and Economics*, 1(1): 5–28.

Milward, A. (1992). *The European Rescue of the Nation-State*, Berkeley/Calif.: University of California Press.

Mitchell, R. B. (1996). 'Compliance Theory: An Overview', in: J. Cameron, J. Werksman, and P. Roderick (eds.), *Improving Compliance with International Environmental Law*, London: Earthscan.

Mitrany, D. (1943). *A Working Peace System*, Chicago: Quadrangle Books.

Moravcsik, A. (1994). 'Why the European Community Strengthens the State: Domestic Politics and International Cooperation', *Harvard University Center for European Studies Working Paper Series*, 52.

Moravcsik, A. (1998). *The Choice for Europe: Social Purposes and State Power from Messina to Maastricht*, Ithaca: Cornell University Press.

Moravcsik, A. (2002). 'In Defence of the "Democratic Deficit": Reassessing Legitimacy in the European Union', *Journal of Common Market Studies*, 40(4): 603–24.

Morgan, G. (2005). *The Idea of a European Superstate: Public Justification and European Integration*, Princeton/N.J.: Princeton University Press.

Morgenthau, H. J. (1948). *Politics among Nations. The Struggle for Power and Peace*, New York: Alfred Knopf.

Müller, H. (2001). 'International Relations as Communicative Action', in: K. Fierke, and K. E. Jorgensen (eds.), *Constructing International Relations: The Next Generation*, New York: M. E. Sharpe.

Müller, H. (2007). 'Internationale Verhandlungen, Argumente und Verständigungshandeln. Verteidigung, Befunde, Warnung', in: P. Niesen, and B. Herborth (eds.), *Anarchie der kommunikativen Freiheit. Jürgen Habermas und die Theorie der internationalen Politik*, Frankfurt am Main: Suhrkamp.

Müller, J. -W. (2011). 'The Promise of "Demoi-Cracy": Democracy, Diversity, and Domination in the European Public Order', in: J. Neyer, and A. Wiener (eds.), *Political Theory of the European Union*, Oxford: Oxford University Press.

Münch, R. (2001). *Nation and Citizenship in the Global Age. From National to Transnational Ties and Identities*, Houndmills/Basingstoke: Palgrave.

Nagel, T. (2005). 'The Problem of Global Justice', *Philosophy and Public Affairs*, 33(2): 113–47.

Nanz, P., and J. Steffek (2005). 'Assessing the Democratic Quality of Deliberation in International Governance—Criteria and Research Strategies', *Acta Politica*, 40(3): 368–83.

Neyer, J., and A. Wiener (eds.) (2011). *Political Theory of the European Union*, Oxford: Oxford University Press.

Nicol, D. (2012). 'Can Justice Dethrone Democracy in the European Union? A Reply to Jürgen Neyer', *Journal of Common Market Studies* 50(3): 508–522.

Bibliography

Nicolaides K., and R. Howse (eds.) (2001). *The Federal Vision. Legitimacy and Levels of Governance in the United States and the European Union*, Oxford: Oxford University Press.

Nicolaïdis, K. (2007). 'Trusting the Poles' in the *Journal of European Public Policy* 14(5): 682–98.

Norton, P. (1996). 'Introduction: The Institution of Parliaments', in P. Norton (ed.), *Parliaments and Governments in Western Europe*, London: Frank Cass.

Nugent, N. (1999). *The Government and Politics of the European Union* [Forth Edition], Durham: Duke University Press.

Nwobike, J. (2005). 'The Application of Human Rights in African Caribbean and Pacific–European Union Development and Trade Partnership', *German Law Journal*, 6(10): 1381–406.

O'Brennan, J., and T. Raunio (eds.) (2007). *National Parliaments within the Enlarged European Union: From 'Victims' of Integration to Competitive Actors?* London: Routledge Chapman & Hall.

Page, S. (2003). 'Developing Countries: Victims or Participants. Their Changing Role in International Negotiations', Online Publication, London: Overseas Development Institute/Globalisation and Poverty Programme.

Papadopoulos, Y. (2010). 'Accountability and Multi-Level Governance: More Accountability, Less Democracy?', *West European Politics*, 33(5): 1030–49.

Pardo, S. (2007). 'Does the EU have a Value-Driven Vision of the World?', *The International Spectator: Italian Journal of International Affairs*, 42(1): 141–3.

Parijs, P. van (2011). *Just Democracy: The Rawls-Machiavelli Programme*, Colchester: ECPR Press.

Pedersen, J. (2008). 'Habermas' Method: Rational Reconstruction', *Philosophy of the Social Sciences*, 38(4): 457–85.

Peter, J., C. H. de Vreese (2004). 'In Search of Europe: A Cross-National Comparative Study of the European Union in National Television News', *Harvard International Journal of Press/Politics*, 9(4): 3–24.

Peters, R. (2006). 'Roadblock to Reform: The Persistence of Agricultural Export Subsidies', *Policy Issues in International Trade and Commodities Study Series of the United Nations Conference on Trade and Development*, 32.

Peterson, J. (1995). 'Decision-Making in the European Union: Towards a Framework for Analysis', *Journal of European Public Policy*, 2(1): 69–93.

Philip, M. (2009). 'Delimiting Democratic Accountability', *Political Studies*, 57(1): 28–53.

Pogge, T. (1994). 'An Egalitarian Law of Peoples', *Philosophy and Public Affairs*, 23(3): 195–224.

Pogge, T. (1998). 'A Global Resources Dividend', in: D. Crocker, and T. Linden (eds.), *Ethics of Consumption. The Good Life, Justice, and Global Stewardship*, New York: Rowman and Littlefield.

Pogge, T. (2002). 'Moral Universalism and Global Economic Justice', *Politics, Philosophy, and Economics*, 1(1): 29–58.

Polanyi, M. (1966). *The Tacit Dimension*, New York: Anchor Day Books.

Pollack, M. A. (1997). 'Delegation, Agency, and Agenda Setting in the European Community', *International Organization*, 51(1): 99–134.

Pollak, J. (2007). *Repräsentation ohne Demokratie. Kollidierende Modi der Repräsentation in der Europäischen Union*, Wien/New York: Springer.

Pollak, J., and P. Slominski (2003). 'Influencing EU Politics? The Case of the Austrian Parliament', *Journal of Common Market Studies*, 41(4): 707–29.

Pollak, J., and P. Slominski (2011). 'The Silence of the Shepherds: the Austrian Parliament's Modest Attempts to Communicate Europe', Paper presented at the Humboldt-Viadrina School of Governance—Workshop on National Parliaments in the European Union, Berlin, April 2011.

Przeworski, A. (1998). 'Deliberation and Ideological Domination', in: J. Elster (ed.), *Deliberative Democracy*, Cambridge: Cambridge University Press.

Puetter, U. (2012). 'Europe's Deliberative Intergovernmentalism: the Role of the Council and European Council in EU Economic Governance', *Journal of European Public Policy*, 19(2): 161–78.

Putnam, R. (1988). 'Diplomacy and Domestic Politics. The Logic of Two-Level Games', *International Organization*, 42(2): 427–60.

Raunio, T. (2009). 'National Parliaments and European Integration: What We Know and Agenda for Future Research', *Journal of Legislative Studies*, 15(4): 317–34.

Rawls, J. (1993). *Political Liberalism*, New York: Columbia University Press.

Rawls, J. (1997). *Die Idee des politischen Liberalismus, Aufsätze 1978–1989*, Frankfurt am Main: Suhrkamp.

Rawls, J. (1999a). *A Theory of Justice* [Second Edition], Oxford: Oxford University Press.

Rawls, J. (1999b). *The Law of Peoples*, Cambridge/Mass.: Harvard University Press.

Risse, T. (2000). ' "Let's Argue!": Communicative Action in World Politics', *International Organization*, 54(1): 1–39.

Risse, T. (2010). *A Community of Europeans? Transnational Identities and Public Spheres*, Ithaca/London: Cornell University Press.

Risse, T., and M. Kleine (2010). 'Deliberation in International Negotiations', *Journal of European Public Policy*, 17(5): 708–26.

Risse, T., and M. van den Steeg (2003). 'An Emerging European Public Sphere? Empirical Evidence and Theoretical Clarifications', Paper presented at the Science Center Berlin—Conference on the 'Europeanization of Public Spheres, Political Mobilisation, Public Communication and the European Union', Berlin, June 2003.

Rittberger, B. (2003). 'The Creation and Empowerment of the European Parliament', *Journal of Common Market Studies*, 41(2): 203–25.

Rittberger, B. (2005). *Building Europe's Parliament. Democratic Representation beyond the Nation-State*, Oxford: Oxford University Press.

Rittberger, B., and A. Wonka (2011). 'Introduction: Agency Governance in the European Union', *Journal of European Public Policy*, 18(6): 780–9.

Rittberger, B., and Berthold (2012). 'Institutionalizing Representative Democracy in the European Union: The Case of the European Parliament', *Journal of Common Market Studies*, 50th Anniversary Special Issue, 50: 18–37.

Rosamond, B. (2000). *Theories of European Integration*, Basingstoke: Macmillan.

Ruggie, J. (2002). 'The Theory and Practice of Learning Networks. Corporate Social Responsibility and the Global Compact', *Journal of Corporate Citizenship*, 5: 27–36.

Sabia, D. (2010). 'Defending Immanent Critique', *Political Theory*, 38(5): 684–711.

Bibliography

Schäfer, A. (2006). *Die neue Unverbindlichkeit. Wirtschaftspolitische Koordinierung in Europa*, Frankfurt am Main/New York: Campus.

Scharpf, F. W. (1999). *Governing in Europe: Democratic and Effective?* Oxford: Oxford University Press.

Scharpf, F. W. (2002). 'The European Social Model. Coping with the Challenges of Diversity', *Journal of Common Market Studies*, 40(4): 645–70.

Scharpf, F. W. (2009). 'Legitimacy in the Multilevel European Polity', *European Political Science Review*, 1(2): 173–204.

Scharpf, F. W. (2010a). 'The Asymmetry of European integration, or Why the EU Cannot Be a "Social Market Economy"', *Socio-Economic Review*, 8(2): 211–50.

Scharpf, F. W. (2010b). 'Legitimacy in the Multi-Level European Polity', in: P. Dobner, and M. Loughlin (eds.), *The Twilight of Constitutionalism?* Oxford: Oxford University Press.

Schilling, T. (1996). 'The Autonomy of the Community Legal Order', *Harvard International Law Journal*, 37(2): 389–410.

Schimmelfennig, F. (2008). 'EU Political Conditionality after the 2004 Enlargement: Consistency and Effectiveness', *Journal of European Public Policy*, 15(6): 918–37.

Schimmelfennig, F., and S. Lavenex (2009). 'EU Rules Beyond EU Borders: Theorizing External Governance in European Politics', *Journal of European Public Policy*, 16(6): 791–812.

Schmalz-Bruns, R. (2007). 'The Euro-Polity in Perspective: Some Normative Lessons from Deliberative Democracy', in: B. Rittberger, and B. Kohler-Koch (eds.), *Debating the Democratic Legitimacy of the EU,* Lanham/Md.: Rowman & Littlefield.

Schmidt, S. K. (2007). 'Mutual Recognition as a New Mode of Governance', *Journal of European Public Policy*, 14(5): 667–81.

Schmidt, V. (2006). *Democracy in Europe: The EU and National Polities*, Oxford: Oxford University Press.

Sen, A. (1999). *Development as Freedom*, New York: Anchor Books.

Sen, A. (2009). *The Idea of Justice*, Harvard: Harvard University Press.

Sifft, S., M. Brüggemann, K. Kleinen-v. Königslöw, B. Peters, and A. Wimmel (2007). 'Segmented Europeanization: Exploring the Legitimacy of the European Union from a Public Discourse Perspective', *Journal of Common Market Studies*, 45(1): 127–55.

Sjursen, H. (2006). 'The EU as a "Normative" Power: How Can This Be?', *Journal of European Public Policy*, 13(2): 235–51.

Slaughter, A. -M. (2004). *A New World Order*, Princeton: Princeton University Press.

Smith, K. E. (2006). *European Union Foreign Policy in a Changing World* [Third Edition], Cambridge: Polity Press.

Steinberg, R. H. (2002). 'In the Shadow of Law or Power? Consensus-Based Bargaining and Outcomes in the GATT/WTO', *International Organization*, 56(2): 339–74.

Steinberg, R. H. (2006). 'The Transformation of European Trading States', in: J. D. Levy (ed.), *The State after Statism: New State Activities in the Age of Liberalization*, Harvard: Harvard University Press.

Tallberg, J. (2007). 'Bargaining Power in the European Council', *Swedish Institute for European Policy Studies SIEPS*, 2007(1).

Thatcher, M. (1988). 'Speech to the College of Europe ("The Bruges Speech")', available at: http://www.margaretthatcher.org/document/107332, last accessed: 15/12/2011.
Tönnies, F. (1887/2005). *Gemeinschaft und Gesellschaft. Grundbegriffe der reinen Soziologie* [Fourth Unrevised Edition], Darmstadt: Wissenschaftliche Buchgesellschaft.
Valentini, L. (2011). 'Coercion and (Global) Justice', *American Political Science Review*, 105(1): 205–20.
Verhofstadt, G. (2006). *The United States of Europe*, London: Federal Trust.
Vetters, R., E. Jentges, and H. -J. Trenz (2009). 'Whose Project is it? Media Debates on the Ratification of the EU Constitutional Treaty', *Journal of European Public Policy*, 16(3): 412–30.
Vosskuhle, A. (2011). Mehr Europa lässt das Grundgesetz nicht zu', *Frankfurter Allgemeine Sonntagszeitung*, 25/09/2011.
Wallace, W. (1983). 'Less Than a Federation, More than a Regime: The European Community as a Political System', in: H. Wallace et al. (eds.), *Policy Making in the European Community*, Chichester: Wiley.
Wallace, W., and J. Smith (1995). 'Democracy or Technocracy? European Integration and the Problem of Popular Consent', *West European Politics*, 18(3): 137–57.
Waltz, K. (1979). *Theory of International Relations*, Reading Addison-Wesley.
Walzer, M. (1977). *Just and Unjust Wars*, New York: Basic Books.
Walzer, M. (1983a). *The Spheres of Justice*, Oxford: Basil Blackwell.
Walzer, M. (1983b). 'Spheres of Justice: An Exchange', *The New York Review of Books*, 21: 43–6.
Watson, R., and M. Shackleton (2008). 'Organized Interests and Lobbying', in: E. Bomberg, J. Peterson, and A. Stubb (eds.), *The European Union: How Does it Work?* Oxford: Oxford University Press.
Weiler, J. H. H. (1981). 'The Community System: The Dual Character of Supranationalism', *Yearbook of European Law*, 1(1): 267–306.
Weiler, J. H. H. (1999). 'Epilogue: "Comitology" as Revolution—Infranationalism, Constitutionalism and Democracy', in: C. Joerges, and E. Vos (eds.), *EU Committees: Social Regulation, Law and Politics*, Oxford: Hart.
Weiler, J. H. H. (2000). 'Federalism and Constitutionalism: Europe's Sonderweg', *Harvard Jean Monnet Working Paper*, 00(10).
Weiler, J. H. H. (2003). 'In Defence of the Status Quo: Europe's Constitutional Sonderweg', in: J. H. H. Weiler, and M. Wind (eds.), *European Constitutionalism beyond the State*, Cambridge: Cambridge University Press.
Weiler, J. H. H., and U. R. Haltern (1996). 'The Autonomy of the Community Legal Order—Through the Looking Glass', *Harvard International Law Journal*, 37(2): 411–48.
Wendt, A. (1992). 'Anarchy is What States Make of it', *International Organization*, 46(2): 391–425.
Wendt, A. (1999). *Social Theory of International Politics*, Cambridge: Cambridge University Press.
White, J., L. Ypi (2011). 'On Partisan Political Justification', *American Political Science Review*, 105(2): 381–97.
Wiener, A., and T. Diez (eds.) (2005). *European Integration Theory* [Reprint], Oxford: Oxford University Press.

Bibliography

Wolf, K. -D. (1999). The New Raison d'État as a Problem for Democracy in World Society', *European Journal of International Relations*, 5(3): 333–63.

World Bank (2001). *World Development Report 2002: Building Institutions for Markets*, Washington D.C.: Oxford University Press for World Bank.

World Bank [P. Chuhan-Pole, and M. Angwafo (eds.)] (2011). *Yes Africa Can: Success Stories from a Dynamic Continent*, Washington D.C.: The World Bank.

Young, A. (2005). 'Picking the Wrong Fight: Why Attacks on the World Trade Organization Pose the Real Threat to Environmental and Public Health Protection', *Global Environmental Politics*, 5(4): 47–72.

Zielonka, J. (2006). *Europe as Empire. The Nature of the Enlarged Union*, Oxford: Oxford University Press.

Zielonka, J. (2007). 'The Quality of Democracy after Joining the European Union', *East European Politics & Societies*, 21(1): 162–80.

Zielonka, J. (2008). 'Europe as a Global Actor: Empire by Example', *International Affairs*, 84(3): 471–84.

Zimmermann, H. (2007). 'Realist Power Europe? The EU in the Negotiations about China's and Russia's WTO Accession', *Journal of Common Market Studies*, 45(5): 813–32.

Zürn, M. (2005). 'Law and Compliance at Different Levels', in: M. Zürn, C. Joerges (eds.), *Law and Governance in Postnational Europe. Compliance beyond the Nation-State*, Cambridge: Cambridge University Press.

Zürn, M., and J. Neyer (2005). 'Conclusions. The Conditions of Compliance', in: M. Zürn, and C. Joerges (eds.), *Law and Governance in Postnational Europe. Compliance beyond the Nation-State*, Cambridge: Cambridge University Press.

Index

absolute gains 170
accountability 3, 20, 56, 76, 107–11, 141, 145, 183
  democratic 23, 105
ACP countries 177
acquis communautaire 77, 95, 148
actorness 171, 190
Amnesty International 137
anarchy 14, 49, 116, 151, 195
  international 39, 134, 191
  untamed 9, 188
arguing 5, 10, 15, 20, 35, 38, 43, 89, 92, 122, 172
Asia-Pacific Economic Cooperation (APEC) 12
authority 19, 23, 24, 43, 44, 46, 47, 49, 50–1, 52, 55, 56, 69, 73, 81, 86, 105, 108, 123, 126, 134, 137, 141, 146, 155, 167, 183, 187
  ECJ 119
  EP 161
  law-making 8, 193
  legal 36, 39, 42, 50
  political 4, 12, 55, 66, 77, 80, 86, 108, 109, 138, 140, 164

Barber, B. 6
bargaining 15, 20, 37, 54, 89, 94, 105, 118–19, 122, 126, 133, 153, 170, 182
  arguing and 5, 10, 38, 172
  diplomatic 155
  intergovernmental 9, 17, 20, 167–8, 188
  international 30, 115, 134, 151, 188
  power 16, 118
Beck, U. 22, 24, 173
Beitz, C. 74, 76, 193
biofuel(s) 180, 183
Bohmann, J. 194
Bologna declaration 136
Bosnia and Herzegovina 175–6
Bundesrat 60, 141
Bundestag 137, 141–42

cardinal laws 157
Cassis de Dijon 131
Central and Eastern European Countries (CEEC) 104, 175

CFSP 50, 160, 171
Charter of Fundamental Rights 139
checks and balances 3, 12, 108
China 11, 102, 195
Christian 75, 81, 83
civil power 169
civil rights 139
civil society 16, 62, 101, 166, 167, 194
Civil Society Organization (CSE) 166, 194
civilizing force of hypocrisy 93
Codex Alimentarius Commission 142
coercion 6, 24, 36, 52–5, 174
  monopoly of 4, 6, 19, 67, 190, 191, 195
  legitimate monopoly of 14, 39
coercive order 14
collective goods 10, 18
comitology 52, 53
Commission 8, 36, 44, 45, 49, 51–5, 62–64, 65, 66, 104–5, 106, 109–10, 111, 125, 127–9, 131, 139, 140, 143, 144, 145, 146, 147–8, 153, 154, 157, 163, 167, 171, 174, 175, 176, 179
  Codex Alimentarius 142
Committee of the Regions 127
Common Agricultural Policy (CAP) 171, 179
Common Foreign and Security Policy 95, 160, 171, 189
communication function 166
competition 50, 52, 65, 66, 69, 125, 129, 130, 182
  competition policy 50, 51, 65, 69, 129
compliance 14, 15, 16, 29, 41, 42, 45, 46, 47, 49, 54, 55, 66–8, 110, 139, 146, 177, 181, 188, 193, 195
  compliance pull 9, 188, 195
  non-compliance 9, 55, 188, 195
concentration of power 21
conciliation committee 53
conflict 16, 29, 40, 42, 45, 55, 65, 66, 67, 68, 78, 86, 87, 115, 118, 122, 130, 145, 175, 178, 191
  interstate 6, 60
constitutional asymmetry 20, 65
constitutional convention 154
constitutional tolerance 5, 21, 24
constitutional treaty 41, 154, 155

211

Index

constitutionalization 9, 46, 156, 188
contextualism 74, 78–84
control
  parliamentary 6, 160, 165
  cooperation
  coordination 12, 101, 104, 118, 126, 163
  corruption 102, 108
COSAC 8, 17, 167–8, 189
cosmopolitan polity 170, 184
Cosmopolitanism 77–8
Cotonou Agreement 177
Council 8, 41, 44, 50, 52–3, 60, 62, 65–6, 104–6, 109, 127, 129, 139, 140, 148, 160, 163, 167, 171
  European *see* European Council
  General Affairs and External Relation 106
  Federal Council of Germany 59–60, 141
Council of Europe 157, 171
Croatia 21
culture 24, 48, 59, 63, 83, 89, 116, 165, 189
  political 5, 62, 77, 191

Dahl, R. 57, 58, 59, 77
de Gaulle 125
decision-making
  transparent 8, 104
delegation
deliberation 20, 30, 56, 96, 152, 163, 194
  democratic 66, 69
  parliamentary 167
  public 61, 156
  transnational 151
deliberative problem-solving 147
democracy 3–9, 12–14, 22–4, 26, 56–70, 73–4, 77, 93, 106, 134, 138, 141, 158–62, 169, 171, 174–5, 177, 188–9, 191, 194–5
  deliberative 121
  domestic 156, 158, 162, 175
  European 143, 159, 160–1
  German 42, 47
  global 19, 143, 194
  imperfect 155–158
  media 166
  national 8–9, 18, 188
  transnational 154
democracy standard 7, 23
democratic deficit 4, 7, 23, 37, 57, 68, 70, 73, 161
demoi-cracy 21
demos 24, 61, 64
  European 5, 21, 160, 161
Denmark 21, 54, 96, 164–6
dependence 144
Deutsch 82
developing countries 99, 101, 102, 170, 175, 178–80, 190, 195
development aid 45, 46, 123, 169
Development Assistance Committee 100
Difference Principle 97–8

diffuse social interests 145
diplomacy 12, 94, 106, 107, 122, 153, 178
direct effect 25, 35, 36, 38, 40, 41, 43–6, 67, 68
discourse
  deliberative 152
  justificatory 5, 8, 9, 16, 17, 18, 30, 87, 89, 92, 93, 97, 98, 99, 100, 107, 120–142, 151, 165, 188, 189
dispute settlement body 116, 123
distributive justice 97–104
domestic ratification 136
domestic scrutiny 37, 138
domination 59, 98, 174
Dryzek, J.S. 19, 143, 194
dualism 14, 30, 38, 120
Dworkin, R. 81, 152

Early Warning System 159
European Court of Justice (ECJ) 35, 65–6, 68, 95, 119, 128, 131, 139, 163, 168, 189
Economic and Social Committee 127
economic rights 139
education 39, 59, 61, 98, 99, 102, 111, 127, 177, 193
  educational achievement 58
  higher 136–7
  ministers of 136
  policy 136
elite 3, 36, 58, 59, 61
  élite pluralism 145
  political 117, 154
Elster, J. 92–3, 118
energy policy 68, 172
enlargement 50, 125, 175, 176
EP 26, 62–4, 117, 140, 146, 160–2
epistemic communities 61, 82, 96
European arrest warrant 165
European Central Bank 50, 108
European Convention for the Protection of Human Rights and Freedoms 139
European Council 8, 49–50, 53, 60, 62, 104, 107, 125–6, 153, 171
European Development Fund 177
European Neighbourhood Policy 176
European Parliament (EP) 26, 62–4, 117, 140, 146, 160–2
European statehood 4
European-wide media 3, 61, 157
Europeanization 8, 12, 62, 162, 188
expert communities 96–7
expertise 49, 50, 98, 99, 128, 136, 143–5
  bureaucratic 25
  scientific 126
expert 12, 26, 57, 61, 122
  expert communities 96–7
  experts 26, 96, 97, 105, 143, 176
exploitation 80, 101, 194
export subsidies 179

212

Index

external effects 4, 5, 8, 9, 109, 132, 172, 183–4, 187–8, 193
external governance 175

fairness 76, 81, 122
fascism 48
federal state 6, 21, 47
  European 191
federalism 20–2, 26, 160
financial crisis 11
Fischer, J. 23, 161
fishing agreements 180–1
Folketing 141, 163–6
Forst, R. 7, 9, 13, 85–6, 88, 110, 151–2
four freedoms 65–6, 168
France 24, 60, 111, 119, 124–6, 153, 154, 155, 171
freedom 6, 18, 65, 75, 80, 86, 93, 110, 128, 158, 171
  individual 8, 5, 97, 109, 111
  restriction/limitation 8, 13, 15, 80, 81, 85, 91, 109, 111, 120, 181

GATT 46, 131, 132, 178
gender 26, 29, 58, 77, 127, 128
German Federal Constitutional Court 41, 67, 162, 165
Germany 22, 48, 60, 68, 93, 103, 111, 118, 119, 124–6, 137, 153, 171
  constitutional order of 42
  democracy in 47
  federal states of 59–60, 141
Giscard d'Estaing 154–5
global democracy 19, 143, 194
global division of labour 180
global parliamentary assembly 77
global tax regime 181–2
globalization 11, 80, 134
Greece 65, 83
  ancient 106
greenhouse gas 99, 110, 171
Greenpeace 137, 180

Haas, E. B. 25, 36, 82, 90, 96, 118
Habermas, J. 3, 5, 6, 11, 13, 22, 23, 29, 57, 82, 88, 89, 90, 94, 121
Held, D. 76, 193
House of Representatives 60
human rights 10, 28, 75, 77, 104, 130, 139, 169, 170, 172, 174, 175, 177, 195
  respect for 64, 158, 174, 177
  protection 139, 143
  violation 152
Hungary 104, 157, 158
Huntington, S. P. 80

Iceland 21–2
ideal worlds 19
IMF 101–3, 136

immoral act 88
inclusion 5, 22, 56, 140, 144, 145, 157, 177, 194
inclusionary 15, 67, 69, 157
India 102, 180
Indonesia 102
informal networks 20
informational disadvantages 136
infringement 45, 54–5, 90, 92, 111
  illegitimate 15, 86, 109
  of/on liberty/freedom 15, 86, 90, 91–2, 109, 110
  proceedings 54–5
interdependence 5, 10, 39, 69, 171, 187
  conditions of 4, 9, 18, 68, 172, 188
  normative 120
  transnational 173
Intergovernmental Conference 153–5
intergovernmentalism 36, 37, 161
international organization(s) 5, 10, 11, 12, 13, 16, 35, 38, 39, 44, 47, 50, 76, 100, 116, 117, 136, 142, 153, 169, 187, 190, 194
Interparliamentary Constitutional Assembly 17, 167, 193
Iraq 172
Italy 65, 103, 157–8

Juncker, J.-C. 65, 154
jurisdiction 11 12, 36, 41, 68, 192, 193

Kant, I. 6, 79
Kelsen, H. 78–9
Keohane, R. O. 10, 27, 69, 120
Kosovo 175–6

Laeken Declaration 154–5
legal integration 5, 35, 38–9, 128, 130, 170, 188
legalization 10, 95, 100
legitimacy 14, 15, 20, 39, 47, 49, 56–7, 62, 64, 68–70, 73, 87, 92, 93, 110, 117, 130–2, 143, 156, 195
  democratic 117, 159, 162
  EU 3, 5–9, 23, 30, 47, 107, 115, 151, 161–2, 188, 191
  prima facie 36
less-developed countries 179
liberty 86, 110, 139
  individual 13, 25, 56, 86, 109, 139
  infringement of 86, 90, 91–2, 109, 110
  limitation of 86, 98, 109, 111
Luxembourg 52, 60, 65, 125, 154
  Luxembourg Compromise 52

Macedonia 21
Majone, G. 3, 25, 66
maladministration 140, 145–6
malnutrition 181
market-correcting 65
market-making 50, 65, 132, 177

213

Index

media control 107, 157
media
   European-wide 3, 61, 157
   national 37
Mercosur 12
migration policy 39, 50, 107, 189, 193
military interventions 169
Mill, J. S. 89, 166
Miller, D. 74, 79
Mitrany, D. 118
modernity 87
monetary policy 10, 12, 22, 68, 69, 97, 193
Monnet 25
   Monnet method 25
monopoly of coercion 4, 6, 19, 67, 190, 191
   global 195
   legitimate 14, 39
moral obligation 76
Moravcsik, A. 3, 10, 20, 37, 48, 52, 69, 124, 162
Morgenthau, H.J. 78
most-favoured nations-principle 95
multi-level governance 8, 106, 107, 188
Muslim 75
mutual recognition 21, 38, 128, 131–2, 187

NAFTA 12
Nagel, T. 80–1
national parliaments 3, 8, 9,16, 17, 22, 23, 25, 40, 76, 77, 105, 135–6, 138, 140–1, 153, 158–168, 189
nationalism 5, 7, 48, 191
NATO 171
negative integration 3, 57, 64–6, 68
neofunctionalism 36–7
nepotism 102
new *raison d'état* 137
non-discrimination 69, 131, 132
non-governmental actors 8, 44, 134, 137, 143
non-imperial empire 17, 173, 184
North American Free Trade Area *see* NAFTA
normative heterogeneity 18
normative power 170, 172, 183
normative realism 7, 13, 15, 19–31, 73, 88, 89, 152, 190–2
Norway 21–2

Organisation for Economic Cooperation and Development (OECD) 100, 136, 179, 181–2
Organization for Security and Cooperation in Europe (OSCE) 171
Organization of American States (OAS) 177

participation 22, 37, 56, 59, 144, 152, 154, 183
   cross-boarder 76
   lack of 3
   legislative 142
   parliamentary 160, 164, 189
   political 58, 59, 98

stake-holder 107, 128, 144
party system 3, 64
peer review 107
performative contradiction 91
Pogge, T. 75, 76, 101
Poland 21, 24, 94, 104, 139, 155
policy deliberation 20, 30, 144
political culture(s) 5, 24, 62, 77, 83, 191
   different 94, 95
political equality 57, 58–61, 144, 145
   individual 4, 6, 14, 61, 68, 161, 187
political integration 5, 38, 126, 195
pooling 36, 48, 50–2, 142
positive integration 57, 64–5, 68
postnational constellation 11, 22
power asymmetries 7, 18, 120, 126, 128, 131, 151, 161
   influence 89, 131
   vertical 9, 188
power play 117, 118, 153, 178
pragmatism 25, 190
precedence 35, 40–1, 42, 46, 67
preliminary ruling procedure 43–4, 49
principal-agent analysis 108–9
principle of conferral 138
principle of subsidiarity *see* subsidiarity
problem-solving capacity 10, 14, 57, 58, 64–8, 189
procedural justice 99
proportionality 42, 60, 138–9, 163, 184, 194
public discourse 13, 61, 62, 63, 65, 166, 194
   critical 3, 93
   European 3, 24, 62, 161, 167
   European-wide 49, 57
   justificatory 62, 167
   legally structured 184
public goods 30, 172, 183
public scrutiny 36, 134, 137, 138, 156, 166, 189
public sphere 14, 61, 92, 93, 99, 144, 156
   European 62–64

rational reconstruction 29–30
Rawls, J. 13, 28–9, 73, 75–6, 83, 85, 97
   Rawlsian 30, 75–6, 85, 97, 98
realist power 169–73
reason-giving 89, 92, 98, 153
reciprocity 81, 88, 95, 116, 131
redistribution 76, 98, 101, 103
redistributive policies 25
referendum 153, 155, 164
reflective equilibrium 28–30
regulatory agency 25
representation 3, 12, 69, 132, 144, 145, 156
   mode of 9, 16, 144, 145, 188
   political 16
retaliatory action 45, 116
Romania 22
rule of law 5, 10, 23, 46, 104, 158, 174, 175, 177

Index

acceptance of 116
principles of 41
standards of 41

Scharpf, F.W. 3 n., 20, 57, 64, 66, 161
Schengen Agreement 22
self-interest 18, 79, 87, 92
  self-interested 89, 90, 93
Sen, A. 85, 102
Senate of the United States 59–60
separation of power 12
Serbia 21, 176
  Berlusconi, S. 157–8
Singapore 103
Single European Act (SEA) 52, 117
Solange II 67
South Korea 103
sovereignty 47, 48, 51, 60, 159, 149, 174
  national 10, 61, 116, 189
  of a European people 5
  political 39
  popular 23
  supranational 42
  tax 182
Spain 65, 155
special and differential treatment 102
special interests 127, 128
spill-over 24, 25, 36, 187
stake holders 107, 152
subsidiarity 140, 184
  principle 128, 140, 159, 163
subsidies 45, 51, 69, 129, 179, 183
super-majority 105
supranational democracy 56–69, 189
supremacy 28, 36, 38–9, 40–42, 44, 124, 139
Switzerland 22

tacit knowledge 29–31, 115–20, 126
Taiwan 103
taxation 24, 64, 66, 107, 129, 168, 181
  capital 182
  rates 182
Thatcher, M. 118
Tönnies, F. 82
Trade Policy Review Body (TPRB) 123
Trade Related Intellectual Property Rights *see* TRIPS
Trade Related Investment Measures *see* TRIMS
Transatlantic Business Dialogue 142
transnational democracy 154
transnational justice 8–9, 16, 80, 188
transnational publics 194
transparency 56, 104–7, 128, 134, 145, 154
  lack of 3, 157
Treaties of Rome 5, 35
Treaty of Lisbon 5, 41, 49, 57, 139–42, 147, 153, 158, 159, 160, 162, 163

Treaty of Maastricht 9, 42, 141
Treaty of Nice 154
TRIMS 178–9
TRIPS 53, 178–9
truth 29, 67, 84, 87, 90, 93
  objective 87, 88, 89, 90
  truthfully 79
truth-seeking 89–90, 92
Turkey 21–2

unanimity 50, 50, 65, 96, 152
  intergovernmental 17, 168
  the principle of 60, 126
United Kingdom 21, 22, 24, 48, 54, 62, 111, 125
United Nations 10, 12
  United Nations Charter 174
  United Nations Conference on Trade and Development (UNCTAD) 101
  United Nations Development Programme (UNDP) 101
United States Trade Representative 44
universalism 74–84
unjustified non-policies 181
US 45, 46, 124
USA 44, 102, 103, 120, 178
utopian wishful thinking 73

Van Gend en Loos 43
veil of ignorance 75–6, 85
Venice Commission of the Council of Europe 157
Versailles 118
veto 77, 105, 125, 136, 155
  qualified 86, 110

war 5, 6, 10, 60, 75, 118, 175
  post-war 37, 48, 59
  war-criminals 110
  warfare 173
weak states 8–9, 124, 188
wealth 75, 79, 101, 102, 133, 182
  (re)distribution of 20, 76, 101
  economic 23
  global 183
  independent/irrespective of 58, 59
Weiler, J. 5, 14, 21, 37–9, 42, 47, 61, 64
welfare 24, 64 99, 128
  welfare state 59, 66, 86, 97
working agreement 87–8, 94, 133
World Bank 95, 101–3, 136, 142
World Trade Organizaion (WTO) 10, 100–3, 116, 123, 131–2, 142–3, 153, 170, 178–9, 190, 193, 195

Yugoslavia 175

Zürn, M. 67